W9-BRN-853

Feelings

"This is a remarkable book, sage, witty, emphatic, and humane. Highly recommended."
—*Library Journal*

"One effect of these essays is paramount. They make us think about our feelings as if they were objective realities. By the very act of doing so, we are bound to feel enriched in self-knowledge."
—Christopher Lehmann-Haupt

"Provocative and refreshing . . . *Feelings* is a delightful book, imaginative, judicious and exceptionally well written."
—*New York Times Book Review*

"[Gaylin] moves man out of the psychoanalytic cave into the sunlight of common sense and vigorous endorsement. . . . An Aristotelian genius for taxonomy . . . Gaylin's treatment of feeling upset I find a tour de force."
—*Best Sellers*

Other books by Willard Gaylin, M.D.

Doing Good: The Limits of Benevolence
(with I. Glasser, S. Marcus, and D. Rothman)

Caring

Partial Justice: A Study of Bias in Sentencing

In the Service of Their Country: War Resisters in Prison

The Meaning of Despair

The Rage Within: Anger in Modern Life

Rediscovering Love

The Killing of Bonnie Garland: A Question of Justice

Feelings

Our Vital Signs

Willard Gaylin, M.D.

PERENNIAL LIBRARY

Harper & Row, Publishers, New York
Cambridge, Philadelphia, San Francisco, Washington
London, Mexico City, São Paulo, Singapore, Sydney

Copyright acknowledgments begin on page 253.

FEELINGS: OUR VITAL SIGNS. Copyright © 1979 by Willard Gaylin. All rights reserved. Printed in the United States of America. No part of this book may be used or reproduced in any manner whatsoever without written permission except in the case of brief quotations embodied in critical articles and reviews. For information address Harper & Row, Publishers, Inc., 10 East 53rd Street, New York, N.Y. 10022. Published simultaneously in Canada by Fitzhenry & Whiteside Limited, Toronto.

First PERENNIAL LIBRARY edition published 1988.

Designed by Gloria Adelson

Library of Congress Cataloging in Publication Data

Gaylin, Willard.
  Feelings.

  "Perennial Library"

  Bibliography: p.
  Includes index.
  1. Emotions. I. Title.
BF561.G39 1988   152.4   78-2130
ISBN 0-06-091480-7 (pbk.)

88 89 90 91 92 MPC 10 9 8 7 6 5 4 3 2 1

Dedicated to my new sons
Andrew Heyward
and
Clinton Brandon Smith

Contents

The Waking

I wake to sleep, and take my waking slow.
I feel my fate in what I cannot fear.
I learn by going where I have to go.

We think by feeling. What is there to know?
I hear my being dance from ear to ear.
I wake to sleep, and take my waking slow.

Of those so close beside me, which are you?
God bless the Ground! I shall walk softly there,
And learn by going where I have to go.

Light takes the Tree; but who can tell us how?
The lowly worm climbs up a winding stair;
I wake to sleep, and take my waking slow.

Great Nature has another thing to do
To you and me; so take the lively air,
And, lovely, learn by going where to go.

This shaking keeps me steady. I should know.
What falls away is always. And is near.
I wake to sleep, and take my waking slow.
I learn by going where I have to go.

—Theodore Roethke

Preface and Acknowledgments

M Y PROFESSIONAL INTEREST in feelings coincided with my entering the fields of psychiatry and psychoanalysis. I was fortunate to have as one of my teachers a brilliant psychoanalytic thinker and critic, Sandor Rado. Rado, in his mature years, wrote little and not well. His name therefore is little known outside of psychoanalytic circles. His primary influence was as a teacher. While Rado was interested in the central role of emotions, for the most part he focused on fear and rage. Those who have read Rado will recognize the term guilty fear as used in this volume as being a primary reference of his.

My interest in writing a book about feelings emerged—perversely—while occupied with writing another book. During an examination of dependency and the need of the human infant for caring I became interested in the emotional experiences of love and caring. Certain of my concepts—particularly on being touched and feeling hurt—were first presented in that context.

Despite the fact that I have stated in the body of this book that my primary concern is with the subjective aspect of emotions, that is, the feelings, I am fully aware of the importance of the other aspects of emotion. I have, therefore, expanded the bibliography to include materials that go well beyond feelings (indeed, feelings occupy little of the literature of emotions). Because the titles of many articles give no indication of the emotions with which they deal, I have also included an index to the bibliography to help those who seek further information in this field.

In the course of writing a book I have an almost compulsive need to test new ideas, theories or definitions on my colleagues. I am therefore particularly indebted to Dan Callahan and the rest of the staff at the Hastings Center, Institute of Society, Ethics and the Life Sciences for creating the kind of environment that encourages communication across disciplines.

In a community in which everyone is always writing something, the reading of manuscripts is low enough on the popularity scale to be just barely above computing income taxes. I am, therefore, particularly indebted to those good friends who were prepared to make the ultimate academic sacrifice of reading my rough first drafts. So thank you all who have done this service for me: Jody and Andrew Heyward, Verena and Robert Michels, Margaret and Peter Steinfels, and my editor, Erwin Glikes.

To my wife—beyond gratitude—my love.

Feelings

Feeling Free to Feel

ONE DAY YOU FEEL GOOD and the next you feel bad, and between those two poles are compressed all the joys of heaven and the anguish of hell. The events that prompt feelings, the justification for the feelings, even the reality of the perceptions that lead to them are all unimportant. It is the feeling that counts.

Despite its importance, there is an incredible amount of confusion about feelings and emotions in both the minds of the public and the attention of the "experts." Even the nomenclature presents a problem. Generally speaking, the field of psychology has settled down to the use of three terms: "emotion" is the general term which encompasses the feeling tone, the biophysiological state, and even the chemical changes we are beginning to understand underlie the sensations we experience; "affect," introduced from psychoanalysis, is used to describe the dominant emotional tone of an individual, and is particularly used in relationship to our recognition of the feelings of others; "feeling" is our subjective awareness of our own emotional state. It is that which we experience; that which we know about our current emotional condition.

Given the central importance of feelings in our everyday life, you would think that the psychological and psychoanalytical literature would be dominated by them. It is not so. Perhaps it is unsettling in a scientific and logical age to place much value on such a subjective, unmeasurable—such an "irresponsible"—subject as feelings. Perhaps feelings are too close to our vulnerable central core to allow for comfortable evaluation. Perhaps it is simply that in a technological society, which values the measurable, the visible, the palpable, and the objectifiable, feelings embarrass us by defying our most respected current tools of investigation.

As a result, we have been exhorted by so many academic prophets with their own contradictory visions of truth, preached to by so many ministers of misinformation, that the culture at large—and the individual within it—is confused about the nature, the meaning, and even the respectability of feelings. Are they the antagonist of intelligence or the special attributes of the only truly intelligent animal; are they the sign of the undisciplined or the evidence of personal liberation from the constrictive inhibitions of society; are they the symptoms of neurosis or the measures of emotional freedom?

Obviously, different cultures, and the individuals within them, vary in their attitudes about feelings. What is emotionally acceptable in the streets of Palermo would seem aberrant in the cool reserve of Stockholm. There is significant difference even in even more similar cultures, such as Germany and England, as Naomi Bliven comments:

My reading has given me the impression that Germans have been more tolerant than English-speakers of men who throw tantrums, get into flaps, and publicly exhibit wide swings of emotion.

She then compares the acceptance of Wilhelm II by German people with English attitudes, and notes that

Wilhelm II was always giving offense in England, though his own subjects seem not to have found him unstable or even notably unattractive. It is difficult to imagine someone as lacking in self-control and good manners as Ludendorff achieving high command in an English-speaking army—the English used to send gifted but temperamental military men, like Gordon and Wingate, to places like the Sudan and Burma, the boondocks of empire.*

She is particularly horrified that the Germans were said to have found Hitler charming. Here she is not of course referring to the monstrous political actions of Hitler, toward which the word "charm" is almost obscenely juxtaposed, but to his public personality. She is incredulous that the Germans "found charm in a man who gobbled sweets, made disgusting comments on food at the table, engaged in staring matches, bragged about his intelligence, and flew into a rage when anybody questioned one of his statements." She wisely recognizes that cultural attitudes about the display of public emotion are permitted to vary when she concludes: "Perhaps it is a matter of other places, other mores." While we may differ in our cultural attitudes toward display of emotion, no culture can afford to disparage the importance of feelings.

Feeling is—if not all—almost all. It serves utility and sensuality. Feelings are the fine instruments which shape decision-making in an animal cursed and blessed with intelligence, and the freedom which is its corollary. They are signals directing us toward goodness, safety, pleasure, and group survival.

Feelings can, like every other aspect of our humanity, be corrupted from their original purposes. As hunger drove the primitive man to the nurture required for life, gluttony can drive modern man to the obesity that destroys. So, too, with feelings. Jealousy, which serves the struggle for survival, can deteriorate into the envy which draws defeat even from victory. We can be overwhelmed by inappropriate guilt, anxiety, shame, and the like. Mental illness is usually a mere disarray of the ingredients of survival. All that is necessary is rearrange-

---

* Naomi Bliven, book review of "The Psychopathic God: Adolf Hitler," by Robert G. L. Waite. *The New Yorker*, Aug. 29, 1977, p. 84.

ment. Feelings are internal directives essential for human life. In addition, and not just in passing, they are their own rewards. They are the means and the ends. All goodness and pleasure must be ultimately perceived in the realm of feelings. It is in the balance of small passions of daily existence that we measure and value our lives.

Yet the public at large is confused about the meaning of feelings and the propriety of their public expression. The confusion is exploited by the continuing flow of "how to" books which guide the perplexed and despairing to inner peace via conflicting and contradictory pathways. On the one hand, there is the "emotions are bad" school, which sees them as stormy intruders on the tranquil sea of life. Here shame and guilt are the most frequently denounced as unnecessary and "neurotic." But shame and guilt are noble emotions essential in the maintenance of civilized society, and vital for the development of some of the most refined and elegant qualities of human potential—generosity, service, self-sacrifice, unselfishness, and duty.

Then there is the theory that accepts emotions as perfectly permissible signs of the healthy body's response to distress, provided they are not contained. In this school of thought, emotions are obliged to be discharged into the environment. This is the "emotions as pus" concept. You must bring your anger to a head—and if you cannot the good doctor will lance the boil and discharge the venom. What must be expressed is almost always anger—occasionally, anxiety. It is a principle that has found particular favor in a time and a subculture that have glorified self-expression. Its credo is captured by the vulgar but descriptive expression "Let it all hang out." I have never felt that people's inner feelings have some claim to public recognition.* Quite the contrary; for the most part, the private life of the narcissist, like the private parts of the exhibitionist, ought not be hung out—uninvited—in the public space.

---

* See Willard Gaylin, "Putting It Back Where It Belongs," *The Hastings Center Report* 7, no. 1 (February, 1977).

It was my daughter who first suggested to me that bad temper was a form of public littering, and indicated that she would as soon have a casual acquaintance drop her dirty Kleenex on her as her foul language and ill-humor. I am at a loss to explain why it is that the very same individual who is so vigilant in his protection of the environment of material wastes will often have an absolute compulsion to contaminate it with the spiritual droppings of his personal catharsis. I myself feel we have a responsibility—not only to the social unit, which demands a certain amount of evasion, reserve, and dissembling, but also to our personal dignity—to keep "it" in.

Even if one does accept the concept that the discharged emotion has a particular moral standing, I do not understand how one moves from this assumption to the next, that self-improvement can be achieved by generating the emotion so that it may later be relieved. In other words, if one accepts the fact that fevers are bad and ought to be reduced by dissipating the heat into the environment through cold-water immersion, alcohol rubs, or aspirin, this hardly means that there is something therapeutic in generating a fever in the first place just so that dissipation can occur. The problem with people who have pent-up emotions is usually not their inability to express them but their incredible capacity to generate them. They do not need a weekend marathon of provocation and humiliation to express the very emotions that they generate to excess *without* provocation.

Obviously, the cathartic, howling, and confrontation theories arise from a sloppy reading of early Freud. In his first speculations in the *Studies in Hysteria* (1893), Freud postulated with his colleague Breuer that neurosis was due to the accidental encapsulation of emotion that failed to be discharged. Even in that first treatise, he was not so naïve as to assume that the simple discharge of the emotion by whatever means would alleviate the condition. At any rate, Freud spent the next fifty years of his life modifying that position, recognizing its oversimplification, and building the theory of psychoanalysis that saw behavior as purposive, dynamic, defensive, and meaningful. He grew to see the accidental encapsulation of emotion, like a foreign body, as a grossly oversimplified concept of the etiology of neurosis.

In the twentieth century there gradually emerged a general theory of behavior which progressively reinforced the sense of the "wisdom of the body." More and more it became apparent that behavior was purposeful and goal-directed—even seemingly "foolish" or discomforting behavioral symptoms which were originally viewed *as* the disease were proved to be defenses *against* the disease. Fever is not a sickness but the body's adaptive mechanism to increase the rate of biochemical defenses by increasing the temperature. Similarly, phobias, obsessions, and delusions are attempts to control, limit, and cope with unbearable emotional states.

Obviously, specific feelings serve multiple and varied purposes, depending on the nature of the feelings. But more important is the general recognition that emotions are useful and serve adaptive purposes.

Why do people have emotions and feelings? What good are they? Perhaps here the analogy with pain is important. We know by the nature of their crude nervous system that certain lower forms of life cannot experience emotions. They have no brain or central nervous system. They do, however, have a built-in stimulus-response mechanism, so that when something noxious is touched an innate and automatic withdrawal mechanism occurs. An emotion therefore is not essential to trigger a protective maneuver. Even when the subjective feeling of pain is present, it need not be the initiator of the response. In simple situations the response is simultaneous with the feeling, or may even precede it. If pain is severe enough, a momentary sense of shock occurs and the pain is not experienced until well after the contact. So if you put your finger to a hot plate, the withdrawal is likely to occur well before the pain is experienced. When the trauma is sufficient, there is often a surprising absence of pain for a few seconds until the overwhelming flood of painful experience occurs.

What is the purpose of that subjective sense of pain—the feeling, if you will? It is a message to the cognitive processes, to the thinking brain and to our intelligence, which is so often wrongfully seen as the opposite of emotion. It is a signal of danger whose purpose is to direct behavior. It is part of the learning experience. While in the extreme case cited it is not needed to effect the protective maneuver, the experience of pain still serves a purpose. It is stored in memory, and in other cases where there are choices it will be recalled. In either case, it is a guide in determining future behavior.

Feelings, therefore, particularly the complex and subtle range of feelings in human beings, are testament to our capacity for choice and learning. Feelings are the instruments of rationality, not—as some would have it—alternatives to it. Because we are intelligent creatures—meaning that we are freed from instinctive and patterned behavior to a degree unparalleled in the animal kingdom—we are capable of, and dependent on, using rational choice to decide our futures. Feelings become guides to that choice. We are not just passive responders, as some lower life forms are, to that which the environment offers us. We can avoid certain conditions, select out others, and anticipate both, and, moreover, via anticipation we can even modify the nature of the environment. Feelings, then, are fine tunings directing the ways in which we will meet and manipulate our environment.

Feelings of anxiety, boredom, tension, and agitation alert us to the sense of something wrong, and, more importantly, by the subtle distinctions of their messages they indicate something of the nature of the impending danger and direct us to specific kinds of adaptive maneuvers to avoid, prevent, or change the incipient threat. Feelings of guilt allow us to model our behavior against certain ideals and register when we have moved away from those ideals, or have not yet achieved them.

Equally important, because of the pain of the emotion, it will—like a thermostatic control—initiate the very process of moving us back closer to the nature of our ideal.

Of course, emotions and feelings can go out of balance. It is the nature of an animal endowed with free will to design his own future—at least in part. But that freedom allows us to design badly—i.e., maladaptively—as well as to design well.

There is also an expressive side to emotions, and while I am not primarily dealing with that aspect—the part of emotion that is visualized by others—it is important here to see that, like feeling, it also serves a purpose. The affects, in allowing others to view our emotional state, transfer one individual's experience to the group at large and by so doing enhance group survival.

The contagious nature of emotion is essential to a group animal like *Homo sapiens;* it allows us, with our feelings, to forewarn those around us. Each individual becomes an extension of the group, serving the mutual needs of the whole. If one lone "scout" perceives a danger, his very emotion advertises the fact. Words are not necessary. Affects are simple alternatives to the spoken word and, as such, the "language" of most herding animals. When one member perceives that which the group has yet to perceive, it serves as an early-warning system.

While we are not technically herding animals, like cattle or sheep, we are also not isolates. We must live in groups; other people are like nutrients for us, and are absolutely essential for our survival. Certain feelings like shame force us to forgo selfish pleasures for the benefit of the group at large. They indicate our unwitting sense that all individual survival is dependent on, and therefore must defer to, group survival. Even without knowing why, we respond to the feelings of others. Emotions are contagious. Anxiety moves like a ripple through a crowd. Tears evoke tears, even when the content or cause of the original distress is unknown.

Because of the public function of emotions, their absence

also seems to be important. Certain conditions call for a response. When it is not forthcoming, we question the significance or importance of the event. We do want signs from the people around us. The absence of an emotional response where it is expected seems to diminish the importance of the event. A poignant metaphoric expression of this is seen in Larry Woiwode's description of a young man burying his father on an isolated Midwestern farm. He lays out the body himself, tends it himself, builds the coffin, all the while attempting to cope with his father's death. Alone with his sister and the hired hand (no mourners are present), he prepares to seal the coffin and lower it into the grave.

Charles stared at the coffin lid, at the crucifix, the oval with his father's name countersunk into it, at the nails along the lid, each with its black shadow, at the hammer beside the lid, and felt such an uncharacteristic and malevolent bitterness that he had to lock his knees to feel his legs beneath him. He wanted to see lightning across the entire sky, a violent storm, falling snow, or a dove burst from his father's breast and fly off from the coffin—some sign that his father's life and good deeds had not gone unnoticed on earth, not for his father's sake or his own sake, but so his sons and daughters would always feel he believed in a just and reasonable God.*

In such a way we judge the importance of our activities. We want to feel pride and joy, but we also want to sense others' delight, love, appreciation, and respect. Emotions, then, are not just directives to ourselves, but directives from others to us, indicating that we have been seen; that we have been understood; that we have been appreciated; that we have made contact.

Unfortunately, we are confused about the very purpose and value of emotion. We have gotten into the bind of not being sure whether the healthy person is emotion-free, emotionally

---

* Larry Woiwode, *Beyond the Bedroom Wall: A Family Album* (New York: Farrar, Straus & Giroux, 1975), p. 55.

open, a person with minimal emotion, or a person with certain select emotions. We are often ashamed of the wrong emotions. In our concern for power and assertion, we overvalue rage and demean guilt.

Granted the importance of emotions and our confusion about them, they are worth a reexamination, particularly that elusive, neglected aspect of emotions called "feelings." To do so, we must fly in the face of the experts' advice—eschew objective analysis and return to the shadow world of the inexact, the poetic, and the subjective. What is necessary, then, is to start the process over again, return to the period before the scientific revolution of the late nineteenth century to attempt once again a descriptive approach to feelings.

When researchers utilize such an approach, they often defensively employ impressive jargon to describe these methods—to no avail. What they describe as "phenomenological" is inevitably labeled "anecdotal" or "subjective" by their critics anyhow. It is time to unapologetically acknowledge that the anecdotal and the descriptive can be worthy, respectable, and in some areas absolutely essential.

Feelings are mushy, difficult, non-palpable, slippery things even by definition. In that sense they are immune to the kind of analysis to which most behavior is typically exposed. They are difficult to quantify, difficult to communicate, difficult even to distinguish within ourselves one from the other. With feelings, there is also a sloppiness in public usage that follows closely on the difficulty of definition. People know how they feel, and therefore assume that others feel the same. Communication, they assume, need only be suggested, so the language of feelings is imprecise to the point of making generalization hazardous.

In order to overcome this, we resort to drawing on shared experience, thus avoiding the labeling process altogether. People use the expression "You know how you feel when . . ." But it is intriguing to find out how often people do *not* agree "how they feel when," and how they even confuse and misunderstand the nature of the emotion they may be experiencing.

The degree of misunderstanding tends to vary with the emotion. Most people recognize fear. On the other hand, as a psychoanalyst, I have noticed how often people seem visibly and obviously angry, and yet have no genuine awareness that they are angry; or, worse, they misinterpret their anger for another emotion. It is not uncommon to hear a clearly angry patient talk about feeling "agitated" or "anxious." One patient when angry felt a unique kind of internal "pressure" of the most unpleasant sort, which he assumed to be some form of abdominal spasm. He could not "honestly say that it was painful"; "gnawing, unpleasant" were close. "Something akin to hunger," he once said. This was as near to acknowledgment of the emotional state that this reserved man could allow. In time, it became clear that this emotion, perceived as a physiological and physical phenomenon, was indeed anger that he somehow denied entrance into his world of recognition.

When we leave the more basic and primitive emotions and enter into the range of more subtle, more specifically and exclusively human emotions, of shame, embarrassment, guilt, pride, and so forth, we find how confused people are in the labeling of even their own feelings.

In this book, my primary concern, then, is not the emotions but the feelings, and even here not the grand passions but the small ones. Out of the dozens of complex feelings that shape and define the elegant range of human sensation, I have taken a select group for primary analysis. It is not intended to be an exhaustive list. I have divided the feelings into three groups. The first represents that range of feelings which direct us toward individual survival and the obligations of group living. One significant feeling that certainly has pre-eminence in this group is that of anger. It was omitted because it, indeed, has been attended to and addressed with adequacy and completeness in both technical and general literature. If anything, in recent times it has been elevated to a primacy which distorts its role in the balance of feelings.

The second group is representative of that category of feelings which warn us of malfunction. They are the indicators that we are not achieving our goals, not serving our ends, or are depleting our resources. They are cautionary, warning, and directive to attend to a way of life that needs modification.

The third set of emotions includes those that acknowledge the fact that survival of the individual and the group must have meaning beyond the mere fact of surviving. Life is to be enjoyed, not simply endured. Pleasure and goodness and joy support the pursuit of survival.

In each of the groups there are of course many and diverse feelings which warrant evaluation. These represent a beginning—and, as such, a selection. The more psychoanalytically oriented may see in my selection a reflection of my personal taste, and perhaps so. With this in mind I was surprised and somewhat distressed to find that I seem more involved with painful feelings than joyous ones. I was not comforted when I realized that in Descartes's list of six primitive emotions—admiration, love, hate, desire, joy, and sadness—at least four are positive. To protect my own pride, I therefore turn to other possible explanations for this selection beyond a personal proclivity toward pain, which I am reluctant to embrace.

Perhaps it is not a reflection on my psyche, but a reflection on our time. Perhaps the twentieth century lends itself better to pain than to pleasure.

Or perhaps it is the psychiatric tradition from which I come. We are part of the larger field of medicine, and medicine in general moves more comfortably amid pain than pleasure. Health is, after all, only the ideal of medicine. Disease is its business.

Or perhaps it is simply that the ways of pain are more varied than the ways of pleasure. This is not to deny some variability in the experiencing of pleasure. Surely there are recognizable differences in the quality of good feelings: there is that cluster of feelings around pride; another cluster around joy; and at least a third cluster around loving. But generally speaking, when we feel good, we feel good. There are some differences of modality in feeling good, and of context, but the feeling of goodness is a diffuse phenomenon, a feeling that crosses over even the few arbitrary divisions afforded it.

In sharp contrast there is a large repertoire of ways of feeling bad, all discreet and different. Guilt is no better, or worse, or more tolerable, or less intense than despair. But guilt and despair are different. Rage can consume us as equally as terror—but we do not equate them. The tortures of the negative emotions are unique, disparate, and idiosyncratic.

With the negative feelings, quantity also seems more important. There is a direct continuum in the good feelings. A little bit of joy is welcome, and a little more, more welcome. If one thinks of negative feelings, they seem to change character with intensity. Quantity alters quality. A certain amount of fear can almost be fun. Pregame anxiety for a competitive athlete, while still anxiety, is an excitement he often relishes and is obviously quite different from the intense fear of the nightmare.

Finally, it may simply be that evil is more interesting than goodness, or simply easier to talk about. At any rate, I will occupy myself only with the small passions, the feelings of everyday life, approaching them descriptively, subjectively, and speculatively—taking care to end with feeling good.

PART I

Signals for Survival

Serving Self and Group

Feeling Anxious

ൟ 1

FEAR IN ANY OF ITS MANIFESTATIONS is the ideal area in which to begin to examine feelings. In practical example it readily demonstrates the uses of emotions that previously have been described only theoretically. That we have all known fear compensates somewhat for the absence of objective means of defining it. Nonetheless, incredible difficulty exists in communicating even so commonly experienced a feeling. The dictionary helps us to a certain degree by showing common roots and by relating it to common synonyms. We still remain like a group of blind people exchanging their ideas about color. The blind can exchange all the information they wish on places in the spectrum of various colors and they are still not sure that the experience of color exists or that if it does exist, it is a shared experience. The ultimate test—the "You know how you feel when . . ."—assumes that there is a commonness of experience, and that we tend to feel the same in similar situations. With anxiety we feel most confidently so. In dealing with anxiety an author at least has the reassurance that every one of his readers has not only experienced it but probably recognizes the feeling.

The word "anxiety" has become confused. It has so many meanings in so many languages, compounded by bad usage and bad translation, that in some circles it has simply come to be a synonym for the generic term "fear." Much of the trouble probably arose from the early translation of Freud in which the German word *Angst* was translated into "anxiety" on the basis of its derivative rather than its emotional implication. The real meaning of *Angst* is closer to our concept of terror. Think of a nightmare. To describe that terror as anxiety, or anxiousness, seems inadequate. It is too pale and small. It is inappropriate. Unfortunately, the popularization of psychoanalysis has introduced into common parlance such terms as "castration anxiety" and "separation anxiety," thus further confusing the language of emotion.

If one looks beyond popular usage and into semantic roots, again there is not much objective help. The mere fact that "anguish" and "anxious" are etymologically related shows us the limit of this approach. When you feel anxious, you do not feel anguished. I feel safe in assuming across these pages that those two words are as disparate and distinct in your experience as in mine, even though neither of us may be capable of articulating an objective distinction.

In addition, English is such a deliciously complex and undisciplined language, we can bend, fuse, distort words to all our purposes. We give old words new meanings, and we borrow new words from any language that intrudes into our intellectual environment. The one definitive aspect of anxiety is that it is a component of fear; a special kind, occurring in a special way and reserved for special situational usage. Even here there are some complications. We have come to use anxious in a non-fearful way, as in "I'm anxious to start my vacation." While popular usage seems to have accepted "anxious" here, most of us would prefer to use "eager" in this context.

Since anxiousness is a component of fear, let us look at the broader emotion *per se*. There are of course different qualities of fears and different quantities, and as I suggested before, the quantitative distinction in many of the emotions makes a qualitative difference. With the richness of the English language, we are free to range from trepidation to terror, from dismay to dread, from perturbation to panic, from anxiety to alarm. But the basic emotion that all these words modify is fear.

Fear and anger are generally viewed as the two basic emotions to support our behavior in emergencies. They are part of the biological response mechanisms built into each human animal to enhance survival. They are the servants of security.

Fear and anger are emotions which we share with most of the higher animals—not with all animals, however, for a certain developmental level must be reached before one can experience even fear.

Distance yourself from your own experiences for a moment and try to visualize what life must be like for the simplest creature on earth, the amoeba, a one-celled animal, which has managed to have a survival mechanism—as simple as it is— that puts to shame its more complicated relatives. The amoeba, it is fair to assume, is free of emotions. It survives by ingesting particles around it in a haphazard fashion and with less discrimination than the most indiscriminate adolescent. That which is nutrient is broken down and absorbed; that which is noxious is repelled and rejected.

As one moves up the scale of animals, one sees an increasingly complicated regulating mechanism, built on pain and pleasure, which helps to insure survival of the organism. In order to distinguish between pain and pleasure, one requires an increasingly elaborate nervous system with receptors and mediating organisms.

The pain-pleasure apparatus regulates survival by serving as indicators of proper adaptive behavior. These go beyond sensations; telling us what is good (lifesaving) and what is bad— they direct us to the proper course. That which is painful is survival-endangering, and we avoid it, and that which is pleasurable is survival-enhancing, and we seek it.

It is not necessary to anticipate an intelligent design in this, although one is free to do so. One can simply recognize the Darwinian principle of selection. An animal could have developed in which destructive impulses were enjoyable and nourishing, and sustaining ones were disgusting. In that case he would not have long survived. To a certain extent one can postulate that our technological society is leading the human creature to such an end—and to the degree that is true we are in for trouble.

Pain and pleasure, then, are the common mediators of survival in many forms of animals. To call it pain and pleasure— in some of the lower animals, at least—is to indulge in projection of our own feelings. The fact that an animal will avoid a noxious stimulus does not necessarily imply any perception of what we would call pain. It is unlikely, for example, that the oyster we swallow feels distress even as he is being digested. Indeed, such tropisms and avoidances occur in plants, and we do not ascribe to them sensual perception. It is survival, not vanity, that directs the flower to the sun.

It is probably reasonable to assume that pain occurs somewhat lower in the animal line than does pleasure. Pain, however, is still not fear. Pain requires immediate contact and, as such, it may help one avoid ingesting the wrong things, but it is not much help in avoiding one's being ingested. Pain has limited escape value. By the time the jaws of the predator are on us so that we can feel the pain, the perception does us little good. There must be some way to anticipate the predator, as there must similarly be some way beyond the willy-nilly meandering of the amoeba to direct our search for nourishment. With the emergence of senses of smell, audition, and vision, the so-called distance receptors (as distinguished from touch and pain, which require actual contact), we gain this edge in the battles of survival. These distance receptors allow us to locate, before physical contact, that which is about to destroy us or be destroyed by us. They enlarge our environment; they expand our awareness, and improve our control over an increasingly bigger and bigger world. Distance receptors make possible anticipation. And anticipation is an incredible instrument in the struggle for survival.

When can we assume an animal is capable of feeling fear? The first essential is the biological development of distant receptors. Fear, then, is the anticipation of a painful—in the broadest sense of that word—experience.

The feeling of fear is one part of the larger emotional complex which mobilizes the individual for action. When we feel fear of a potential impending disaster, the feeling is part of a set of multiple physiological changes that prepare us for either flight from the danger or an attack on it. This concept of a fight-flight mechanism as an inbuilt part of the emergency response of the organism was most eloquently expressed in the pioneering work of the American physiologist Walter Cannon. It led us to greater understanding of stress reactions and a recognition of the positive value of even so-called negative emotions. Many of these responses are controlled through the mediation of the autonomic nervous system.

Within the human organism, a whole set of responses is under direct voluntary control. This is a system that serves our conscious needs. As you turn the page of the book, an automatic set of responses is directed by you to muscles to be flexed in the fingers and others to be extended to perform the act. Even though this is done automatically, it is part of what we call the voluntary system. But in addition, if a light is dimming in the room as you read, the dilatation of the pupils that accommodates for this is automatically directed by a largely involuntary system of neuro-control mechanisms called the autonomic system. It is the autonomic system that determines that adrenalin be pumped into your blood, palms get sweaty, pupils dilate, blood flow be redirected, sphincters controlled during moments of fear.

All of these responses facilitated survival in that primitive stage of our cultural development when life depended on fight or flight. It is, of course, not just man that experiences fear or has autonomic systems. To observe a cat threatened by a dog is to be able to visualize objectively much of the function of an autonomic system, albeit only that of the external body: the arching of the back, the crouching for flight, the dilation of the pupils—all are conducted mechanically and involuntarily as part of the alerting fear mechanism. The feeling of the emotion is but one aspect of the total response.

To feel anxious is somewhat different, however, from feeling frightened, and it is anxiety which is our concern here. Fear tends to be direct, object or event oriented, specific, and conscious. When we feel anxious, it is usually vague and indirect, with no particular source, and more unconsciously oriented. It is not only that anxiousness is generally a slighter emotion than some of the other descriptive components of fear; the context in which it will arise, and the quality of the feeling, and the conditions to which it directs us are all different. Think of another small derivative of fear—worry. When we feel the same quantitative equivalence of anxiety, but in relationship to a specific known subject, we tend, I think, to use the word "worry." When we do not know why we are anxious, and someone reminds us of the impending airplane flight tomorrow, the emotion of anxiety becomes fixed to the subject, and then we tend to switch to the use of the word "worry." Of course, all these generalizations are subject to the idiosyncrasies of each person's vocabulary, so we tend to talk interchangeably about being anxious or worried. Most of us, however, tend to worry *about* something, whereas we tend to feel anxious in that vague, disturbing way that almost hungers for a subject of attachment.

Worry is easier to handle. We can tell ourselves to stop worrying because it *is* about something. It is harder to direct ourselves to stop feeling anxious when the emotion seems so arbitrary and unfocused. Worry we can all understand, particularly when it is about such universals as health, money, success, and love. Anxiousness, with its lack of a specific contextual focus, seems more mysterious—and we may find our anxiety worrisome. To understand the sources of anxiety, we must examine some aspects of the human condition.

There are so many ways in which man is unique from all the lower forms of animals, and almost all of them make us uniquely susceptible to feelings of anxiousness. Our imagination and reasoning powers facilitate anxiety; the anxious feeling is precipitated not by an absolute impending threat—such as the worry about an examination, a speech, travel—but rather by the symbolic and often unconscious representations. We do not have to be experiencing a potential danger. We can experience something related to it. We can recall, through our incredible memories, the original symbolic sense of vulnerability in childhood and suffer the feeling attached to that. We can even recall the original memory and still be stuck with the emotion— which is then compounded by its seemingly irrational quality at this time. It is not just the fear of death which pains us, but the anticipation of it; or the anniversary of a specific death; or a street, a hospital, a time of day, a color, a flower, a symbol associated with a death.

The capacity for symbol formation permits us to learn from the past, but also to anticipate the future. It is the foundation of so much that makes our humanness. Speech and language are facilitated by this capacity for symbolization. It is an extraordinarily useful adaptive device. We need not wait for the predator to charge us; we need not even wait to see it on the horizon. We can utilize symbols, signs, or antecedents of the event as though they were the actual occurrences.

Of course, this is a mixed blessing. Often what we see as the symbol of the danger is not a true prediction, but represents a distortion introduced by our own past and our own sensitivities. If we have experienced something too strongly in the past, we may anticipate it where we ought not, and perceive it where it does not exist. If, for example, we were intimidated by a punitive father who terrified us, we may approach *all* authority figures with the bias of that early dominant memory. The memory of that authority may possess a greater reality to us than the actual authority figure with whom we were involved. Regardless of how gentle and unchallenging the authority figure is, we may approach each teacher, each employer as though he had both the power and the personality of that dominant father who once ruled our life.

Because of this particular capacity to recall sharply our past and to construct a future based on the symbolic meanings of that past, we each occupy a different—even when shared— present. No individual ever quite experiences the same environmental stimuli as that person standing near him who seems to be occupying the same time and space. For this and related reasons, human responses will never be predictable by computer, and are never completely predictable by psychologists or psychiatrists. Each stimulus has very special, often ineluctable meanings when viewed through the complex, distorting lens of our past environments and experience.

The same capacity for symbolization permits an anticipation of the future unparalleled among animals. Such anticipation allows for strength and stability beyond sheer weight, size, and normal power. The obvious advantages of anticipation and prediction in matters of survival are not only to prepare ourselves for the assault or run from it, but indeed to modify the situation so there is no assault at all. We can build defenses, institute preventive measures (quench the fire, dam the stream, support the collapsing tree, mollify the antagonist, ingratiate the boss, lie, cajole, seduce, and so on). Unlike most animals, who use their anticipation only for fight or flight—i.e., to escape or conquer a fixed reality—we have the recourse of changing the reality itself. We are in a sense, therefore, co-authors with nature (and chance) of our future; we are not merely passive subjects of it.

Our intelligence is that step beyond distance receptors. As distance receptors gave us an advantage over simple tactile responses, intelligence can be seen as super-distance receptors. Our imagination, our synthetic reasoning, permits us even during periods of maximum security to anticipate danger; to recognize that there are seasons, that the balm and security of summer will, in a fixed period of time, inevitably give way to the cold threats of winter. And because of our intelligence and imagination we need not see the first frost before we store the harvest.

Like the other great adaptive maneuvers, this also leaves us vulnerable to false alarms. What we anticipate may be false. The anxiety we feel may be triggered by an unreal danger, an echo of a similar but not identical situation from the past whose relevance no longer operates. And the future we fear may only be of our imagination. It may once again be a product of distortions from our past. We may end up "protecting" ourselves against that which will never come.

> I always have felt strange when we come home
> To the dark house after so long an absence
> And the key rattled loudly into place
> Seemed to warn someone to be getting out
> At one door as we entered at another.*

This vague feeling of fear, particularly when unprovoked, is a classic example of feeling anxious.

When the same self-generated emotion is more intense, "anx-

---

* Robert Frost, "The Fear," *Collected Poems* (New York: Henry Holt & Co., 1930), p. 112.

iety" seems an inappropriate term. Jane Eyre, locked in a room she believes haunted, sees a beam of light which she assumes to be a ghost.

My heart beat thick, my head grew hot; a sound filled my ears, which I deemed the rushing of wings; something seemed near me; I was oppressed, suffocated; endurance broke down; I rushed to the door and shook the lock in desperate effort.*

No one would describe Jane as anxious—the emotion is too intense. It is horror that she is experiencing.

We do, then, live in a world partly of our own creation— not just in our imagination.

We are capable of actually facilitating that which we dread through defensive maneuvers that are both unnecessary and self-destructive. The suspicious, paranoid person, always expecting to be taken advantage of, always assuming he is, whether he is or not, eventually invites exploitation. He asks for it—and we are inclined to oblige.

Because we have the power to create the world that we will be forced to live in, our anticipation can be a dangerous instrument. The effectiveness of our defensive maneuvers is one of the simplest distinctions between neurosis and health. The mechanisms of both are the same. It is the adaptive value of the mechanism in influencing our future that decides whether we will call it healthy or not.

While all forms of fear are future-oriented, the vague feeling of anxiousness with which we are concerned, this non-specific emotion which often baffles us, is as equally past-oriented as future-oriented. We may be anxious in anticipation of some future danger, but how we define or visualize that danger is often shaped by the lessons of our early past. In the conditions of modern society most anxiety is not generated by the anticipation of an actual danger in the environment. We do not feel

---

* Charlotte Brontë, *Jane Eyre* (New York: W. W. Norton & Co., 1971), p. 14.

threatened by the specific presence of the predator; our culture has already removed most of the predators except those of our own kind. More often than not, anxiety is generated from a change in our sense of self, rather than a change in the environment. In a world where survival is always seen as a struggle, and in which some pitfalls always exist, if something brings into question our confidence in our own coping ability, it will threaten our safety.

We need not see any actual danger or threat, then, but can feel anxious simply by recognizing certain shifts in the power balances in the world in which we operate. Anything which weakens us, which threatens our sense of our own strength, which attacks our pride, our self-confidence, and our self-esteem, can be seen as making us more helpless and more vulnerable. To understand why we feel anxious in non-threatening situations, we must understand those conditions of early-childhood experiences which dominate our unconscious and our memory.

The term "castration anxiety" pervades much of the psychoanalytic literature and has become a cliché of everyday life. It is grossly misunderstood, because psychoanalysts in communicating among themselves will use a shorthand which, when taken literally, is at best an oversimplification and at worst not at all what they intended to say. Obviously, any young man seeing someone approaching his genitals with a carving knife will feel castration terror. To use a word like "anxiety" at that time becomes ludicrous. The term "castration anxiety," as it is currently used, covers the entire gamut of threats to our potency and power. It is a term which inevitably derived from a male-dominant society. To be a "man" is to be strong and powerful. To lose your manhood is to lose position and power. The ultimate instrument of power and dominance is symbolized by the male genital; the ultimate reduction is the removal from the masculine role.

Castration anxiety, therefore, has come to be used, for male or female, as a sense of some threat to competitive and survival powers. Anything that seems to diminish us—our strength, our intelligence, our security—will produce anxiety. We feel anxiety about job performance because money is social position, is power, is survival in our society. A man may feel anxious over a receding hairline because of what aging usually means in the whole power position of the business or professional world in which he operates. A woman is intimidated by aging because what money has been to the man, beauty has traditionally been to her—the leverage point for social gain and social acceptance.

The threat that produces anxiety may be as indirect as an invitation not received, an offer not made. The threat may be even more indirect. It may not even be addressed to us, but to our kind or our category. The first heart attack in that forty-year-old age group threatens every colleague of the man who has it. It is a reminder of their weakness and vulnerability. Therefore, any of the symbolic indirect events of the day which threaten us either directly or indirectly by analogy can produce that vague and strange sense of anxiousness. "I don't know why I feel so anxious today" is the most common plaint about anxiety.

Another strong focus about which anxiety can polarize—beyond power and strength, but also drawn from our earliest experience—is the concept of approval and acceptance. This has been traditionally listed by psychiatrists as a derivative of separation anxiety. It really precedes castration anxiety. Historically, the first organized sense of fear we experience is probably related to separation. One of the earliest lessons we learn is that weakness does not mean destruction, for were that so, none of us would have survived. We are born incredibly weak, and will remain so for a long period of time.

Biologists have long remarked at how strikingly different human development is from that of all other species. Relatively uncomplicated, undifferentiated animals are born with a short gestation period and are born ready to face life alone. Generally speaking, the more complicated the animal the longer the gestation period, so that by the time we reach the relatively high mammals we have—as in the case of the elephant—a gestation period of twenty-two months. But man, the most complicated of the animals, has a relatively short gestation period. Beyond that, he will be born, unlike most mammals, in a ridiculously helpless state.

How is it that man is born so helpless and with practically no instinctual capacities for survival? It is part of that necessary combination which also gives us our intelligence and imagination, the extraordinary human brain. The brain, necessary to encompass the demands of humanity, is, by normal animal standards, enormous. It weighs roughly 350 grams (¾ pound) at birth, but by the end of the first year of life it will be fully 825 grams (1½ pounds)! If the fetus is not delivered—ready or not—that huge head will not be able to pass through the relatively narrow pelvis supplied the mother by our developmental "decision" to adopt an erect posture. Even though at nine months the animal is but a helpless fetus, it is essential that that fetus be delivered into the real world unprepared. This means that by comparison with all other animals it is born at incredible disadvantage—shockingly vulnerable and helpless.

Many biologists consider gestation to continue beyond the point of actual birth; they speak of the first year of life as an extrauterine fetal year. But surely that defines a strange kind of gestation, for it is the gestation of an *aware* fetus who, while helpless to act, is not helpless to perceive and is managing to learn lessons he will never forget—lessons that will dominate his adult behavior. And among those lessons the most crucial is the link between helplessness, care, and survival.

If we return once again to the fight-or-flight theory of emergence behavior, we become aware that there is a limitation on this concept when applied to human beings. Neither flight nor fight is an available mechanism of defense or survival for the human infant. The infant obviously cannot perceive his survival in avoiding the source of danger himself. He is often incapable of even recognizing the danger. Just as surely, he cannot possibly see survival in terms of overcoming the danger. Therefore survival is never originally visualized in terms of personal strength. Since that is not the model of early survival, it is unlikely that our first anxieties would be in relation to the diminution of personal strength which never existed at all. The first method of survival is not fight or flight, but clutch or cling.

The infant in the first few weeks of life may not be at all aware of any environment. In this early undifferentiated state where he does not see himself as separated from his environment, he may have some delusional sense of his own power. Indeed, he may think of himself as magically omnipotent. Since all of his needs somehow get satisfied, and since he cannot be aware of the mechanisms that go into his feeding and care, he may assume them to be the magical products of his wishes. He feels the pain of hunger in his belly, screams, and hocus-pocus a flow of warm fluid eases his hunger. The child may see the milk as the *product* of his scream, and himself as the master of his needs.

Once the infant begins the differentiation process of self from environment, he will then have to confront his own helplessness. He is not magically omnipotent. The truth is that he is a totally powerless creature, incapable of insuring any of his creature comforts, let alone the essential needs for his survival. One would expect the poor infant to go into a depression. Indeed, the distinguished British child psychologist, Melanie Klein, assumed he did precisely that.

If the child does despair, he need not. For soon he will recognize the presence in the environment of figures who are powerful. Psychiatrists are apt to see this phase as the period of delegated omnipotence. If I am helpless, the child may feel, those attending me are all-powerful. The parents are the gods of survival. In the following scene, a mother is falling apart from fear. Since she is unable to adjust to a new life without a husband, her anxiety is fast approaching terror. Her fear is contrasted with her symbolic role as a parent.

My spirit I could now measure in grains and it was running out faster and faster onto the sand whereon my house was built instead of rock—well, you understand—real, not pretend problems; no money, and what to do with the babies so I could go to school so I could learn to do something practical so that I could take care of the babies— a circular difficulty seemingly impossible of solution, and the roof of the house, that principal symbolic structure, actually leaked, and all the machines, the washer and toaster, rusted and stopped. . . . There's nothing bleaker than when your machines stop, when even machines desert you, and also the telephone rings in the cold night, and salesmen, somehow knowing about you, seedy salesmen assault the doors. . . . Nothing would work right. A swarm of termites came up one day through the windowsill and lay in the sun shedding their wings. Such arrogance, you are so powerless even frail insects defy you. But my children seemed to trust me as before, held my hands when we crossed the street, didn't seem at all to know I had no powers any more.*

This tendency to romanticize the parents, to see them as all-knowing and all-powerful, extends—in residue, at least— well into childhood. Its presence for so long a time often captivates and deludes the very parents who should know better. They begin to accept the child's adulation as reasonable, and are inevitably unprepared when the sophisticated adolescent begins to withdraw his overvaluations. The parent has been seduced by his own best public-relations man and is unprepared then for the "betrayal" from within. But to return to infancy— in time, the child will begin to see he has, if not direct power, at least derivative power via his influence on these adult figures. After all, it is not sufficient that the parents have the *capacity*

---

* Diane Johnson, *The Shadow Knows* (New York: Alfred A. Knopf, 1975), pp. 102–3.

to supply his needs; they must also be *willing* to supply those needs. The child then learns that their willingness is related to their feelings about him. As long as they love him, cherish him, and value him, they will take care of him. This awareness initiates a set of mental associations which will link dependency—through love—to survival. To be helpless is not necessarily to be in jeopardy. The impotent can be strong if their very helplessness generates protective feelings in the powerful defenders. Thus the power of lovability becomes firmly established in the child's mind.

The abiding lesson of the first year of life is that he who is loved is safe. Our power is a vicarious one expressed in our capacity to endear or ingratiate that all-powerful figure, the parent. If that is so, then the first fear experienced by the individual in relationship to his environment must be separation anxiety. The most dangerous thing is not to be weak, but to be unloved.

Separation from our loving protectors will continue through childhood to be a major source of fear and anxiety. Think of the poignant scenes that inevitably occur on the first day of class at nursery schools and kindergartens. If separation from those who love us produces insecurity, it is compounded if we fear there is no one who loves us.

Unlovability becomes the second major focus in adult life for events that instill feelings of insecurity and anxiousness. All that is necessary is the most fleeting, the most imagined, the most derivative, the most incidental, the most accidental, the most insignificant of assaults on the sense of our lovability to engender feelings of anxiety.

Why in the world should you feel anxious when you have been criticized with the full knowledge that the criticism is wrong? If survival were dependent only on your capacities and abilities, they would not be undermined, but if it is dependent in some way on approval by the group or representatives of the group, then it matters not that their judgment is wrong.

It is the judgment that threatens your survival, not the fact.

Obviously, certain personality types are more dependent than others on these cues of survival and worth. To some, at the most extreme, it is not necessary that a negative response of worth be directed to them. Their own sense of vulnerability is so great, their sense of passivity is so entrenched, they need a constant stream of reassurance from the environment—a procession of signs of affection and approval—to sustain them through the day. Any interruption in the flow of approval is like cutting the current on a respirator case. They are the applause seekers of the world, and it is not surprising that actors, fairly or not, have been characterized as being so in high order. The current popular term in psychoanalysis "narcissism" includes, among others of its aspects, such needs for external approval. "Narcissism" is a peculiar word, with its implication of self-love. More often than not, it is quite the opposite. It is because of the absence of self-love that constant reassurance, center-stage seeking, the public declaration of approvability, and insistent focus on self are necessary. The "Look at me, Ma" phenomenon is the sign of the immature and insecure, not the self-loving.

Disapproval, even simply absence of positive signs of approval, then, can be seen like signs of weakness, as increasing our vulnerability. As such, they generate anxiety.

The third source of our everyday anxiety stems from the awareness of our inevitable vulnerability. By mere dint of being a human being, we are aware of all the inherent problems of our species, independent of any specific threat. Unlike God or the amoeba, we are not immortal. We share with the large range of creatures in between the fact of a limited existence. But, unlike any of the other creatures doomed to the same fate of a short term on earth, we alone are aware of the ephemeral nature of our existence. Our capacity to anticipate serves us perhaps least well in the capacity to visualize our own death.

It is unlikely that any other animal has a sense of personal mortality. It is a crushing burden for many of us. So much so that the most common means of handling it is by denying the validity of our intelligence. We know that "of course, we are going to die," but operationally we do not know. We do not believe it. "Of all the world's wonders, which is the most wonderful?" the Bhagavad-Gita asks, and answers, "That each man, though he sees others dying all around him, never believes that he himself will die."

We pay a price for this denial. Since we cannot face death where it exists, we see it everywhere else. We see death not directly but "through a glass darkly." We see it "in a handful of dust." We cannot accept this incredible anticlimax of nothingness as the inevitable concluding paragraph of our own lives. It cannot be so. Religion has flourished on the promise that "it really isn't so." Take your pick: reincarnation, Valhalla, fusion with Christ. Each promises that there is no end, only a transition. Indeed, each tends to promise an appreciative change and so, like Old Black Joe, we will only be "gone from this earth, to a better land."

And yet the existential anxiety tends to break through. Those things which remind us of our vulnerability produce anxiousness not just because of the insecurity of our role in life but because of the limitations of that role with its implied dreadful end. To be sick is to reduce us to the role of a child and to be frightened, again, not merely because it reminds us of our helplessness but because it goes beyond and reminds us of our ultimate personal finitude.

Anxiety from other sources can—at least to a certain degree—be alleviated by locating the source of the feeling. Since much of the source of our anxiety is symbolic and irrational, the mere identification dissipates the emotion. Sometimes, even without such conscious discovery, we will unconsciously direct ourselves to activities which alleviate the threat by reassurance. With our existential anxiety of death, there are few sources of reassurance. We are here on earth for a limited time, and while time seems unlimited when we are children, the extraordinary brevity becomes apparent to us in our middle years. Here it may be that the only mechanism available to relieve the anxiety is denial. I am not impressed with the current vogue for an almost ruthless insistence on forcing each individual to face the fact of his death. We live in an age that seems to worship candor. Of all the virtues, candor has always seemed to me (with the possible exception of humility) the least attractive. The need to be not merely honest but to impose your awareness of the truth on others is more often an act of violence and aggression than the generous sharing of knowledge that it purports to be.

If denial has its legitimacy anywhere, I suspect it is in the denial of death. I have never been enthusiastic about the potential for such acceptance anyhow, and have found the difficulty somewhat confirmed by recent shifts in attitudes of some thanatologists. It is touching, though regrettable, that the great and gentle champion of truth-telling to the dying, Elisabeth Kübler-Ross, has, in recent years, discovered the afterlife, which to many of us simply seems a return to denial.

Given the changing nature of our world, it would seem we are doomed to lead lives of constant anxiety. And yet for most of us this is not true. We do have mechanisms for avoiding or dissipating anxiety. Despite the fact that much anxiety is unconsciously generated and we are unaware of the sources, we are not defenseless. Obviously, direct assault is not usually possible. Nonetheless, to meet the threats of unconscious automatically determined anxiety, we have unconscious mechanisms of defense. Some work and some do not. When they work, it is well that you not know about them. Insight here can only interfere. When they do not work—i.e., when you pay a bigger price for the defense than for that which is defended against—you have to begin to examine the behavior.

One of the chief ways of handling a fear is to rationalize it. Anxiety, like any fear, is most troublesome when it has the appearance of irrationality, when it seems to be caused by nothing and therefore is inappropriate. With such anxiety, one procedure is to find some cause, even if it is the wrong one. This finding of reasons which are rational and legitimate, even though not correct, is called rationalization. If you are afraid of the elevator, it rarely has much to do with elevation mechanisms. But you can rationalize the fear by stating that twelve hundred people were caught in stalled elevators in 1977, fourteen were killed by falling out of elevators, and so on. But how did you become afraid of elevators in the first place? More often than not, it is a displacement. To feel vague dread, vague fear, vague anxiety of any sort is to leave one defenseless against the sources. To face the true source of our fear may be unbearable because it seems insoluble. (It may be our own aggressiveness we fear.) Better then, when one is feeling anxious, to displace it onto a specific, controllable locus.

This is the mechanism of a phobia, and is seen in its most typical form in the small child who around the age of three to five becomes terrified of the strength and angers of his parent. What in the world is he supposed to do about that? There is no way to conquer *them*. There is no way to win the competitive struggle with the parent. Surely you are smaller and they will destroy you if you allow yourself to be angry with them, but even were you to succeed in destroying them, are they not the bulwarks of your defense, the safeguards of your vulnerability in a hostile world? The power struggle between the child and the parent is always lost by the child, never more so than when the parent allows the child to win. Nor can you avoid the source of anxiety, for it resides in the same persona that you cherish and require.

One of the ways, then, to handle the fear of the parent is to displace it onto a horse, a book, a wolf, the boogeyman, monsters, or what have you. Animal displacements are wonderful. All you need do then to control your anxiety is to make sure to avoid the animal! Displacement not only offers the relief of rationalizing the anxiety—and there is nothing more terrifying than irrational fear—but offers a way of controlling and limiting the fear. How many wolves will a three-year-old encounter in his typical day? The only one he is likely to meet is too preoccupied with Little Red Riding-Hood to attend to him.

Perhaps the most ingenious of solutions to terror and fear are psychotic delusion formations. They are also the most destructive, since they demand a suspension of reality testing. Suppose a man is plagued with irrational terrors of he knows not what. If he delusionally decides that his wife is trying to poison him, the decision offers almost instant relief. No wonder he has been feeling so anxious. He is not crazy—anybody would feel anxious in such circumstances. By doing this he universalizes his experience, thereby making it less onerous. Besides, it is reasonable and rational to be frightened if someone is trying to take your life. He therefore rationalizes the experience, makes it seem reasonable, not crazy. And, finally, he need not feel anxious at all so long as he does not eat at home, or does so with great care and caution. He thereby limits and controls the anxiety by focusing it in one area of life rather than allowing it to spill over and contaminate all areas.

Another device that grants relief from generalized anxiety—somewhat less drastic than delusion formation—is somatization; i.e., the conversion of anxiety into physical symptoms. If we begin to feel the anxiety as though it were the symptoms of a heart attack, a kind of solution to the problem of anxiety is achieved. It rationalizes the anxiety, thereby making it less terrifying. It universalizes it—anyone with heart disease would feel anxious. It dictates certain behavior to limit it: all one need do is go to the doctor, have a checkup and electrocardiogram, and be reassured.

Unfortunately, with the major anxieties such displacements rarely work. Phobias tend to extend until they force the individual into smaller and smaller circles of comfort. There are, however, some individuals with isolated phobias who have found in them a way of life. In these cases, the rash young psychiatrist who goes in to break up a phobia by mechanical means often finds a shattered patient as a result. For the most part, however, phobias and the like work for a limited time and then the anxiety begins to break through. They are then forced to extend the phobia: they start with fear of airplanes, then autos; then simply leaving the house is terrifying. Eventually, the defense becomes worse than the disease.

Short of such symptom formation, these same mechanisms serve us on an *ad hoc* basis with day-to-day anxiety. Since part of what makes everyday anxiety uncomfortable is the unconscious and indeterminate nature of it, the mechanisms previously described provide a focus. Whether the focus is the correct one or not is totally unimportant. It serves to make the anxiety more tolerable. It controls the level of fear. If the incorrect focus resolves the tension without extracting an excessive price in adaptation and adjustment, it serves its purpose. Truth is no particular added virtue here. Since the anxiety itself is often generated by false—i.e., irrational—threats, we must not be fussy in condemning the choice of alleviation.

Beyond these devices for making anxiety seem reasonable, there are in addition mechanisms designed to mitigate the threat by a direct confrontation of its underlying premises. So if the premise is that we are threatened because we are vulnerable (weak, impotent, castrated), one means of controlling it is to do something—anything—to establish our efficiency and strength: we can seek reassurance from friends; get involved with an activity in which we have a sense of proven superiority; spend money with a certain degree of extravagance, thereby implying both our worth and our power emanating from the purse.

Spending money is a particularly gratifying means to alleviate anxiety, especially popular in our country. It seems to straddle both the threats-from-separation anxiety and the castration anxiety. To spend money you have to have it. And to spend money on yourself is a means of proving your lovability by receiving a "gift"—if only from yourself. If one is to judge by the crowds seen—at least in the New York area—in the department stores which are now open on most major holidays, spending money has to be listed as one of the leading entertainments of the American population.

Two other mechanisms particularly suited for self-reassurance during moments of anxiety involve oral gratification and sexual gratification. There is no question that sex is one of the great palliatives. Much of the sexual activity of both men and women these days is designed not just for sexual pleasure but to prove worth, lovability, and entitlement. Even in the days before our more libertarian attitude toward sexual activities, masturbation was a popular tranquilizer and the leading non-prescription soporific—and still one of the best. Masturbation is probably more often used as a means of allaying anxieties than as a gratification of the sexual impulse. The idea to masturbate often intrudes on a worried mind well before any sexual passion is present.

Oral gratification is another great favorite ataractic. The close association between feeling, sucking, and mouthing and the early-dependency period is obvious. The child at the breast is the ultimate symbol of peace and contentment, security and love. It is no wonder, then, that in moments of tension and anxiety orality of one sort or another is seen as both a sign of safety and a sign of worth. Perhaps the most prevalent way of relieving anxiety is to stuff something in your mouth. It explains in great part the obesity of the population at large as well as the popularity of so many worthless drugs.

Feeding is, in addition, a form of self-reward. It is not just chance that people on diets have specific hungers usually involving treats and sweets. It is a proving of our worthiness by resorting to the rewards of childhood. The nipple, the thumb, the pacifier, and the cigarette represent the direct line of primitive, infantile reassurance. It is interesting to see the sophistication of cigarette advertisers preying on the insecurity of the adolescent. It is paradoxical that in most of this advertising the vestigial behavior left over from the sucking infants is usually sold commercially to the gullible susceptible adolescent boy as a sign of manhood and power. The cigarette is of course, not an extra phallus, merely an adult pacifier.

Finally, what is to be made of those specific behaviors—seemingly so irrational to others—of driving ourselves into trivial work in an obsessive attempt to afford relief from anxiety? Shining shoes, the polishing of cars, tidying the house, straightening up drawers, fixing the desk, even scrubbing floors and washing windows, while usually seen as drudge operations, are often sought out by individuals. In certain times of tension these spit-and-polish activities offer a degree of relaxation. It is not just chance that they tend to be exactly the kinds of cleanliness behavior that guaranteed the approval of certain loving parents.

We must also remember that anxiety and "tension" do often serve to drive one into concrete and productive work habits. Certain students are aware they must first build a level of anxiety before they can begin studying. And certain writers find that after every pencil in the house is sharpened, and the desk has been cleansed like an altar, and when the last research paper has been read, it is only the generation of anxiety that overcomes the resistance to the blank page.

Anxiety is a primary signal of potential distress; it is a directive to action; it is a serviceable instrument of adaptation. Sometimes, however, anxiety can spill over and actually diminish our adaptive capacity and deprive us of the pleasure of existence. Then we are dealing with pathological anxiety. This is a clinical condition and not to be taken lightly. But here we are talking about feelings, the small passions that are part of the fabric of our unpredictable lives. These anxieties will never be completely assuaged, nor should they be. Only the kind of predictability of fixed instinctual life allows for an anxiety-free existence. Anxiety is a product of and a tribute to our imagination, our intelligence, our memory, our individuality, our courage, our variability, our power, and our uniqueness. We endure anxiety for the privilege of freedom. Like most everyday emotions, it serves a purpose. It alerts us, buoys us, and motivates us. Fear and pain are no more enemies than love and pleasure. They are part of the regulating mechanisms necessary in so intricate a function as human life.

~§ 2
Feeling Guilty

I N ONE OF THE RECENT BOOKS supplying prescriptions for happiness, a chapter heading reads: "The Useless Emotions— Guilt and Worry." Since worry here is used to mean all anxiety, the author has managed with this title to dismiss the basic props for individual survival and group responsibility.

Guilt is not only a uniquely human experience; its cultivation in people—along with shame—serves the noblest, most generous and humane character traits that distinguish our species.

We can assume that everyone has felt anxiety; with guilt we are in a different situation. First, there are people who have never experienced the feeling of guilt. They are not, however, the lucky ones, nor are we fortunate in having them in our midst. The failure to feel guilt is the basic flaw in the psychopath, or antisocial person, who is capable of committing crimes of the vilest sort without remorse or contrition.

Another difficulty in writing about guilt is that even those who have experienced the feeling do not readily distinguish it from such differing emotions as fear and anger. In addition, it is confused with certain like emotions (shame and guilty fear), so that people are never quite sure—in feeling as well as usage—whether they are experiencing guilt or the related emotions. Again, a rush to the dictionary is no help. Quite to the contrary, it may confound you. It was with some chagrin that after having already completed a paper on conscience in which I talked about the feeling of guilt, I discovered that the most intimidating and authoritative of lexicons, the Oxford English Dictionary, does not allow that guilt *is* an emotion. I was chastised by the O.E.D., which in its usual generous way acknowledged dozens of definitions of guilt, none of which included the emotional state. It sees guilt exclusively as an act or state of wrongdoing: a failure, offense, crime, delinquency, a culpability—not an emotion! It specifically cautions against "misuse for 'sense of guilt.'" As is its wont, it then cites for eternal shame down through the centuries a Reverend Tillotson, who committed the error of confusing the state of guilt with the sense of guilt—i.e., the feeling. In this case, I stand with Reverend Tillotson, rather than the O.E.D., and I will accept his definition of guilt as "nothing else but trouble arising in our mind from our consciousness of having done contrary to what we are verily perswaded was our Duty."

What, then, is the feeling of guilt? More often than not, it is confused with two other closely related emotions. One is shame (which I will deal with later), and the second is something that is best called "guilty fear." If you were to ask a typical group of people to define a situation in which they recently felt guilty, it is probable that at least half would not describe guilt, but rather guilty fear. I have tried this experiment in classrooms and social situations and the results were always the same. Some of the answers that indicate guilty fear are the "I was caught in the act of" category. A larger percentage might be classified as the "I was about to be caught." Everyone knows that panicky feeling when we are in the process of an immoral, illegal, or disapproved action, and we feel the hot breath of authority down our necks. When we assume that we will be imminently apprehended, we have this rush of sickening feeling which is not guilt, but guilty fear. The primary emotion is fear. It is *guilty* fear because it is fear that is clearly related to some wrongdoing we acknowledge. If you are casually driving at sixty-five miles per hour (when you know that fifty-five is the legal limit) and suddenly hear the sound of a siren as you catch a glimpse of the highway patrol in your rear-view mirror, that slightly nauseating rush of feeling through your chest is guilty fear. It is fear you are experiencing.

Here "guilt" is only the modifier, the adjective to describe the kind of fear that is felt. If we can experience unjustified fear and irrational fear, we are also free to feel fear which we know stems from our having done something that will elicit punishment. The emotion is related not to the act of having been bad but to the fear of getting what we deserve for it, or fear of getting caught.

To return to that scene on the highway: as you apprehensively watch the approaching police car, you are amazed to find that he passes you by to flag down the Porsche which whizzed past you only moments before. What do you feel? If it is relief, then the emotion experienced with the first sound of the siren was guilty fear. If there are a few strange ones among you who are disappointed, then I grant you felt true guilt.

The distinguishing test between the two is in its relation to exposure and apprehension. When guilty fear alone is present, getting away with it—the avoidance of punishment—brings immediate relief and delight. Guilt, however, wants exposure; it needs expiation and forgiveness.

Maxine Kingston, in her memoir, describes guilt as an unbearably constrictive feeling in her throat. (I myself always experience guilt as a nauseating feeling somewhere between the upper chest, reserved for fear, and the abdomen.) The only relief for this feeling is to confront the individual who is both responsible for the feeling and capable of relieving it—to the child, almost invariably the parent:

. . . I had grown inside me a list of over two hundred things that I had to tell my mother so that she would know the true things about me and to stop the pain in my throat. When I first started counting, I had only thirty-six items. . . . If only I could let my mother know the list, she—and the world—would become more like me, and I would never be alone again. I would pick a time of day when my mother was alone and tell her one item a day; I'd be finished in less than a year. If the telling got excruciating and her anger too bad, I'd tell five items once a week like the Catholic girls; and I'd still be through in a year, maybe ten months. . . . I had decided to start with the earliest item—when I had smashed a spider against the white side of the house: it was the first thing I killed. I said, clearly, "I killed a spider," and it was nothing; she did not hit me or throw hot starch at me. It sounded like nothing to me too. . . . Relieved because she said nothing but only continued squeezing the starch, I went away feeling pretty good. Just two hundred and six more items to go.*

I first realized the oppositional nature of guilty fear to guilt in one of the most vivid memories of early life—involving what I then considered a revelation. Being the eldest of three boys, I was often left "in charge" for small periods of time. Even when not in charge, I would assume authority or privilege. Obviously, as the eldest, I possessed a whole repertoire of tormenting and manipulative devices, and characteristically the only retaliative device of merit left to the younger ones was "I'm going to tell Daddy on you." I remember now with a chilling awareness—although the nature of the heinous crimes I had committed has long since been comfortably forgotten—

---

* Maxine Hong Kingston, *The Woman Warrior: Memoirs of a Girlhood Among Ghosts* (New York: Alfred A. Knopf, 1977), pp. 197, 198, 199.

a moment when my younger brother said precisely that over something evil enough to insure wrath and punishment. I had that sick rushing, chesty feeling which is the mark of guilty fear. At that moment I experienced one of the few epiphanies (if not the only) in my personal life. He is going to tell Daddy that I did that, I thought. But Daddy is not here. I can tell Daddy that I did *not* do it. It had never occurred to me before that reality could be modified, that indeed the past only existed in the relating of it. I had discovered lying! I had such a sense of power, joy, and delight that its parallel in life is hard to recall. A powerful new tool had been handed me. It filled me with an indescribable sense of pleasure and freedom.

Only later in life would I experience true guilt and it is surely not coincidence that it was also in relation to lying; to this day there is nothing that can invoke true guilt more readily in me than telling a lie, even a white lie. One of my first memories of the torture of guilt was when I had lied to that same father, whom I adored and to whom lying was anathema. The Saturday afternoon movies were a tradition for the prepubescents in our neighborhood. Everybody went, and always to the local neighborhood movie (no "big" streets to cross). I had left my sweater at the movies—a reversible tragedy—but somehow when I was asked where my sweater was, I said, "Grandma's." Surely I was old enough to realize that the lie would be exposed. This doting grandmother, after all, was acquainted with my father. It was a gratuitous lie bound to be detected, and about something which could not have concerned my father less. The longest day of my young life was waiting for him to come home so that I could blurt out my confession.

Guilty fear is relieved when the threat of punishment disappears. True guilt seeks, indeed embraces, punishment. Guilt represents the noblest and most painful of struggles. It is between us and ourselves. It is alleviated or mitigated by acts of expiation. Consider that most endearing of Jane Austen's heroines, Emma Woodhouse. She has just been chastised by

Mr. Knightley for being unkind to an admittedly boring and garrulous elderly woman.

> ". . . How could you be so insolent in your wit to a woman of her character, age, and situation? Emma, I had not thought it possible."*

Emma blushes, tries to laugh it off, and attempts to apologize, but before she has an opportunity Mr. Knightley leaves. The frustration at not having the opportunity to acknowledge her wrongdoing leaves her feeling progressively more guilty.

> . . . Never had she felt so agitated, mortified, grieved at any circumstance in her life. . . . The truth of his representation there was no denying. She felt it at her heart. How could she have been so brutal, so cruel to Miss Bates! . . . Time did not compose her. As she reflected more, she seemed but to feel it more.

Poor Emma. All the pleasures of the day seemed only to compound her misery and wretchedness. But finally comfort does come; she discovers expiation! While a whole morning of would-be pleasures caused misery,

> . . . A whole evening of backgammon with her father was felicity to it. *There*, indeed, lay real pleasure, for there she was giving up the sweetest hours of the twenty-four to his comfort. . . .

This is the turning point for this indomitable young woman, and she proceeds to move from guilt into determination.

> Miss Bates should never happen again—no never! If attention in future could do away with past she might hope to be forgiven. She had often been remiss, her conscience told her so; remiss, perhaps, more in thought than fact; scornful, ungracious. But it should be so no more. In the warmth of true contrition she would call upon her the very next morning and it should be the beginning, on her side, of a regular, equal, kindly intercourse.†

---

* Jane Austen, *Emma*, in *The Complete Novels of Jane Austen* (New York: Random House, Modern Library), p. 992.
† Ibid., p. 993.

When guilt is sufficiently extreme, there exists such self-disgust and self-contempt that even the expiation of punishment will not alleviate it. Chekhov expresses it beautifully in this short passage. (Olga Ivanovna is married to a virtuous man who has been a kind and good husband to her. She has been unfaithful to him and she is now watching him die of diphtheria.)

Olga Ivanovna sat in her room and reflected that God was punishing her for deceiving her husband. That silent, uncomplaining, inexplicable man—impersonified, it seemed, on his sofa and suffered alone, uttering no groan. . . . She no longer thought of the moonlight Volga night, the love avowal, the romance of life in the peasant's hut; she remembered only that from caprice and selfishness she had smeared herself from head to feet with something vile and sticky which no washing would wash away.*

It is interesting that guilt is so often related as being contaminated, fouled, marked, soiled, or, as with Lady Macbeth, stained. But, like Lady Macbeth, it is all the more typically guilt when the stain is only visible to ourselves.

Guilt is the most personal of emotion. It is internalized and intensely so. I can see your fear and your anger; you can hide it assuredly, but when it is intense enough I can see it. I cannot always interpret your guilt.

Guilt is also exclusively a human emotion. Guilty fear is obviously not. It is most evident in household pets. I have had more trouble in the writing of this book with my wife and daughters over the one relatively unimportant point of whether animals can experience an emotion such as guilt. In the dozens of times my wife has come across this section, she is offended by the assertion that animals never feel guilty, and inevitably offers as proof the behavior of a disreputable dog, one Mr. Dooley. Dooley is a Kerry blue terrier and, as such, has all the expansiveness of the Irish and rambunctiousness of his terrier breeding. He is therefore constantly, but only

---

* Anton Chekhov, "La Cigale," *The Stories of Anton Chekhov* (New York: Modern Library, 1932), p. 99.

metaphorically, "in the doghouse." That slinky, slippery, slithering, ingratiating, tail-between-the-legs, whimpering, and altogether disgusting behavior which follows his typical outrage is, my wife and children are convinced, the ultimate expression of guilt. It inevitably reduces them to a state of forgiveness—and amnesia. Gone is the outrage and out comes the sympathy. His miserable behavior being interpreted as guilt, and therefore implying contrition, demands forgiveness.

I, on the other hand, remain unconvinced. I have never noticed Dooley approaching me "asking" to be punished. If anything, quite the contrary. I know immediately when he has violated the code of canine conduct. He is nowhere to be found, hiding under, or in, or behind, some barricade. I have never found that this presumed "guilty" feeling and behavior has been diminished by punishment, nor has the behavior been compounded by love, as guilt would be. But my family remains unconvinced. I have resorted to the one-upmanship of quoting "higher sources," amongst whom who could be higher than Martin Buber? In his discussion on guilt he states:

Conscience means to us the capacity and tendency of man radically to distinguish between those of his past and future actions which should be approved and those which should be disapproved. . . . Conscience can, naturally, distinguish and if necessary condemn . . . not merely deeds but also omissions, not merely decisions but also failures to decide, indeed even images and wishes that have just arisen or are remembered. . . . One must bear in mind that among all living beings known to us, *man alone* (emphasis mine) is able to set at a distance not only his environment but also himself. As a result, he becomes for himself a detached object about which he can not only "reflect," but which he can from time to time confirm as well as condemn.*

One would think that psychoanalysis would have early dealt with the concept of guilt, but it did not. Freud was long in discovering a way to integrate guilt into conscience mecha-

* Martin Buber as quoted in *The Knowledge of Man,* M. Friedman, ed. (London: George Allen & Unwin, 1965), p. 133.

nisms. As early as the 1890s, Freud was aware there were certain counterforces that kept our natural drives for pleasure in check. He correctly located them in the emotions well before he was prepared to elaborate any theory of conscience. He referred to the feelings of shame, disgust, revulsion, loathing as counterforces which limited and controlled our drives for pleasure.

His first full attempt to deal with conscience did not occur until 1913 when he wrote *Totem and Taboo*. Building on his recognition that group living was an essential survival mechanism for the individual, Freud concluded that certain conscience mechanisms could not be simply learned anew in each generation, but were essentially part of the genetic nature of the human being. Conscience here was still regulated by fear, and still was always, inevitably oriented toward the figure of authority. We acted as though the punitive parent were within us and therefore cognizant of all our wrongdoing. The controller—even though within us—was always some other, some punishing figure. Good behavior then served the purposes of avoiding punishment and retaliation. The only mechanism visualized at this time was guilty fear, and the driving force which kept us from selfishly pursuing individual aims was an internalized image of the father. Later, that all-knowing presence of power and authority would be assigned to God—or Father in Heaven.

That marvelous modern moralist Philip Roth has young Portnoy visualize this in terms of his seeing all women authority figures as his ubiquitous mother.

She was so deeply imbedded in my consciousness that for the first year of school I seem to have believed that each of my teachers was my mother in disguise. As soon as the last bell had sounded, I would rush off for home, wondering as I ran if I could possibly make it to our apartment before she had succeeded in transforming herself. Invariably she was already in the kitchen by the time I arrived, and setting out my milk and cookies. Instead of causing me to give up my delusions, however, the feat merely intensified my respect for her powers. And then it was always a relief not to have caught her between incarnations anyway—even if I never stopped trying. . . . The burden of betrayal that I imagined would fall to me if I ever came upon her unawares was more than I wanted to bear at the age of five. I think I even feared that I might have to be done away with were I to catch sight of her flying in from school through the bedroom window, or making herself emerge, limb by limb, out of an invisible state and into her apron. . . . Of course, when she asked me to tell her all about my day at kindergarten, I did so scrupulously. I didn't pretend to understand all the implications of her ubiquity, but that it had to do with finding out the kind of little boy I was when I thought she wasn't around—that was indisputable. One consequence of this fantasy, which survived (in this particular form) into the first grade, was that seeing as I had no choice, I became honest.*

According to this view of conscience, we behave well because whether the punitive parent is present or not we have the sense of him within us. We assume that, like the view of God entertained by some children, the parent is an omniscient Peeping Tom, who in seeing all is prepared to expose all, and punish the same.

Later, as Freud began to get more and more involved with the concept of identification, leading him close to, but never quite to, a point of discovering love, he began to acknowledge a distinction between guilt and guilty fear. Identification became the vehicle for incorporating guilt into the processes of conscience.

Identification is a peculiar phenomenon. We have all experienced it. It is, in great part, what makes you, whether you like it or not, like your parent—at least in certain respects. Identification is seen as literally internalizing—swallowing up—another person and his attributes, or, if not that person, some idealized image of the way you thought he was, or the way he ought to have been.

Identification becomes a marvelous device for learning that

---

* Philip Roth, *Portnoy's Complaint* (New York: Random House, 1967), pp. 3, 4.

shortcuts all the small experiences of tedious conditioning. It is not imitation, although it may lead to it. It is much more an unconscious and unwilled process. Identification leads to manners, form, taste, attitudes—all of the behavior which makes little English boys seem so English, and French boys preciously Gallic. The same procedure allows us to incorporate a model of proper moral behavior. This model exists—in our unconscious, unbeknownst to our conscious self—as an ideal against which we will measure ourselves. This ego ideal becomes fundamental to the self-respect mechanisms of the individual. In this final conception of conscience, Freud continues to be impressed with the importance of guilty fear and the internalized parent, but in addition he postulates that there is an internalized ideal of behavior by which we, our actual selves (our Ego), judge our own behavior—and in our failures experience true guilt. Guilt, then, is a form of self-disappointment. It is the sense of anguish that we did not achieve our standards of what we ought to be. We have fallen short. We have somehow or other betrayed some internal sense of potential self. This is why guilt is the most internalized and personal of emotions. You-against-you allows no buffer—and no villains except oneself. Even when guilty fear is internalized, it is as if someone else were there. But with guilt, it is like tearing apart our internal structure. It is why guilt is so painful to endure.

Guilt is not only *not* a "useless" emotion, it is the emotion that shapes so much of our goodness and generosity. It signals us when we have transgressed from codes of behavior which we personally want to sustain. Feeling guilty informs us that we have failed our own ideals. As Paul Ricoeur has so eloquently stated:

Guilt becomes a way of putting oneself before a sort of invisible tribunal which measures the offense, pronouncing the condemnation, and inflicts the punishment; at the extreme point of interiorization, moral consciousness is a look which watches, judges, and condemns; the sentiment of guilt is therefore the consciousness of being inculcated and incriminated by this interior tribunal.*

The readiness to avoid the emotion is testament to the discomfort, and therefore the driving force of the feeling. To avoid it, we may avoid the behavior that generates it—or, short of that, expiate for it. At times the avoidance takes the form of an almost childish avoidance. This results in the "hot potato" game, which probably leads to more domestic quarreling than any other emotion.

It is much easier to feel anger than guilt. As a result, when something goes wrong, there is often an immediate tendency to attribute fault to some other—to protect against its being assigned to us. The irony is that even when there is no fault at all, we defensively assume "someone" must be to blame— for the car breakdown, the canceled performance, the rained-out picnic. "If *you* hadn't told me . . ." "I told you we should have . . ." "*You* had to insist on . . ." The fear that the guilt will be passed on to oneself often makes us angry with whoever happens to be sharing the scene of the accident. A typical example of the hot-potato syndrome whereby guilt is converted into blame is the following. The husband is going out to mail a letter. On the way to mailing the letter he will pass a grocery store. Wife to husband: "Would you mind picking up a quart of milk?" Husband to wife: "Certainly not. I'm passing right by." Husband goes to post office; stops at grocery store; buys the milk; leaves his wallet on the counter. On the way home he realizes the loss; goes back—no wallet.

He has his choice then. He can feel guilty for having done something "stupid"—i.e., wrong. It is he who has betrayed himself and he will feel guilty. It is not guilty fear. No one is going

---

* Paul Ricoeur, "Guilt, Ethics and Religion," in *Conscience: Theological and Psychological Perspectives*, C. Ellis Nelson (New York: Newman Press, 1973), pp. 15, 16.

to punish him. (I am here assuming a gentle and loving wife.)
More often than not, however, the husband will come home
not with contrition or guilt but with a "you and your damn
milk" comment.

This phenomenon is so universal it is possible to see it when
even a no-fault chance event occurs. Because of the fear that
somehow we may have had some responsibility, because of
the readiness by certain people to assume guilt for almost any
disaster, we defensively fix responsibilities somewhere other
than ourselves even where no responsibility is involved.

For the most part, these maneuvers prove ineffectual. We
feel the guilt; we have been—even if only in our anxious illu-
sions—responsible for a wrong.

It is obvious, then, that guilt is of a different order of emotion
from fear. Fear and rage, as Cannon pointed out, are emotions
oriented to the survival of the organism. They serve you as
an individual, or at least they did in the days before civilization.
In the primitive society there was predator and prey. In that
struggle for survival, the emotion, fear or rage, signaled
whether it was appropriate to flee or flight. Guilt seems so
unself-serving, so peculiar an emotion. But it is not alone among
the emotions in its other-serving goals.

Love is not (or should not be) a singular activity, and is also
an unselfish emotion. It involves communication between people and, as such, involves reciprocity. What survival purpose
is served by emotions like guilt, love, and caring? Would we
not survive more adequately if, unencumbered by such emotions, we fought for each scrap of food even to the point of
personal greed and gluttony and the starvation of our weaker
neighbor?

The conscience mechanisms and the emotions that serve
them are testament to the fact that for *Homo sapiens* community is not an ideal, but a biological necessity. There is no
such thing as individual survival. The human being is human
because of the nurture of other human beings, and absent this,

will not survive. Or if the love and caring are supplied only minimally, he may survive as a biological entity without the qualities of humanness which elevate him above the common animal host. Even after development, if at any key point an individual is withdrawn from contact with his kind, he may re-create social relationships in his imagination that sustain him for a time, but he suffers the risk of being reduced to an animal indistinguishable from lower forms.

We are so constructed that we must serve the social good— on which we are dependent for our own survival—and when we do not, we suffer the pangs of guilt. In that sense, guilt parallels the sexual drive. Here one sees the most primitive, the most central and essential fusion between individual pleasure and group needs. Pleasure and procreation are bound intensely together, so that even while the individual serves his own pleasure he guarantees the survival of the species. Similarly, guilt and its fellow emotions of caring, loving, shame, compassion, empathy, and pity bind us to those who are needed for our own survival. These seemingly unselfish acts serve the self in a way that is not always apparent in the everyday individual battle for survival. Guilt is a guardian of our goodness.

~§ 3

Feeling Ashamed

S HAME IS THE SISTER of guilt and is often confused in usage with guilt. They serve the same purposes: both facilitate the socially acceptable behavior required for group living; both deal with transgression and wrongdoing against codes of conduct and are supporting pillars of the social structure. But whereas guilt is the most inner-directed of emotions, shame incorporates the community, the group, the other directly into the feelings.

Shame may be defined as pain or disturbance in regard to bad things [often translated misdeeds], whether present, past, or future, which seem likely to involve us in discredit [often dishonour] . . . we feel shame at such bad things as we think are disgraceful to ourselves or to those we care for.*

---

* Aristotle, *Rhetoric,* bk. II, chap. 6, in *Basic Works of Aristotle,* ed. Richard McKeon (New York: Random House), p. 1992.

Bad things, misdeeds, discredit, dishonor, disgrace—all reflect the live elements that define shame: the misdeed and its exposure. Shame requires an audience, if not realistically, then symbolically. Shame is a public exhibition of wrongdoing or the fear of being exposed in front of the group. Guilt, on the other hand, often drives us to seek exposure. After having committed a wrong, most of us cannot wait to divulge it to those with whom we share our lives. The ideal person to whom to confess is either someone who might share the injury or someone in authority. What is hoped for is absolution, but we will even accept punishment. Either will relieve the unpleasant experience of guilt. But shame begs for privacy—and it is not just chance that the first recorded example of shame in the Western tradition is in terms of the nakedness of Adam and Eve. Shame retreats into privacy for repair; communication is the alleviation of guilt.

In that masterpiece of American writing on shame *The Scarlet Letter,* Hawthorne succinctly captures the sense of public agony. Hester Prynne is an accused and convicted adulteress. As her punishment, she must wear the scarlet letter "A" so that she may be publicly recognized and her crime publicly acknowledged.

Continually, and in a thousand other ways, did she feel the innumerable throbs of anguish that had been so cunningly contrived for her by the undying, the ever-active sentence of the Puritan tribunal. Clergymen paused in the street to address words of exhortation, that brought a crowd, with its mingled grin and frown, around the poor, sinful woman. . . . She grew to have a dread of children; for they had imbibed from their parents a vague idea of something horrible in this dreary woman . . . first allowing her to pass, they pursued her at a distance with shrill cries, and the utterance of a word that had no distinct purport to their own minds, but was none the less terrible to her, as proceeding from lips that babbled it unconsciously. It seemed to argue so wide a diffusion of her shame, that all nature knew of it; it could have caused her no deeper pang, had the leaves of the trees whispered the dark story among themselves—had the

summer breeze murmured about it,—had the wintry blast shrieked
it aloud! Another peculiar torture was felt in the gaze of a new eye.
When strangers looked curiously at the scarlet letter—and none ever
failed to do so—they branded it afresh into Hester's soul; so that,
oftentimes, she could scarcely refrain, yet always did refrain, from
covering the symbol with her hand. From first to last, in short, Hester
Prynne had always this dreadful agony in feeling a human eye upon
the token; the spot never grew callous; it seemed, on the contrary,
to grow more sensitive with daily torture.*

Shame inevitably involves (if only in our imagination) exposure, but, unlike guilty fear, what we dread is not the results
of the exposure but the exposure itself. "Shame," as Aristotle
said, "is a mental picture of disgrace in which we shrink from
the disgrace itself and *not* [my emphasis] from its consequences."

While Hester is exposed to public humiliation and shame,
her partner in adultery, the Reverend Dimmesdale, suffers in
silent guilt. To my knowledge, no better contrast exists in literature between the feelings and context of shame and guilt than
in this brilliant articulation of public and private agonies.

Shame therefore serves in the most direct way the purpose
of preserving the community. It is the enforcement of community standards and community judgment, and requires for its
effectiveness a respect for the community. It also tends to see
good as being in respect to the community as well as the individual; shame therefore allows the community to join in the
enforcement of moral behavior rather than leaving it exclusively in the hands of individual responsibility.

One of the characteristics of shame is that it is felt most
urgently in groups with strong community or cultural identity.
It is not only a product of strong group identity, but a force
for it. Once that group identity is established, it will expand
our boundaries of shame. An interesting example occurred dur-

---

* Nathaniel Hawthorne, *The Scarlet Letter* (New York: Washington Square
Press, 1955), pp. 85, 86.

ing the writing of this chapter. The entire New York area had been fixated for weeks on a psychopathic murderer of young women, labeled the "Forty-Four Caliber Killer," or "Son of Sam." It was one of those aberrant cases of crime that tend to be romanticized later in movies and to influence dozens of television programs, even though they represent a freakish minority in the cavalcade of antisocial and heinous crimes of our day. Such cases frighten and threaten us because of their purposelessness and irrationality, preying on our terror of the unpredictable and unknowable.

Shortly after the news of the apprehension of the suspect was made public, I was talking with a friend, a sophisticated, educated, cultivated, mature woman, who was appalled by her own reaction. The primary emotion she felt on hearing of the "apprehension of the perpetrator"—even before relief from anxiety—was one of shame. The arrested man was Jewish and so was she, which was about the only conceivable linkage one could make between these two disparate people. The sense of identity is so strong in the Jewish community, so vital, so keenly linked to group survival as to generate even this far-fetched extension of responsibility. The identity as an individual Jew is inexorably combined with the identity of the group— both through the forces of anti-Semitism, which always sees a Jew as a Jew first and a person second, and through the very moral tradition of Judaism, which places community good in a most central position. A "shandah fur die goyim"—to be shamed before the Gentiles—is an expression that is known internationally by the Jewish community. It implies not just the identity, through faith and survival, of each individual *with* the group, but in addition a personally felt responsibility *for* the group as a whole—and, beyond that, even an identification with each member of the group who, through his behavior, might reflect on the body as a whole. To the poor Jewish ghetto occupant, the commission of any crime by a totally unrelated Jew thousands of miles away in another city and in other circumstances can be felt as a personal shame. My friend, in her shame, acknowledged kinship with the Son of Sam.

This responsibility for the group, as well as to the group, is the burden and strength of such communities, and can be seen, in this case, as part of a recorded history of five thousand years. When David, having fled from the wrath of Saul, was presented by a courier with the knowledge of Saul's death and the crown which was now his, there was no rejoicing. There was no public celebration. David would not countenance it. David denounced public exultation:

Tell it not in Gath, publish it not in the streets of Askelon; lest the daughters of the Philistines rejoice.*

Despite all, he who had died, though enemy of David, was still the king of *Israel,* the anointed of the Lord.

Cultures which place great emphasis on community, on family, on tribe often hold shame higher than guilt in the controlling and civilizing chronology of emotions. Certainly it is almost a cliché to discuss the Japanese concept of face, which seems so alien, so "unnatural" when first encountered by an individual-oriented, autonomy-worshiping culture such as exists in the United States today.

One of the best contrasts between shame and guilt is in comparison between the primary thrusts of the New and the Old Testaments. The theology of the New Testament, with its emphasis on individual salvation, is dominated by guilt; but the Old Testament in its preoccupation with duty and responsibility, with its need to serve as a guide for survival for a *community,* elevates shame to the highest position.

Excepting perhaps delight or innocence (if these are emotions), the first expressed feeling in the Old Testament is shame. "And they were both naked, the man and his wife, and were not ashamed," the Bible tells us of Adam and Eve. But after

---

* II Samuel 1:20.

the transgression and the eating of the fruit: "And the eyes
of them both were opened, and they knew that they were
naked; and they sewed fig leaves together, and made themselves aprons." It was then Adam felt the primary humiliation
of shame in the presence of the Lord.

And the Lord God called unto Adam, and said unto him, Where
art thou?
And he said, I heard thy voice in the garden and I was afraid,
because I was *naked;* and I hid myself.
And He said, Who told thee that thou was naked?*

There are no prophets of guilt in the Old Testament that
are in any way equivalent to St. Paul. The New Testament
in its emphasis on individuals and individualistic salvation requires a humanlike godhead, a prototype for the individual
to emulate, and guilt therefore becomes the primary mediator
of morality. The focus of the New Testament is a model and
a model life, whereas the focus of the Old Testament is a code
of conduct. Jesus dominates Christian ethics as the Torah does
Jewish morality. It is respect for *the* way versus respect for
the group and its laws. Guilt is the mediator of individual conscience, as shame is the primary mediator of community-ori-
ented conscience. Obviously, a people charged with the responsibility for sustaining the law and the moral code places a great
emphasis on the survival of the group burdened with this holy
charge. The responsibility was to the group over the individual.

Even the nature of heroes differs between the two traditions;
it is the difference between the perfect and the flawed heroes.
Jesus is an ideal, and therefore can serve as the ego ideal which
Freud found necessary for the establishment of true guilt. We
swallow up the ego ideal, and in that sense it can be seen
how the Christian communion in the Eucharist literally aug-
ments the symbolic concept of Christ inside ourselves.

The heroes of the Old Testament represent people we could

---

* Genesis 3:9–11.

be. They are purposely and seriously flawed. Christ will lead the way to the Kingdom of Heaven, but Moses will not be allowed to step into the Promised Land. The great leaders of the Old Testament are great sinners. David must pay the price of losing his favorite son for the heinous sin of destroying a trusted colleague out of lust for his wife. There is one true path to Christianity, while there are multiple paths in the Old Testament, since its heroes offer alternative life styles. Different times require different heroes because different attributes are required to preserve the group during changing historic conditions. The ideal is in the law. Jeremiah is not Micah, although they share the same profession. Nor is David Saul. Multiple heroes are possible, indeed necessary, because there are multiple ways in which citizens serve the community, particularly in changing times with changing conditions for survival.

When one is serving an ideal of perfection, failure to achieve the ideal is forgivable, understandable, and not a sin. The Christian is expected to emulate Christ, the model of perfection, yet is never completely expected to fulfill the ideal. The ideal is one way of motivating behavior; we move toward something we can never achieve. As a standard of perfection, it enhances and directs the energy of good behavior. We aspire to Christ, but are not really expected to become like him. Guilt is invoked in the failure of aspiration, not achievement.

The laws of the Old Testament, however, are meant to be obeyed, not aspired to. The commandments (with the exception of the first, which establishes that all that is to follow is derivative to our acknowledging the primacy of God) are specific rules of social behavior. Do this and not that. Indeed for the most part they are injunctions—the "shalt nots" outnumber the positive instructions. Most of us could, with difficulty, I grant, fulfill all Ten Commandments. I suspect none of us could really obey the injunction to love our enemy.

The emphasis on responsibility to the community in the Old Testament at times seems to transcend even the responsibility to God. In actuality, it is simply that our obligations to God are for the most part defined in our relationship to our fellows. The original transgression against God's injunctions not to eat of the fruit of the tree was *not* labeled a sin. According to Biblical scholars, the Hebrew word for sin, in any of its multiple forms, is never used in the account of the Fall. It is to Cain that the label is first applied.

The Lord asks of Cain: "Why is thy countenance fallen? If thou doest well, shall it not be lifteth up? An if thou doest not well, sin coucheth at the door; and unto thee is its desire, that thou mayest rule over it."* The Lord has forewarned Cain and has given him opportunity to choose good, but Cain chooses the course of evil, slays his brother, and faces the judgment of God. The judgment is a terrible one and Cain answers: "My punishment is greater than I can bear." Some Biblical scholars have said that the word translated as "punishment" is an inaccuracy; that the word, *"avon,"* is actually a combination of guilt and culpability, which is better translated as sin, and the better reading of the line is "My sin is greater than I can bear."

For purposes of understanding shame, the Biblical marking of Cain by the Lord is perhaps the most interesting. In most laymen's minds the mark of Cain has come to mean the stain or the mark of a shamed man. It is equated with Hester Prynne's scarlet letter. But even the most cursory reading of the Old Testament indicates that the purpose of the mark on Cain was to *protect* him. "Sevenfold" would the Lord harm anyone who attempted to take vengeance on Cain, and to protect him he marked him.

That most of us today see the mark as part of the *punishment* reflects an understanding of the metaphoric meaning of the story. It indicates, beyond the responsibility of man to his brother, the role of the social recognition of evil. It was the

---

* Genesis 4:6, 7, Holy Scriptures (Philadelphia: Jewish Publication Society, 1955).

crime against one's fellow rather than the transgression against God that created the first major sinner in Cain, and he would suffer the shame of recognition throughout his life.

In the post-World War II period, the shaving of the head of collaborationist women was seen as imposing an unbearable punishment. Surely no physical harm was done to the women. If fashion had dictated the same shearing of the locks, women would have flaunted their bare heads. But it represented in the most graphic way the community's contempt, and forced them to bear the shame of the group they had betrayed. Their sexual involvement with the occupying soldiers may not have been *a positive* evil in the same way that the activities of the Nazis themselves were, but it was a betrayal of the community and was therefore deemed appropriate to be marked by the community, and before the community. It is terrible to feel the disgrace of the community which is our moral and social world. We feel for Cassio when he cries: "Reputation, reputation, reputation! O, I have lost my reputation! . . . My reputation, Iago, my reputation!"*

In homogeneous societies, with generally shared traditions and ideals, shame is an influential and potent force for good. The power of shame is minimized in a heterogeneous society, where minorities isolated from general acceptance and privilege may only identify with their subculture. We do not betray the group if we are not privileged with true membership in it. The burden for social behavior then will rest even heavier on a personal and individual sense of guilt—and even the nature of that which warrants guilt may differ from the norms of the majority.

With dependence on guilt for moral order, the necessity for heroes is particularly vital. They give form to the models that are essential in constructing our ideals. The paucity of heroes in modern culture, and the ready ascription of heroic

---

* *Othello*, Act II, Scene 3, lines 259–62.

status to the unworthy, is therefore a serious social problem. When, in addition, the controlling power of shame is undermined by the destruction of community pride, or the alienation of the individual from any sense of community, antisocial behavior is facilitated.

One current example comes to mind. In the summer of 1977 the city of New York suffered a total blackout, extending in most areas for over twelve hours. Secondary to the blackout, a rampage of looting and arson occurred that shocked the entire community. In the immediate aftermath, in an exceedingly sensitive and prescient editorial, the *Amsterdam News,* a leading Harlem paper, acknowledged as one of the key forces in the tragedy of that riot the failure of leadership to supply ideals, to support values, and to bind the group of individuals into a community. More graphic, however, were the television interviewees. One adolescent described it as "the best day of my life, like Christmas with everything free." When asked whether he felt there was anything wrong in looting, his answer was extraordinarily revealing. He said, the police couldn't do anything because everybody was doing it, even "old women and pregnant ladies."

In this perception—whether true or not—we see the undermining of the major forces for social responsibility. "The police couldn't do anything," therefore there was no guilty fear; "everybody was doing it," therefore whatever guilt may have been felt was mitigated by the sense that it was a communal standard of behavior; and no shame of public exposure may be feared when even "old ladies and pregnant women," those two most hallowed symbols of propriety and goodness—the matriarch and the madonna—support the activity.

It is not the purpose here to go into the whole complexity of civil unrest, but it was obvious that while the looters were not hungry, what they were deprived of may be as important as food. They had been denied that sense of identity with the larger community which affords them status, and respect, and the *hope* which alone makes adversity and deprivation bearable. They were, in fact, evidently not violating standards of *their* community.

The public ceremony is a historic and necessary part of the shame mechanism. Certain rituals have a kind of universality about them. When I inform you that "Johnny is a stinker," and ask you to sing that out loud, every reader will use the same melody. This melody of derision, which I have found to be identical among all my friends, I am now told by a more sophisticated traveler is a transcultural one, so that little Indians, Japanese, and Africans, despite cultural differences, will all sing:

The same melody can be used for almost any derisive, shame-attributing jingle. One of the more popular of my childhood was one that at its simplest went "Shame, shame on Willy," and was usually accompanied by a peculiar gesture which involved pointing the index finger of the left hand at the person while the index finger of the right hand stroked across the dorsal surface of the left.

I have tested this out on so many of my friends tht I am beginning to feel that it, too, has a universality, although when I ask what it means, I get (aside from the general acknowledgment that it is an attribution of shame) a multitude of explanations. The most frequent is that it is the pointing of the finger of guilt while shoveling the shame onto the individual. Another common attribution is to assume it is linked to masturbatory guilt and shame, and that the action is both pointing the finger and a metaphor for masturbation.

One of my personal memories involving the jingle is "Shame, shame, everybody knows your name." I have a vivid recall of this as accurate, even though the concept seems patent nonsense. Could it have been a corruption in recall of "Shame, shame, everybody knows your game," which certainly would have made sense, meaning everybody knows what you are up to? Perhaps. But the memory is so distinct, and I have found a few corroborators. Unless we are all having the same memory defect (in which case—psychoanalytically, at least—it is granted validity), it must have some legitimate meaning and may speak to an essential division between the private and the public sphere. There are cultures where the knowledge of one's name is kept secret. In the Chinese culture or in certain Indian tribes, there is a magic assigned to one's name which must be protected. Even here the name suggests the metaphoric sense of the inner self which is never truly revealed. To know "one's name" is to know "who you are" at the most basic level; to expose our name is to expose that core of ourselves for which we have no public responsibility and which need not be popularly shared. This private self may set the limits of shame. It represents that most personal area of our unconscious and our fantasy life for which we neither owe public accountability nor need public apology. On the other hand, the "everybody" knowing may simply imply notoriety—always easier to achieve than fame.

This private self introduces a different sense of shame which caused me some confusion. An example of shame generally mentioned by classicists is the story of Gyges. In the first book of *The History of Herodotus,* Herodotus tells the story of a certain king of Sardis, called Candaules:

Now it happened that this Candaules was in love with his own wife; and not only so, but thought her the fairest woman in the whole world. This fancy had strange consequences.*

---

* *The History of Herodotus,* translation by George Rawlinson, edited by Manuel Komroff (New York: Tudor Publishing Co.), 1956, Book I, p. 3.

Candaules is so proud of his wife's beauty that he insists that
his favorite lieutenant, Gyges, view his naked wife. Gyges is
most reluctant, and only on the pressure of his king is forced
into a position of secretly entering the bedchamber in which
the royal couple slept.

A moment later the Queen followed. She came in, and laid her
garments on the chair, and Gyges gazed on her. . . . As he was passing
out, however, she saw him, and instantly divining what had happened,
she never screamed as her shame impelled her, nor even appeared
to have noticed anything, but purposing to take vengeance upon her
husband who so affronted her. For among the Lydians, and indeed
among the barbarians generally, it is reckoned a deep disgrace, even
to a man, to be seen naked.*

The following day, the Queen commands Gyges to her presence:

"Take your choice, Gyges, two courses which are open to you. Slay
Candaules, and thereby become my Lord, and obtain the Lydian
throne, or die this moment in his room. It must needs be, that either
he perish by whose counsel this thing was done, or you, who saw
me naked, and so did break our usages."†

Gyges chooses to kill rather than be killed, and asks how it is
to be done.

"Let him be attacked on that spot where I was by him shown naked
to you, and let the assault be made when he is asleep."‡

I must admit that on first examination this did not strike
me as an example of shame at all, but rather of its close relative
humiliation. Shame is the sense of exposure *before* someone;
humiliation is the sense of exposure *by* someone. Shame carries
with it always a small kernel of guilt; it is the public exposure
of some failing; it implies a lack of adequacy or responsibility.
Humiliation is fused with anger; the exposure is done to us.
If there is no implication of either wrongdoing or humiliation

---

* Ibid., p. 4.
†Ibid., p. 4.
‡ Ibid., p. 4.

by another, we are dealing with still another related emotion—embarrassment. It is obvious that there are situations in which any of these emotions can occur in combination with the other.

It later occurred to me that what is illustrated in this chapter is not *the feeling of* shame (i.e., being ashamed) but the sense of shame. The sense of shame also contains within it specific emotional feelings, and it is related to the feeling of being ashamed, but it is a different feeling.

A sense of shame arises out of our conviction that certain things *are* and *ought* to be private; it guards these areas from public view and protects the public space from contamination by private matters. It is we ourselves who must be the primary guardians of our private self. It *is* related to the feeling of shame in that both are dominated by the concept of exposure of that which ought not be exposed. In the feeling of shame it is our misdeed or wrongdoing or deficiency that is exposed. In the sense of shame it is some part of ourselves—often our bodies (but not necessarily so).

It is crucial to distinguish between "being or feeling ashamed" and a "sense of shame."

With the sense of shame, that which is exposed may not itself be a fault; here it is the exposure that is deemed morally wrong. With the exposure we are apt to feel some culpability in that each individual is seen as the keeper of his own privacy. A sense of shame is bound closely to the now old-fashioned concept of modesty. A sense of shame may encompass a multitude of feelings: guilt, even if unwarranted; humiliation when we are exposed by others; embarrassment when chance is the only culprit.

I recall a particularly poignant demonstration of the distinctions and interrelationships involved with shame when I was visiting prisons interviewing a group of young conscientious objectors who had chosen prison over service in the Vietnam War. Among the many hardships of prison life for these young men was the deprivation of sexual outlet. This was a young group, at their prime sexually and still young enough so that their sexual identity and confidence had not yet been firmly established. With no opportunity for sexual intercourse and eschewing the homosexuality that is rampant in most prisons, the only obvious sexual release was masturbation. These men discussed their masturbation with me and their masturbatory fantasies, and almost to a man they bemoaned the fact of the lack of privacy which made masturbation so difficult. Unlike the image most people have of prison with its terrifying implication of being locked in a cell, few prisoners are still locked in individual cells. This is particularly true in federal prisons and minimum-security facilities. More often than not, the problem is precisely the opposite of isolation. There is no place to retreat—no sense of privacy, no escape. Barracks are the traditional prison fare.

These men, while knowing and indeed discussing among themselves their need for masturbation, would lie awake at night each waiting for the others to fall asleep, so that they could masturbate in private. They expressed their feeling that they were not guilty about the masturbation. They certainly talked about it freely, but they were ashamed to do it in public. There are certain things reserved for the private sphere of our activities. Here we see a contrast between guilt and the sense of shame. They certainly did not suffer the kind of internal guilt one prisoner did when he broke a group fast. There was little shame in this; it was a difficult thing they had undertaken, and there was the recognition by the group that not all would be able to continue a fast. This was a particularly non-judging, non-judgmental community of fellows. Yet the one C.O. who broke the fast suffered internally enormously for it.

There may have been some feeling of "being ashamed" if caught masturbating; with masturbation there is almost an inevitable residual sense of guilt owing to the profound cultural injunctions against it. But there was no "sense of shame" in the acknowledgment of the activity to the group. The Lydian queen (who is not honored by a name in Herodotus) shows none of the manifestations of shame. She is outraged, and she is vengeful. She uses the word "shame" in relationship to her nakedness. It is the announcement of *a shame* done to her.

This is the sense of shame, not the feeling of being ashamed. Embarrassed, humiliated, outraged, but not—this noble queen—ashamed.

How much the sense of shame is an inbuilt mechanism and how much culturally determined and taught to the child have always been open to question. In either case, the sense of shame is generally very closely tied to sexuality. We see this in the examples from Adam and Eve, Herodotus, and the young prisoners. Sexuality, in almost all cultures, is a private affair. To enforce this privacy and to protect the public sphere, the sense of shame is extended beyond the act of sexuality to the organs of sexuality—and beyond that, in a form of shame "by association," to the entire pudendal (from Latin, *pudendus*—ashamed) area. The sense of shame as applied to the exposure of the genitals has traditionally been viewed as a controlling mechanism in tribal societies, and particularly as a protection against incest. In *Totem and Taboo,* Freud viewed all rituals of propriety, regardless of how powerful they might appear, as derivatives and extensions of the taboo against incestual sexuality. Freud assumed this incest dread to be universal and genetically fixed.

It is a debate that has gone on in anthropology and psychoanalysis for years. Certain anthropologists have described cultures where no sexual guilt was apparent, and Abram Kardiner pointed out anthropological cases where shame was not at all directed toward genital exposure, nakedness, or even excretion, but was reserved for the eating ritual.* One thinks of the Trobriand Islanders, where eating must be done back-to-back.

---

* Abram Kardiner, *The Individual and His Society* (New York: Columbia University Press, 1939).

Whether there is an inbuilt mechanism or not, what is clear is that the two kinds of shame have a certain relationship both in protecting the public space from contamination and in defining for the individual the distinctions between public and private.

Pornography is an attempt to violate that distinction. Central to the concept of pornography is an *intention* to shock us with its insistence on blurring the boundaries between private and public. Those who defend unlimited free expression often neglect the importance of the equally respected right to be left alone. George Steiner has said: "Sexual relations are, or should be, one of the citadels of privacy. . . . The new pornographers subvert this last vital privacy. They do our imagining for us, they take away the words that were of the night and shout them over the rooftops, making them hollow. The image of our lovemaking, the stammering we resort to in intimacy, come prepackaged."*

In either case, whether it is the feeling of being ashamed or the sense of shame, there is an awareness of something being exposed which ought not be, and in its exposure reflecting badly on us. With feeling ashamed, it is our own wrongdoing, inadequacy, deficiency which are exposed. In the sense of shame, guilt is not primary, although we may still feel some culpability; the injunctions to separate private from public have been violated if only by our own lack of vigilance. Even when the violation is by assault, we may still feel ashamed because of a vestigial sense that what has been exposed somehow or other does disservice to us. In this last case we see that in classifying things as private, we run the risk of adding a negative and pejorative connotation to things which ought not be so perceived.

We often equate "private" with "dirty." Most of us are, I am afraid, indelibly tinged with a sense of the pejorative nature

---

* George Steiner, "Night Words," *Encounter*, September, 1965, p. 18.

of our genitals and our sexual activity, and, by association, our excretory activity, our secretions, and our body parts, extending far beyond the original sexual locus for such feeling. This has led to one of the more serious misreadings of psychoanalysis.

When psychoanalysis insisted that certain sexual feeling and behavior ought be accepted without guilt (i.e., without the feeling of their being wrong or dirty, if you will), that did not automatically mean they ought then be made public, or there ought not be a primary sense of privacy. To make public what should not be made public can be wrong even when what is made public is not itself wrong.

For some people, the feeling of privacy extends itself into a generalized modesty which includes every form of self-presentation. All public attention is a form of exposure, a kind of nakedness; every public event in which they are featured is painful. This acute discomfort experienced with public attention—independent of the nature of the public reaction—is embarrassment. The shy person will feel that embarrassment with praise as well as censure. When we are exposed nude, it does not relieve the sense of shame if in our consternation we also notice that the glance received was an admiring one. Shyness sees all eyes as penetrating a layer of protective privacy—and feels embarrassment with any unexpected attention. Guilt need play no role here.

Humiliation also may involve minimal, or no, guilt. When there is little or no sense of our personal responsibility in our exposure, when it is clearly the hostile imposed act of another, we feel humiliation. It is the distinction between our revealing a defect and the sense of being used in such a way as to make us feel defective. It is the user of us who imposes the condition rather than exposing a secret pre-existing one.

There is an intriguing mechanism by which shame is converted into humiliation, humiliation evidently being for many a more acceptable emotion. The mechanism is projection, and it is the basic maneuver of paranoia. When we feel something of which we are ashamed—sexual fantasies, homosexual feelings, masochistic tendencies—we can project these feelings onto those around us and claim not that we wish these things but that they are being forced on us by some other. We can then feel outrage and fear, and be relieved from feeling guilty of the feeling or ashamed of its potential exposure. The actual paranoid, then, must manufacture a conspiratorial world in which everyone is plotting his personal humiliation. Better humiliation than shame: at least then he can be the noble warrior in his own defense, and attack the conspirators.

Sense of shame, being ashamed, humiliation, embarrassment, and guilt—all are discrete and separate feelings. And yet whenever we are dealing with something as subjective as feelings in an organism as complicated as *Homo sapiens,* there is such a confluence and amalgamation that no one can be too arrogant in assuming which exists when and in what condition. The peculiar fusion of emotions often makes for our most painful moments. James Joyce, in *A Portrait of the Artist as a Young Man,* describes an episode when his young hero, Stephen, is about to beaten for breaking his glasses accidentally:

Stephen closed his eyes and held out in the air his trembling hand with the palm upwards. He felt the prefect of studies touch it for a moment at the fingers to straighten it and then the swish of the sleeve of the soutane as the pandybat was lifted to strike. . . . The scalding water burst forth from his eyes and, burning with shame and agony and fear, he drew back his shaking arm in terror and burst out into a whine of pain. His body shook with a palsy of fright and in shame and rage he felt the scalding cry come from his throat and the scalding tears falling out of his eyes and down his flaming cheeks.*

Surely in these circumstances Stephen has nothing to be ashamed of; there is no source of guilt for him here. On the other hand, the fear itself, and the impotence of his rage, and

---

* James Joyce, *A Portrait of the Artist as a Young Man* (New York: Viking Press, 1969), p. 50.

the position of humiliation and his readiness to endure it are in themselves enough to produce shame.

In general there will always remain the problem of differentiating such similar yet distinct emotions as guilt, shame, humiliation, and embarrassment. Some of it will always be a confusion of semantics. Guilt, after all, was not until recently (and perhaps is not even now, according to some authorities) even considered an emotion. In these most elegant environs, proper usage demands one say "sense of guilt." But that is awkward, and I suspect because of that very awkwardness shame may be incorrectly substituted for guilt. A "sense of guilt" is in itself a distortion. This term tends to give a cognitive emphasis, particularly inappropriate to an emotion like guilt so viscerally felt.

Surely, then, when we are involved with translations from other languages, and literature that spans time, we can only surmise what the particular historic character is feeling. The evocation of the emotion within us—independent of the words used—will be our clearest guide. In separation of guilt from shame, the most valid distinction is still the internal and the external. Guilt is a struggle bound in secrecy but seeking expiation; shame is the public acknowledgment of our wrongdoing.

Yet here, too, it ought to be recognized that man is versatile enough to compound his agonies even beyond those that nature has created for him. It is possible to feel shame without the presence of the group; the imagination and perception of man are capable of the symbolism, internalization, and generalization that allow the group to seem present even when it is not. We need not be exposed to the group. We have familiar analogies from the past to know what group shame and group exposure mean.

The anticipation of shame is different from the anticipation of guilt. I am not even sure that one *can* anticipate guilt. The problem with guilt is that we are never quite able to predict when we are likely to feel it or how terrible the feeling is.

So we commit our minor transgressions and suffer the consequences. When those transgressions may be exposed to the
group, it becomes an added impetus to weigh the cost of the
behavior.

The capacity to anticipate shame is well established, and
much of the criminal justice system is built around public exposure, shame, and its deterrent affect. Unfortunately, the criminal justice system is directed at the criminal, who may be alienated from and indifferent to the public, or even devoid of a
capacity for shame.

In the eighteenth century, Oliver Goldsmith reminds us that
shame and contrition are universal. In reading this quotation
remember that "guilt" is used for the wrongdoing only, not
for the emotion.

> Guilt and Shame, says the allegory, were at first companions, and,
> in the beginning of their journey, inseparably kept together. But their
> union was soon found to be disagreeable and inconvenient to both.
> Guilt gave Shame frequent uneasiness, and Shame often betrayed
> the secret conspiracies of Guilt. After long disagreement, therefore,
> they at length consented to part for ever. Guilt boldly walked forward
> alone, to overtake Fate, that went before in the shape of an execu-
> tioner; but Shame, being naturally timorous, returned back to keep
> company with Virtue, which in the beginning of their journey they
> had left behind. Thus, my children, after men have travelled through
> a few stages of vice, shame forsakes them, and returns back to wait
> upon the few virtues they have still remaining.*

Shame is indeed companion to virtue. Be not ashamed of
feeling shame or scornful of its purposes. These emotions—
guilt and shame—guide us to our better selves and insure our
safety by supporting the group on whom we all ultimately
depend for our survival.

---

* Oliver Goldsmith, *The Vicar of Wakefield* (New York: Washington Square
Press, 1963), pp. 76, 77.

4

Feeling Proud

How in the world did a nice emotion like pride get elected first of the seven deadly sins? Why is not pride one of the cardinal virtues? Self-respect, self-esteem, and self-confidence—all ingredients of pride—are essential elements to adaptation. They serve both the functional and the pleasure purposes of life. Why, then, is pride a sin?

The seven deadly sins were a testament to Hellenic influence on early Christianity. The Greeks, however, only had four primary sins; Christianity managed to add three more for good measure. Pride led both lists. With all deference to St. Gregory, I like pride—but it is certainly a most confusing emotion. It has at least two distinct meanings; it can, in both of its usages, be viewed as either a virtue or a vice; and there has been a distinct shift in our current attitudes about it.

To the Greeks a special form of pride—called "hubris"—
was the cardinal affront to the gods, and the great Greek trage-
dies are dominated by this emotion. Greek tragedy demanded
a mighty hero and his fall. To the powerful, the prime moral
injunction must always be against a misuse of that power. The
danger of power is always arrogance. The warning was clear:
the ruler must identify with the ruled, and to insure this the
great threat to his position was the sin of pride, unforgivable
in the eyes of the gods.

In Aeschylus's play *The Persians,* the ghost of Darius warns
his fellow countrymen: "When arrogance blooms, it bears the
fruit of doomed infatuation, when it reaps a harvest rich in
tears."

It was the emotions of the powerful which interested the
politically oriented Greeks, because their mood established the
nature of life in the state. While cast in terms of a relationship
to the immortals, the purpose of the sin of hubris was to serve
justice, to affirm to the mighty their identity was with man—
even the common man—not the gods. This was particularly
crucial in the hierarchically organized Greek states. Solon
warned that abundance leads to hubris, and hubris to ruin,
and said that man's hubris must pay the punishment for over-
stepping the bounds set by *justice.*

The Christians, however, directed their message not to the
powerful leaders but to the abused masses of the post-classical
period. In a desperate age, where no hope flourishes on this
earth, afterlife becomes the only source of solace. It is comforting to know that humility and poverty are not only our lot,
but a ticket to the beyond. Since we are told that it is "easier
for a camel to go through the eye of a needle, than for a rich
man to enter the kingdom of God," there is a value in poverty.
Whether intended or not, the preaching of pride as a sin and
humility as a virtue led to acceptance and passivity—and served
to protect a social order of inequity.

With the powerful, I suppose, humility still is a requisite

virtue. But times have changed. The number of the securely powerful are few indeed. Modern life has removed all confident security. Anxiety has become the great democratizer. Of course there are still strutting creatures, puffed and filled with smug self-satisfaction, like Wallace Stevens's "Damned universal cock, as if the sun was blackamoor to bear your blazing tail."* But those few arrogant creatures of power who still survive are not, generally, our heroes. They are too removed from our reality to allow for ready identification. We are more likely, these days, to classify ourselves among the unpowerful, the alienated, or the anxious.

In this group it is humility that ought be a sin, for it leads to despair and encourages a tolerance of inequity and injustice. We certainly no longer fear that our overweening pride will offend the gods. For one thing, we have handled that by reducing the gods; and for another, the world which is now viewed as our own creation is in such a mess of uncertainty as to discourage any excessive self-confidence.

It is instructive to trace the change in the meaning of pride in more modern times: to Spinoza, in the seventeenth century, "pride is pleasure arising from a man's thinking too highly of himself"; to Schopenhauer, in the nineteenth century, "pride is an established conviction of one's own paramount worth in some respect"; and to the American Heritage Dictionary, in the twentieth century, pride is simply "a sense of one's own proper dignity or value." In this series of definitions we have moved the definition of pride from an excessive—"too high"— sense of self-worth, to a "paramount" sense, to a "proper" one. As a psychoanalyst in mid-twentieth-century America, I view pride as a virtue and its absence as the deficiency of our time. The restoration of pride is a major goal of treatment. Self-respect and self-value are essential components of the capacity

---

* Wallace Stevens, "Bantams in Pine Woods," *Poems* (New York: Vintage Books, 1959), p. 25.

for pleasure and performance which underlie the healthy (good) life.

In addition, we are here dealing with feelings, and when one thinks of feeling the conflict over meaning of pride is resolved. You cannot deal with feeling "too proud" or, if you do, it ceases to be a prideful feeling. Too proud is a judgment from the outside and even were it a judgment from the inside, then by adding the pejorative "too" we would have destroyed the feeling of pride. In making the judgment that we are excessively proud, we demean ourselves either by the judgment of arrogance or by the judgment of inappropriate self-elevation. In either case it is nothing to feel proud about. When we feel pride, it must, by definition, be a good feeling, a feeling of which we are proud.

There is another set of complications, however, in pride in that it has both a general and a specific feeling form. The first modern dictionary definition (a sense of one's own proper dignity or value) describes the general form. It involves a sense of bearing; a general awareness of one's self; of being worthy, of being decent. In this sense it is synonymous with self-respect. It is a basic attitude which will profoundly influence our general pursuits in life. Such pride involves an overall bearing that normally does not break through into the specific feeling area except on occasions of self-conscious self-appraisal. Pride has been simplistically described by many as the antithesis of shame—but this form of pride at least is almost directly parallel with one of the definitions of shame. "Have you no pride?" is interchangeable with "Have you no shame?" Both imply a self-respect that dictates appropriate demeanor in public. They define our sense of a proper self. The absence of either implies the absence of a decent standard of behavior.

Pride here is self-acceptance and self-value. We wear it with our clothes in public. It sticks out all over us and in its absence we advertise our self-contempt. It affects our bearing, our manner, our aspirations—the way we face defeat and the way we accept victory.

It will also determine how we are treated by others. The self-respect or contempt with which we endow ourselves is like a sign hung around our neck, demanding similar treatment—and usually getting it—from those whom we meet.

The conscious *feeling* of pride, on the other hand, is most often experienced in terms of specific activities. We feel proud when we become aware of having done well. That second feeling is defined by the American Heritage Dictionary as "pleasure or satisfaction taken in one's work, achievements, or possessions."

This self-cosseting feeling of pride is not reserved for the conquest of nations or the grand creations of the select and talented few. It can occur to all of us, and does with each sense of mastery or achievement. We see it in the face of a child when he has completed a task for the first time, even if it be the task of dropping a clothespin into a bottle.

The following quotation from *Great Expectations* demonstrates two feelings of pride: first, Joe's at his incredible achievement; and second, Pip's (the narrator's) in the achievement of his good and kind friend. It is important to have some background of this relationship. Joe, a good, simple, illiterate man, has been kindness personified to young Pip, but when Pip finds out that he is a young man of "great expectations," that he is the heir to some wealthy but unknown patron, Pip becomes a snob. He is embarrassed by Joe and publicly rejects him. Some time later, Pip receives his comeuppance and falls desperately ill. Naturally, it is Joe and his wife, Biddy, who take him in and lovingly restore him to health. It is during this phase of the convalescence that the following scene occurs:

Evidently Biddy had taught Joe to write. As I lay in bed looking at him, it made me, in my weak state, cry again with pleasure to see the pride with which he set about his letter. . . . At my own writing-table, pushed into a corner and cumbered with little bottles, Joe now sat down to his great work, first choosing a pen from the pen-tray as if it were a chest of large tools, and tucking up his sleeves as if he were going to wield a crowbar or sledge-hammer. It was necessary for Joe to hold on heavily to the table with his left elbow, and to get his right leg well out behind him, before he could begin, and when he did begin he made every down-stroke so slowly that it might have been six feet long, while at every upstroke I could hear his pen spluttering extensively. He had a curious idea that the inkstand was on the side of him where it was not, and constantly dipped his pen into space, and seemed quite satisfied with the result. Occasionally, he was tripped up by some orthographical stumbling-block, but on the whole he got on very well indeed, and when he had signed his name, and had removed a finishing blot from the paper to the crown of his head with his two forefingers, he got up and hovered about the table, trying the effect of his performance from various points of view as it lay there, with unbound satisfaction.*

Compare this quotation with another—far better known and more often cited—by the same author, Charles Dickens. In *A Tale of Two Cities,* Sydney Carton is about to die on the guillotine. He has voluntarily substituted himself for the husband of the woman he loves.

I see the lives for which I lay down my life, peaceful, useful, prosperous and happy, in that England which I shall see no more. I see her with a child upon her bosom, who bears my name. I see her father, aged and bent, but otherwise restored, faithful to all men in his healing office, and at peace. . . . I see that I hold a sanctuary in their hearts, and in the hearts of their descendants, generations hence. I see her, an old woman, weeping for me on the anniversary of this day. I see her and her husband, their course done, lying side by side in their last earthly bed, and I know that each was not more honoured and held sacred in the other's soul, than I was in the souls of both.

It is a far, far better thing that I do, than I have ever done; it is a far, far better rest that I go to, than I have ever known.†

---

* Charles Dickens, *Great Expectations* (New York: New American Library, Signet Classics, 1963), p. 498.

† Charles Dickens, *A Tale of Two Cities* (New York: Literary Classics, 1945), p. 401.

Most of us will identify more readily with Joe than with Sydney Carton. For one thing, most of us would not be prepared to make Sydney Carton's sacrifice, nor are we likely to be called upon to do so. But, more important, pride is usually associated with accomplishment, not moral worth. Outside of the literary world, pride is generally felt in the small achievements of our daily endeavor; in the minor measure of our value; in our little victories.

Normal feelings of pride are generally quiet, although warming experiences. They are acknowledged to ourselves by the nod of our head, the shake of our fist, the grin that breaks out with our last stroke of the brush, the last seed planted, the last period on the completed manuscript. Often we are not exactly aware of an emotion—we simply feel good, or gratified.

In an average day we are more likely to be reminded of our inadequacies and our weaknesses than our successes. We are confronted daily with our failures to fulfill the scope of our ambition or our fantasies. It is the nature of fantasies to be unfulfilled. They are used to extend, as well as to supplement, the achievements of life, but, as such, they are a horizon phenomenon; however far we have traveled, they always seem some distance away.

Since we do not necessarily always experience pride as a special feeling in the solitary pursuits that warrant the emotion, the feeling is most readily identified when it is heightened and augmented by public recognition. Recognized feelings of pride, therefore, are often associated with the public acknowledgment of some achievement—with the public recognition of its worth. Achievement, even when not recognized, feeds that general *sense of pride* encompassed in our first definition; in that sense it is most important. Nonetheless, we particularly enjoy the "flush of pride" which accompanies public approval of our product.

Among the "products" most likely to produce pride are our

children. It is of the nature of love anyway to overvalue the object, and most of us see our children through the distorted lens of love. We are proud of them beyond their necessary warrant of pride. Children, being our ultimate products, our best hope for immortality, need do little but exist to produce the feeling of pride.

A parent watching his child perform the most mundane of activity can get a glowing, almost smug look of pride across his face, whether the child is an infant or a balding, middle-aged creature. Very often still photographs taken of a child will catch the parent in the periphery wearing that particular expression that is so identifiable as pride.

We see in our children the expansion of our horizons and time. We assume that they represent the best in us and will go beyond us. We abide frustrations and acknowledge the failures of our dreams if we see these, our surrogates in pleasure and in pain, as our new hopes for fulfillment.

When in addition to their simply being there, they do achieve certain recognizable acknowledgments of their worth, our pride bursts forward in a particularly physical sensation. It is a welling forth, like a fountain of joy, as expressed in the German word Quellung and the Yiddish adaptation, to *kvell*. When the word *kvell* is used, it is almost invariably by a parent in relationship to a child and his achievements.

In the following quotation from D. H. Lawrence's *Sons and Lovers,* we see a scene in which Paul learns he has won a painting competition:

One morning the postman came just as he was washing in the scullery. Suddenly he heard a wild noise from his mother. Rushing into the kitchen, he found her standing on the hearthrug wildly waving a letter and crying "Hurrah!" as if she had gone mad. He was shocked and frightened. "Why mother!" he exclaimed. She flew to him, flung her arms round him for a moment, then waved the letter, crying: "Hurrah, my boy! I knew we should do it!"*

* D. H. Lawrence, *Sons and Lovers* (New York: Viking Press, 1975), p. 253.

In this quote, despite the fact that it is Paul's painting which has won the prize, the pride we sense is that of the mother. "I knew *we* [italics mine] should do it."

Pride is capable of being elicited both by an internal measurement, the self, and by a public acknowledgment. In that sense it combines both the mechanisms of guilt and shame. But it is not quite the antithesis of guilt and shame. Guilt and shame are exclusively moral judgments. They are the emotional signals that we have not done good. Pride tends to be more involved with doing well than doing good. It is true that there can be pride in a moral achievement, but that almost diminishes the moral character of the act. It may indeed be why Sydney Carton's expression of pride seems priggish and pompous in comparison to Joe's. There is a sanctimonious self-righteous quality introduced if one takes pride in having been good. To do good ought be part of the fabric of one's being; one should feel pain in the deviation from the good and simply feel normal in the performance of good. To do good for external approval is goody-good.

Pride is involved with achievement and mastery—the whole area of doing and creating. It is a sign generally not that we are good but that we are competent and more. It supports self-esteem with self-confidence. It is the esteem in a self that we can trust and depend on. Its innate tendency can be seen in the early joy of the child in mastery over small objects. The two-year-old is explorer, builder (and destroyer), and achiever *par excellence.*

The public aspect of pride may or may not be innate. It is always difficult to separate natural genetic tendencies from environmental influences, particularly when the environmental impact is early. Innate tendencies can be either encouraged or discouraged from developing, depending on the responses they elicit from the parents. Similarly, actions of the child will be either rejected or encouraged so artfully and unconsciously as to create the impression that they were "innate" and not taught. The interplay between child and parent is a potent factor in the way the child learns to distinguish between the adaptive ("goodness") and the non-adaptive ("badness") value of his early random behavior. He does something, and almost invariably will look to the mother for approval or disapproval. That *looking* to the mother is surely an organic part of the adaptive process. Anyone who has been in a public place must be aware of the "Look, Mom" phenomenon. For some reason, public swimming pools seem to be the locale I most associate with this. The incredible din that can be generated by the exuberant enthusiasm of children around a swimming pool creates a noise level that, like rock-and-roll, is almost intolerable to people past a certain age. In addition to the general cries and squeals, "Mom, look" and "Look, Mom" are specific and inevitable interjections. So constant is the appeal, particularly with prepubescent children, that "mammaluk-mammaluk" ceases to have an identifiable meaning and becomes a rhythmic background beat before which any attempt at conversation can only be played as melodic counterpoint. Mammaluk is the babaloo of the beach and the doowahdoo of the playground.

Even if the appeal of approval is answered with only the most perfunctory "I'm looking, I'm looking," "That's lovely, dear," the response is required. The ritual must be played out even while the child recognizes the lack of genuine pride and enthusiasm in the mother's intonations.

Externally reinforced pride becomes the initial sign to the child that he has done well. One of the first areas in which the enthusiastic acclaim of the parent over her child's performance is received is in toilet training. In certain cultures and with certain parents, the child is encouraged to "do it for Mommy," and each turd deposited in the appropriate vessel is greeted like an offering on the altar of love. Many people never overcome the sense of their own feces as a gift to be given or retained, and the number of psychosomatic disorders that involve diarrhea and constipation are a tribute to this early association of the lower bowel and rectum with the gift-giving apparatus of the young child.

Fortunately most of our parents have helped direct us to other areas of achievement, and most of us graduate from the point where we consider feces as our greatest creation and area of achievement. Still, more often than not, it is in relationship to our productions and performances that we are likely to feel pride.

Pride is an essential ingredient in maturation. It is our incentive and reward for abandoning the pleasures of dependency. The advantages of being an adored and protected child may be too seductive and the alternative of self-reliance may seem too dry and intellectual for the latter to compete successfully. Pride is the pleasure in achievement that supports independence. It is an added incentive to abandon the ways and pleasures of childhood for the more elusive gratifications of maturity.

Pride, like anxiety, guilt, and shame, is one of our vital signs—those emotions that are basic to the survival apparatus of a thinking and social animal like man—although less obviously so than the others.

Fear (with rage) is, of course, part of the primary emergency responses of many lower animal forms. The feelings are one part of the complex emotional mechanism which prepares the endangered animal for the emergency responses of fight or flight. These stress mechanisms are autonomic and often uncontrollable.

Guilt and shame are also survival-serving emotions. But here we leave the general animal host and enter into the emotional domain assumed to be exclusively human. These emotions guide us to sacrificing selfish immediate interests to serve the standards and the needs of the group. But since we are by nature a social animal, our individual survival is linked to the species.

Why then include pride in this group? In many ways, it belongs in the last section with the emotions of joy and fulfillment.

Yet there is an argument for including pride of achievement with the basic mechanisms of human survival. We are not driven only by mechanisms of pain avoidance; we are also re-ward seekers. But, unlike lesser creatures, our rewards are not simply the nutrients of biological survival. We are aspirers. We crave achievement, mastery, and purpose because this is the stuff which extends the meaning of *human* survival beyond the mere perpetuation of a biological shell.

PART II

Caution Signals

The Center Is Not Holding

5

Feeling Upset

EMOTIONS SUCH AS FEAR AND RAGE are clearly alerting mechanisms warning of and preparing for some impending externally perceived dangers. There are, in addition, a range of feelings whose primary purpose seems to be to warn us about our own state of preparedness—or, more accurately, unpreparedness. These feelings, like the gauges and flashing lights of an automobile dashboard, indicate the state of our resources. They are signs of our internal conditions, indices of our level of functioning. They caution us about our diminishing reserves and warn us that it is time to pull ourselves together.

One of the most common of these caution signals is that strange sense of being upset. Surely we have all at one time or another felt "upset," yet we rarely define the feeling itself as an emotion. It seems to be a description of a state of affairs

not worthy of dignifying with definition. It seems to be happening *to* us—or even *around* us—but surely not *within* us. We
feel upset in such diverse contexts that we deny its specificity
as a feeling. Yet it is a unique emotion and easily communicated
one to another: to say that the boss is upset, Dad is upset, or
the teacher is upset is to warn of a special state of mind, and
to allow the listener to anticipate something which he fully
understands. Yet when you ask anyone to define it—to say
what it really means—you are likely to receive an incoherent
and inconsistent response. It will be tied to and confused with
a wide range of other emotions. This is because "feeling upset"
is always a secondary response to other primary emotions. The
feeling, nonetheless, is special and unto itself.

The central image in the feeling of upset is one of disorder
and disarray. The synonyms for feeling upset all include a sense
of confusion, and an interruption of the normal control and
orderliness of life. We tend to be concrete and physical in
our synonyms. We feel "mixed-up," "disturbed," "shaken up,"
"agitated," "beside ourselves," and "stirred up."

It is precisely this sense of the disruption of our usual operating mechanisms which is the key to the feeling of upset. We
tend to feel upset when we have a sense that our normal orderly
control over our lives is threatened. The feeling of upset suggests a thinness to our defense mechanisms, so that we perceive
ourselves as particularly vulnerable to a shake-up, an explosion,
or an eruption of emotion. Whatever initiated the feeling of
being at sixes and sevens, the risk perceived is not from the
original stimulus but from our sense that we are losing control.

"Upset" in this sense is the psychological equivalent of a
physiological state of high irritability. Irritability, as I am using
it here, refers to the capacity of such tissue as muscle to respond
to stimulus—the sensitivity to stimulation. To be in a state of
high irritability means that a lesser than usual stimulus is able
to elicit a response. The threshold for response has been
lowered.

It is interesting that in our culture "irritable" has come to have the connotation of easily annoyed, or ill-tempered; the emotion about to erupt is assumed to be anger. But that is not the use in the physiology laboratory.

It is true that when we lose control, what frequently emerges is anger—and often to our surprise. But the emergent emotion can equally be tearful distress and anguish. In addition similar responses may be elicited by quite different circumstances. The body has a small repertoire of response to stimuli in general. Physical offenders as varied as bacteria, viruses, toxins, and foreign bodies produce monotonously similar physical reaction—inflammation, fever, pain, and the like. It is what makes diagnosis an art in medicine. Similarly, an incredible variety of psychological assaults lead to the emerging emotions of fear and anger and their derivatives. When we lose control, we give vent to these familiar emotions, masking the fact that the conditions that drove us to the upset point may have been remarkably different.

Similarly, the same feeling can caution of different internal states. Feeling upset warns us that we are stretched thin, that some emotion is about to break through our controls—without necessarily indicating the nature of the emerging emotional response.

We can become upset as a derivative of fear, particularly that special kind of fear called apprehension. When we are preoccupied with an imminent or forthcoming event which makes us worried, we will protect our public image and behavior by concealing the distress and controlling our feelings. We will attempt to maintain the normal façade of functioning. As we get progressively more apprehensive, our adaptive cover is threatened; our behavior patterns become disturbed, our concentration interrupted. We sense that we have diminished authority over our own behavior—and we feel upset. When fear is the emerging emotion, the word "nervous" is used synonymously with "upset."

Upset can also be a derivative of guilt. To have done something wrong without the opportunity to expiate, to ask for forgiveness, to set things right produces an anguish. Guilt, then, drives us to its peculiar end. We want to alleviate the feeling. Confrontation with the injured party is eagerly sought for; although it is painful, it will eventually relieve us of the even more painful emotion of guilt. If we cannot, the emotion begins to dominate our consciousness—just as anxiety does—and we again feel upset.

We can be upset as a derivative of anger. Most often, ironically, it is with the kind of anger for which there is no recourse, no confrontation, and therefore no further real danger. It is specifically in such situations where we may be upset. Here the emotion is not anticipatory but a product of memory and recall. Just thinking of the situation that originally promoted the anger produces a sense of frustration and impotence. The *expression* of anger has a cleansing and refreshing response— unless it precipitates guilt or fear. Unexpressed anger, with its erosive quality, readily upsets us. Sometimes the control of the anger is simply too uncomfortable. We must express it, and here the more specific term of "irritability" indicates the nature of the upset. In such cases we often seek provocations to release an anger whose origins were from other places and other times.

James Joyce describes this painfully and poignantly in *Dubliners*. Farrington, a clerk, has been "obliged to offer an abject apology" to his boss for an "impertinence." It was a day of discontent, and "he was full of smouldering anger and revengefulness. He felt humiliated and discontented." His wife, "a little sharp-faced woman who bullied her husband when he was sober and was bullied by him when he was drunk," is not at home. He is greeted by his little boy, Tom:

"Where's your mother?"
"She's out at the chapel."
"That's right. . . . Did she think of leaving any dinner for me?"

"Yes, pa. I—,"

"Light the lamp. What do you mean by having the place in darkness? Are the other children in bed?"

The man sat down heavily on one of the chairs while the little boy lit the lamp. He began to mimic his son's flat accent, saying half to himself: *"At the chapel. At the chapel, if you please!"* When the lamp was lit he banged his fist on the table and shouted:

"What's for my dinner?"

"I'm going . . . to cook it, pa," said the little boy.

The man jumped up furiously and pointed to the fire.

"On that fire! You let the fire out! By God, I'll teach you to do that again!"

He took a step to the door and seized the walking-stick which was standing behind it.

"I'll teach you to let the fire out!" he said, rolling up his sleeve in order to give his arm free play.

The little boy cried, *"O, pa!"* and ran whimpering round the table, but the man followed him and caught him by the coat. The little boy looked about him wildly but, seeing no way of escape, fell upon his knees.

"Now, you'll let the fire out the next time!" said the man, striking at him viciously with the stick. "Take that, you little whelp!"

The boy uttered a squeal of pain as the stick cut his thigh. He clasped his hands together in the air and his voice shook with fright.

"O, pa!" he cried. "Don't beat me, pa! And I'll . . . I'll say a *Hail Mary* for you . . . I'll say a *Hail Mary* for you, pa, if you don't beat me. . . . I'll say a *Hail Mary.* . . ."*

Just as readily, we can be upset secondarily to feeling hurt. When we feel neglected by someone we love, when the person fails to acknowledge our worth we will feel hurt and disappointed, and often in the following days the memory of that "rejection" may be gone but the vulnerable, unstable condition we call "upset" remains. Here "sensitive" is readily substitutable, and again, as with irritability, we are reminded of the threshold-lowering of which the feeling cautions us. We will say that we wake up "on the wrong side of the bed." All those who depend on our good nature and our good performance

---

* James Joyce, *Dubliners* (New York: Viking Press, 1961), pp.97–98.

for the smooth operation of their lives will sense our upset and, if threatened sufficiently by it, will be upset themselves.

Part of the problem with dealing with the feeling of upset is that the specific event leading to it may not in itself have been recognized or perceived as of sufficient importance to register as an event. The emotion may have been isolated from it or denied and the event repressed. It is a most unsettling experience simply to feel upset without knowing why. Women often say they feel weepy or irritable on certain days. Frequently, this will be tied—rightly sometimes and wrongly in others—to a physiological event such as menstruation. Many women are unquestionably particularly upset and vulnerable in the immediate premenstrual phase. So many that I seriously doubt this can be a purely psychological phenomenon. It has the immediacy and the quality of a physiological event, and I am convinced of an endocrine influence on emotional threshold and lability. It is evidenced by the fact that the feeling of upsetness often precedes the awareness that they are premenstrual. The emotionality is not, then, a response to the idea of menstruation but an adjunct of it.

In any of these described situations, what we have been feeling is the same, and quite different from the primary emotion or event which precipitated it, and with which the feeling of upset may exist. In the following quotation from Henry Roth's book *Call It Sleep,* it is totally irrelevant why the mother is upset. We can still identify the emotion of upset. We can isolate the feeling even while not knowing whether it is an adjunct of guilt, fear, rage, depression, or none of these. The scene is between David and his mother, whom he adores. David is so susceptible to his mother's moods, so used to her attention and her affection, that when her upset intrudes on the traditional relationship, he begins to get a resonant feeling of upset.

He could not help but observe in his mother's actions a concealed nervousness, an irresolution as if under the strain of waiting. Unlike the fluent, methodical way in which she habitually moved about the kitchen, her manner now was disjointed, uncertain. In the midst of doing something or of saying something, she would suddenly utter a curious, suppressed exclamation like a sudden groan of dismay, or lift her hand in an obscure and hopeless gesture, or open her eyes as though staring at perplexity and brush back her hair. Everything she did seemed insecure and unfinished. She went from the sink to the window and left the water running and then remembering it with an odd overhastiness, turned, missed the handkerchief she was pegging to the clothesline and let it fall into the yard. A few minutes later, separating the yolks from the whites of the eggs to make the thick yellow pancakes that were to go with the soup, she cut the film of the yolk with eggshell, lost it in the whites. She stamped her foot, chirped with annoyance and brushed back her hair.*

The child observes the unusual behavior of his mother and then, interestingly, he begins—in his own way, with his own activity—to replicate her behavior of upset.

. . . he remained indoors and occupied himself in a score of ways— now frightening himself by making faces at the pier glass, now staring out of the window, now fingering the haze of breath upon it, now crawling under beds, now scribbling. He spent an hour tying himself to the bed post with a bit of washline and attempting to escape, and another constructing strange devices with his trinkets. He tried to play the four-handed game of manipulating patterns out of a double string with two hands and the leg of a chair. It was difficult, the old patterns slipped before they were clinched, ended in a snarl. The mind too was tangled, apprehensive, pent-up.†

Roth, with the intuitive genius of a fine novelist, includes in the sense of upset the metaphor being tangled, snarled, and out of order. David then continues watching his mother:

Meanwhile he had observed that his mother's nervousness was in-creasing. She seemed neither able to divert her mind nor complete any task other than was absolutely necessary. She had begun to sew the new linen she had bought to make pillow-cases with and had ended by ripping out the thread and throwing the cloth back into

---

* Henry Roth, *Call It Sleep* (New York: Avon Books, 1934), pp. 116–17.
† Ibid., p. 117.

the drawer with a harassed cry. "God knows why I can't make these
stitches any shorter! Six to a yard almost! They'd have parted with a
shroud's wear!" And then later, gave up the attempt to thread a cupful
of large red beads and dropped them into the cup again and shut
her eyes. The newspaper received only a worried glance and was
folded up again and dropped in her lap. After which, she sat for
such a long time staring at him, that David's uneasiness grew
intolerable.*

To a child the disorder of the mother becomes more than
upsetting. It begins to produce real anxiety. After all, his security is dependent on the power, authority, discipline, and order
of the person whose life sustains him. In this specific story,
where the mother is the only defense against a psychotic father,
a particularly intense dependence exists. David attempts to
distract his mother from her mood by asking the typical "why"
questions of childhood. The mother, preoccupied, fails to hear
accurately and seems increasingly separated from the child.
Then, recognizing the situation—with the fierce maternalism
that always pre-empts her own desires—she rouses herself out
of the mood:

"Ach!" Exasperatedly she flung her hand down to her side. "Where
are my senses? What am I doing?" She crouched down before the
stove, buried the poker into the ashes with a provoked stab. "Have
you ever seen your mother so mixed? So lost? God have mercy, my
wits are milling! Ach! I go here and I'm there! I go there and I'm
here. And of a sudden I'm nowhere." She lifted the stove lid, threw
a shovelful of coal into the red pit. "David darling, you were saying—?"
Her voice had become solicitous, penitent. She smiled, "You were
saying what?"†

Can we say that we are upset by the intrusion of a strong
positive emotion? I think not. The word connotes a negative
unraveling. We certainly know that good news can be disrup-
tive, but we will say that we are distracted by it—not distraught.

_____
* Ibid., pp. 117–18.
† Ibid., p. 119.

Even though those two words originally derived from the same root, the feelings are different. The observer may on occasion confuse the two, but the participant does not.

Consider thse two delightful ladies, each of whom has been in receipt of a letter from a beau. One has been proposed to by a man she loves, the other has rejected a proposal, for wrong reasons, and now is apprised of her error.

Here is Elizabeth:

In this perturbed state of mind, with thoughts that could rest on nothing, she walked on; but it would not do; in half a minute the letter was unfolded again, and collecting herself as well as she could, she again began the mortifying perusal of all that related to Wickham, and commanded herself so far as to examine the meaning of every sentence.*

And here is Anne:

The absolute necessity of seeming like herself produced then an immediate struggle; but after a while she could do no more. She began not to understand a word they said, and was obliged to plead indisposition and excuse herself. They could then see that she looked very ill, were shocked and concerned, and would not stir without her for the world. This was dreadful. Would they only have gone away, and left her in the quiet possession of that room it would have been her cure; but to have them all standing or waiting around her was distracting, and in desperation, she said she would go home.†

Which is which? To the observer both will seem similarly "out of sorts." But the ladies themselves are at opposite ends in the arc between hope and despair.

Anne is agitated, preoccupied, even distracted, but not upset. She may look upset, but she would never so describe herself. We reserve that feeling for the breakthrough of painful emotion.

The peculiar emotion of feeling upset, then, is not the same as the painful emotions that elicit it. To "feel upset" is not to

---

* Jane Austen, *Pride and Prejudice,* in *The Complete Novels,* p.354.
† Jane Austen, *Persuasion,* in *The Complete Novels,* p.1355.

feel hurt, anger, depression, or the like, but rather it is the awareness of a change in our threshold. When we feel upset, it is a warning to ourselves that it will take less than in normal circumstances to produce whatever the response. As we advertise our upset, it is also a warning to others to tread lightly. The control mechanism is only partially in effect; the fuse is short; and explosions of emotions—of one sort or another—may be anticipated.

~§ 6

Feeling Tired

WITH ALL ITS PHYSICAL IMPLICATIONS, feeling tired, as typically used, has little to do with physical stress or body fatigue. That we struggle to interpret it in these terms is a sign of the urgency with which we attempt to avoid the psychological meaning of feeling tired.

I am well aware that there is such a feeling of physical tiredness. It rarely, however, contributes to our "feeling tired." Most of us no longer do physical work. We will tend rather to use our body hard in play, and one is not likely to hear a downbeat expression of tiredness after two or three hard sets of tennis, particularly if one is the winner. We may say "I'm *exhausted!*" But when we do, there is an exhilarated tone associated with the use of the words. Often when we comment on physical tiredness after exhausting pleasurable activity, we will use affectionate terms for the feeling: "beat," "bushed," "pooped," and the like. When we are physically spent in an activity of excitement and joy and pleasure, we are likely to be unaware of body tiredness.

Ironically, we are more apt to sense a feeling of tiredness on arising. Surely the body must be, physiologically speaking, at a level of improved tonus, charge, and readiness for work after a night of sleep. Even after a sleepless night when we *really* feel tired, physical fatigue ought not be present, since even the sleepless night imposes a physiological rest on the muscular-skeletal system. The feeling of being tired in all of its multiple dictionary meanings is generally an expression of a psychological state. It is emotionally that we feel "drained," "emptied," "consumed," "worn out," "depleted," and "fatigued."

To feel tired, independent of a source, is as close (excepting grief) as most of us come to the feelings of that clinical state called "depression." Feelings of depression are, I suspect, more often than not misread. Customarily, individuals who are depressed will not even be aware of being in the grip of an emotional state. They are more likely to complain of exhaustion, fatigue, boredom, weariness. When a patient states that he is chronically tired, and then describes the fact that he has had a precipitous weight loss and insomnia, the psychiatrist knows that—barring physical illness—he is getting a classical description of depression.

When one asks any patient who comes for psychiatric help whether he feels depressed, he is likely to look at the questioner as though he were an idiot. It goes without saying that if they feel "bad" it means depressed. To the psychiatrist, clinical depression is not an emotion but a specific disease entity, and the irony of that disease entity is that feeling depressed—i.e., blue, dejected, down—is not necessarily an indication of *being* depressed. The true "feelings" of clinical depression are hopelessness and helplessness—or, worse, no "feeling" at all.

Enter the chilly no-man's land of about
Five o'clock in the morning, the no color void
Where the waking head rubbishes out the draggled lot
of Sulphurous dreamscapes . . . *

Tiredness as a feeling is a transient, prodromal emotion that signals a vulnerability to depression. To understand "feeling tired," we must examine the mechanisms of depression, for tiredness is a mild and ephemeral version of the emotions of depression—and emerges from "depressions" of everyday life which even the soundest of us will have experienced.

"Depression" is a relatively new word for what had been traditionally called "melancholia." In the nineteenth century, psychiatry was almost completely a descriptive discipline. As a result, its descriptions were very good indeed. At the turn of the century psychoanalysis began to probe the mechanisms of mental disorders, seeking for the dynamics that led to breakdowns in healthy adaptation. Psychoanalysis early approached the well-defined condition of melancholia. One of the early analogies made was between the signs and symptoms of melancholia and the traditional mourning pattern. The grief reaction has traditionally been seen as a healthy response to the death of a beloved, but melancholia produces similar behavior despite the fact that no loss may have been endured. Anyone recalling a mourning period, or even the sharing of such with a good friend, will certainly recognize common features. Generally there will be deflation of mood—a sense of sadness and dejection. Next, one commonly experiences a withdrawal of interest from the outside world and the activities that normally occupy our daily life. The image of the mourner sitting hunched—rocking slowly, perhaps—fingering over and over an article in the hands, or simply staring into space, is a prototypic representation. Another sign of both grief and depression is a general

---

* Sylvia Plath, "The Ghost's Leavetaking" in *The Colossus & Other Poems* (New York: Alfred A. Knopf, 1971), pp. 42, 43.

inhibition of physical activity. Finally, a common feature in both is the lack of capacity to feel or relate in a loving way.

There are of course multiple ways of expressing grief shaped by culture, tradition, and personality. There are agitated forms of depression as there may be agitated periods in mourning. Some cultural directives are strong in demanding either the constriction or the expression of emotion. But though one recognizes the variability, there still remains a core of symptoms in the mourning period which seems to cross cultures and individual personalities.

While we still obviously carry the loss of the loved object with us for our lifetime, it is presumed to be normal to pass out of specific mourning in a reasonably short period of time. We will continue to bear our grief, but we will also resume normal experiences and activities, resume the responsibilities and relationships of life. When we do not, one becomes concerned that the grief reaction has slipped into a depression. And, indeed, one of the leading causes of depression is the loss of the loved object.

Depression, however, seems almost a macabre and grotesque parody of grief. It persists too long; it becomes self-destructive; and to the traditional forms of grief it adds a few seemingly irrational additional emotions. The depressed patient seems almost masochistic in demeaning himself, in blaming himself, in finding fault with his life, his functions, and his persona. He seems devoid of all self-esteem and is excessively involved in self-accusations. He has passed beyond the sense of a loss into a state where all is lost.

> . . . I have of late—but wherefore I know not—
> lost all my mirth, forgone all custom of exercises;
> and indeed it goes so heavily with my disposition
> that this goodly frame, the earth, seems to me a
> sterile promontory; this most excellent canopy, the
> air, look you, this brave o'erhanging firmament,
> this majestical roof fretted with golden fire, why,

> it appears no other thing to me than a foul and
> pestilent congregation of vapours.*

This is despair!

Originally, the brilliant German psychoanalyst Karl Abraham
proposed a direct relationship between grief and depression.
This crucial analogy dominated psychoanalytic thinking for at
least sixty years, and it was presumed that all depression represented a symbolic unconscious loss of a loved object. What
may have been lost may explicitly have been a job or even
just a job opportunity, but the assumption was that the individual was grieving as though he had lost his loved object. With
women in our culture, particularly, most depression and most
suicidal attempts do emanate from the loss of a loved object,
either through death or through rejection or abandonment.

Closer examination of the data of depression began to make
it apparent that men rarely were driven to suicide by a real
loss of love. How strange, then, that the symbolic representation would be so much stronger than the actual loss! More
men commit suicide over the loss of a job than the loss of a
wife or child. This does not mean that they necessarily value
one over the other; it would be monstrous to judge it so. What
it means is that the mechanism of depression had been misunderstood and the grievous loss which cannot be borne, which
leads to despair, is not love, but the loss of our sense of confidence in our future.

The fact that women so frequently were driven to depression
by loss of a loved object was because so often in our culture
a woman's future and her value were fused with the male
figures on whom she was forced to be dependent. We now
know that the depression occurs when we lose confidence in
our own coping mechanisms. We become depressed when we
are bankrupt of self-esteem and self-confidence, when we no
longer have the sense of our own capacities to insure either

Hamlet, Act II, Scene 2, lines 300–309.

our actual survival or the worthiness or value of the life which we can sustain.

The two major causes of depression, then, are loss of confidence in ourselves as executives of our futures, and loss of respect for ourselves as suppliers of pleasure in the life that may remain for us. If we become depressed because we have lost a loved object, it is because we have overvalued that loved object in terms of our survival and pleasure. Such depression-prone people carry a childhood sense of their own inadequacy into adult life. They view their capacity to survive—their well-being—as the exclusive product of a relationship with another. The loss of that other therefore means the loss of their *modus vivendi.* Kierkegaard has said:

> Despair is never ultimately over the external object but always over ourselves. A girl loses her sweetheart and she despairs. It is not over the lost sweetheart, but over herself–without–the–sweetheart. And so it is with all cases of loss whether it be money, power, or social rank. The unbearable loss is not really in itself unbearable. What we cannot bear is in being stripped of the external object, we stand denuded and see the intolerable abyss of ourselves.*

It becomes obvious, then, that whatever we overvalue in terms of our pride system will be a potential source of depression if its existence is threatened. It can, indeed, be a lover, but it can also be a job, a fortune, our social position, our beauty, our children, or our professional standing. It can even, ironically, be our neurotic defenses. The young psychiatrist is always shocked to find that as he begins to remove the neurotic symptoms from an individual he may be destroying the patient's reason for existence. One of the first signs of change with a psychoanalytic patient is often the appearance of depression

---

* Sören Kierkegaard, "The Sickness unto Death," as quoted in *Caring,* Willard Gaylin (New York: Alfred Knopf, 1976), p. 157. I had read this particular translation and written it in my journal without noting the source. I find it particularly eloquent in this form and have therefore retained it. A less poetic version appears in Robert Bretall, *A Kierkegaard Anthology* (New York: Modern Library, 1963), p. 343.

as neurotic defense mechanisms are struck down.

When we feel threatened, we can become angry or anxious. These two emotions trigger mechanisms to prepare us to meet the threat. When we become depressed, we abandon both emotions and reserve what anger we have for ourselves. We accept our defeat as inevitable. Depression is not primarily a defensive maneuver, as most neuroses are; it is rather the absence of such maneuvers. It represents the bankruptcy of the individual as announced to himself and the public at large. It is his acceptance of his dismal fate. He sits there helpless and hopeless, beyond reassurance, beyond comfort.

It is interesting to compare two of the most famous quotations traditionally associated with depression. When Hamlet says,

> O, that this too too solid flesh would melt,
> Thaw, and resolve itself into a dew!
> Or that the Everlasting had not fixt
> His canon 'gainst self-slaughter. O God! God!
> How weary, stale, flat, and unprofitable
> Seem to me all the uses of this world!*

that is depression. It is passivity and resignation. "O God! God!" is a lamentation. And "weary, stale, flat, and unprofitable" are the feelings and fabric of depression.

But when Job opened his mouth and cursed the day and said,

Let the day perish wherein I was born, and the night in which it was said, There is a man child conceived.

Let that day be darkness; let not God regard it from above, neither let the light shine upon it.

Let darkness and the shadow of death stain it; let a cloud dwell upon it; let the blackness of the day terrify it. . . .

Why died I not from the womb? Why did I not give up the ghost when I came out of the belly? . . .

For now should I have lain still and been quiet. I should have slept: then had I been at rest. . . .

---

* Act 1, Scene II, lines 129–34.

Wherefore is light given to him that is in misery, and life unto the bitter in soul. . . .*

that is not depression. The passive, languid, melancholic Hamlet is not the contentious, vigorous, and virile Job. Job does not use God's name as a refrain. He is talking to him! Here is an angry man who is still railing against injustice. This is not the accepting martyr. He is demanding answers of God and justification. He is not passive and submissive at this time; otherwise he would not say, "Then *had* I been at rest"—he would have *been* at rest.

What we are seeing in Job is the externally directed rage of a healthy man in grief demanding the whys of an unjust fate. There is nothing flat about Job's articulations. They are crescendo. There is nothing tired in Job, where Hamlet is nothing if not tired.

The depressed patient is at the end of his rope and accepting the end. He is weary and eager for it. He eschews all of the activities that serve pleasure and support life. The depressed patient feels spent and exhausted in the extreme. "Tired" here is too weak a word. But if one re-examines the emotions of depression one sees how closely they relate to these feelings of tiredness. The depressed patient feels drained, emptied, used up. Like the use of the word "fatigue" in relationship to metals, the depressed person has lost the essential components of elasticity, resiliency, and strength that normally characterize human nature.

Obviously, to feel tired is not to feel hopeless and helpless. Those are emotions which require an accretion in time, and depth of experience. They are arrived at only after a steady expenditure of psychic resources. Feeling tired is a transient feeling and a warning of lowered reserves. In the same way that a rush of anxiety is related to, but does not describe, the terror of an "anxiety state," the tired feeling is related to de-

* Job 3: 3–5, 11, 13, 20.

pression. These temporary feelings are signals that alert and mobilize. The chronic states do more than merely increase the quantity of suffering. The whole experience is different because the constancy of the emotion converts it from a warning to a way of life. The way of life adds a qualitative dimension that none of us who are spared its experience can visualize. No number of slaps, bruises, cuts, or abrasions prepare one for the chronic pain of certain malignancies. Building blocks are not buildings and signals are not states of existence.

The signaling emotion, whatever it is, says to us, "Get going." It gives us a taste of what we may be in for. We feel tired when for a moment or even a day we have doubts and questions about our capacity to insure our survival or our capacity to guarantee the value—in terms of pleasure and usefulness—of that survival. It is a product of self-doubt that all of us must feel in a world that demands struggle. When we feel tired, we are having doubts; when we feel depressed, we are no longer having doubts; we are convinced—and convinced in the negative.

In one sense, feeling tired is the opposite of depression. There is a rigidity and fixity to depression; there is absolute conviction that there is no exit.

> I myself am hell;
> nobody's here—
> only skunks. . . .*

The conviction of hopelessness is wrong—but it dominates our perception. When we feel tired, however, by designating it physical (when in our unconscious, at least, we know better) we are reassuring ourselves that psychologically there is nothing wrong. When we use our body hard physically, we know there is a time of exhaustion which demands est. But there is also the comforting reassurance that with rest and nourishment there will be a renascence of strength and energy. The

---

* Robert Lowell, "Skunk Hour," *Life Studies* (New York: Farrar, Straus & Cudahy, 1959), p.89.

physical model reassures our conscious self-deceiving self, while the unconscious psyche registers the true signal of distress and mobilizes proper corrective procedures. When we recognize what is going on, when we consciously feel an erosion of our self-confidence, we experience discouragement. The feeling of discouragement is, more often than not, specific and task-oriented. When we are unaware of our diminishing confidence and it seems to relate to our entire life endeavor, we will somatize the feeling. We will convert our sense of emotional exhaustion into a physical feeling—and we will feel "tired."

When we feel tired, then, we are feeling temporarily used up; when we feel depressed, we feel permanently used up. Because of the hidden source of the tired feeling, the mechanism may be compared to a thermostat rather than an alarm. When it registers at the discomfort threshold we have set, the feeling automatically triggers corrective maneuvers. Even if we mistakenly interpret "tired" as a physical phenomenon, the cures directed toward it are similar to what is necessary when we know we are dealing with exhaustion of psychic energy. In both we recognize our need for spiritual and psychological nourishment; we know that it is now time to be cared for, and to be caring; that it is time for us to indulge our desires—or simply that we are ready for some reward. If we feel tired too often and too unremittingly, it may caution us that it is a prologue to the oppressive exhaustion that constitutes depression.

The feeling of tiredness tells us that we are spending our psychic resources at a greater rate than we are earning. Psychological strength is based on self-confidence and self-esteem. These are built on the prideful awareness of our worth that evolves from doing, giving, loving, achieving—and the rewards inherent in love and work. This reservoir of strength can be drawn on to help us endure the depleting aspects of daily drudgery—the dry seasons of our endeavors. We must restore ourselves through prideful activities to underwrite the unrewarding labors of necessity. The balance is an important and, in modern life, a precarious one. Most people lead lives with psychic reserves as minimal as their economic ones.

The shift in the balance—predicated on such small differences—effects such antithetical results. As the distinguished nineteenth-century economist Wilkins Micawber has said:

"Annual income twenty pounds, annual expenditure nineteen ninety six, result happiness. Annual income twenty pounds, annual expenditure twenty pounds ought and six, result misery."*

And as Micawber's colleague reminded us, "Trifles make the sum of life." We must therefore watch the pence of pain and pleasure.

One peculiar aspect of emotional currency is, however, that it operates on a different cash-flow principle. When we feel tired or depressed, what is needed is *more* activity, not less— or, to be more precise, more activity of a different quality. Energy must be used, not conserved, but used for loving, playing, and doing. Here, spending is saving. We build our reserves through our actions.

Often the feeling of tiredness is specifically directed to an activity, thing, or person, and we then use that peculiar idiom "tired of." We may say that we are tired of travel, tired of television, tired of our job, tired of our husband. Here the meaning is clearly that we are bored, impatient with the specific activity or person. But we do use the metaphor of fatigue and exhaustion—and not by chance. "Tired of" feels different from "bored with." It does literally mean that we no longer have confidence that our involvement with that person or activity will nourish or enrich us. When we say that we are tired of a relationship, it means that the sum total of the involvements has slipped into deficit. It is expenditure, not earning. And it is time to leave—or change the conditions of involvement.

---

* Charles Dickens, *David Copperfield* (New York: Dodd, Mead & Co., 1943), pp. 169–70.

If we modify the conditions, and the feelings still persist, we must begin to question whether we are not simply projecting our internal dissatisfactions onto a convenient external scapegoat situation. This nagging and persistent internal sense of dissatisfaction may be prelude to depression.

When we are depressed, we are, of course, tired of life in all of its available forms and with all of its potential pleasures. Usually, in depression we abandon hope prematurely. It is not life or the nature of existence that we have exhausted—only the narrow segment of our particular life style. We are only tired of certain conditions of our current existence and narcissistically confuse our universe with the universal. We must learn the value of—and have the opportunity for—change.

The relationship between predictability, monotony, boredom, melancholia, ennui, tiredness, and depression becomes apparent with the most cursory examination. Here we see the almost polar relationship between aspects of depression and pride. We build pride on achievements. With pride we raise our levels of self-confidence and self-esteem. With depression— we announce to ourselves our bankruptcy. The feeling of being tired warns of a negative balance, a depletion of these necessary resources.

One need not feel frightened of feeling tired. One ought, perhaps, to feel concerned if one has never felt tired. It may imply a limited reach; a lack of stretching to potential; a protection against failure by settling for less. To strive, to push, to expand life—all require that we be discouraged at times, fail at efforts, and have self-doubts. Feeling tired allows us to acknowledge that we are ready, and needing, to move on. Perhaps the trivial use of so plebeian a word as "tired" is our way of avoiding the implications of the feeling. Unremitting tiredness has the potential to lead to that most painful of psychic conditions—depression. By using a simple word like "tired," we can exploit its physical analogue to reassure ourselves that what we are feeling is ephemeral, reversible, and everyday.

~§ 7

Feeling Bored

B OREDOM IS surely one of the most universal of feelings, and, in an age which has elevated the concept of alienation to an obsession, one of the most written-about of emotions. Why, then, did I find it so elusive, so difficult? Why did I struggle more to capture the essence of this feeling than any of the others? Obviously, I have experienced boredom. I have experienced boredom in the pursuit of boredom. I have experienced boredom by any of the definitions of boredom I have read. What I could not find was the common thread that bound the various definitions of the emotion.

Some of the traditional feelings that have been classified under the general heading of boredom are so antithetical, so at cross-purposes, that there seems no way to unify them into one "thing." Variation is allowable within a group, but there must exist some common root which unifies even the diversity within the group. We have generic classifications for animals and plants which create kinships of the most unlikely sort. The uninitiated may find it bizarre to know that the sweet-scented lily and the pungent onion are close relatives, but the technician who classifies them, knowing the structure that binds them to each other generically, accepts the relationship.

So it is with emotions. Think of the various forms of anger. Irritation, annoyance, rage, resentment, fury, pique, and impatience all conjure up different anecdotes, different situations, different experiences, and different feelings within us. Yet we can find a common root among them. No question that the intensity seriously separates the various categories, but the similarities define a family of feelings called anger.

With boredom, however, I believe we are dealing with two look-alikes (like the day lily and the true lily) which belong to different categories.

The first category is that passive emotion which is in direct descent from *accidie* (or sloth), classically listed as the seventh deadly sin. In its original definition, sloth referred specifically to passivity in religious matters. In these days, where most of us do not take religion with quite the seriousness of our forebears, it may be hard to imagine that at one time even the absence of energy and fervor in religious conviction would be registered as a sin. In the old days it was important not just to be religious but religious with zeal, with action, and with the energy of our minds and bodies. In direct line from this is a whole series of related emotions, from sloth to weariness to dreariness to melancholy and finally to ennui. "Ennui" seems to me an appropriate term to use for this category of boredom. Oblomov is the ultimate symbol of ennui carried to a way of life.

Hardly any outside attractions existed for him, and every day he grew more firmly rooted in his flat. . . . At first he found it irksome to remain dressed all day, then he felt lazy about dining out except with intimate bachelor friends, at whose houses he could take off his tie, unbutton his waistcoat, and even lie down and have an hour's sleep. Evening parties soon wearied him also: one had to put on a dresscoat, to shave every day. . . . His friend Stolz succeeded in making him go and see people . . . but without him Oblomov again wholly abandoned himself to solitude and seclusion that could only be disturbed by something unusual, out of the ordinary routine of life; but nothing of the sort happened or was likely to happen. . . . The flower of life blossomed and bore no fruit. Oblomov sobered down; occasionally, at Stolz's advice, he read this or that book, though without hurry or eagerness, lazily following the lines with his eyes. However interesting the passage he was reading might be, if it was time to go to bed or to have dinner he put the book face downwards. . . . If he was given the first volume of a work he did not, after finishing it, ask for the second, but if the second were brought to him he slowly read it. As years passed he found even a first volume of a work too much for him and spent most of his leisure with his elbow on the table, leaning his head on his arms; sometimes he leaned against the book which Stolz insisted he should read.*

"Ennui" has a romantic and exotic sound to the English ear, and a somewhat alien feeling to the mid-twentieth-century sensibility. It is a nineteenth-century emotion. And it seems appropriate to use this French word, since the French seem to have been particularly captivated by this melancholy languor. From Pascal to Proust, there has been a long tradition of interest in this secular form of sloth that we might as well simply call "ennui."

For the second category I will use the term "boredom." To my ears at least, it is a newer, more abrupt, jazzier, more irritable term, which better describes the fidgety, agitated, jumping-out-of-skin contemporary feeling which I see as deserving of separate representation. Boredom is a more inevitable part of the middle-class American experience than ennui.

Ralph Greenson is one of the few psychiatrists who have devoted significant time and attention to boredom. He was

---

* Ivan Goncharov, *Oblomov* (New York: E. P. Dutton & Co., 1960), pp. 58, 60–62.

cognizant of the two distinct forms, the agitated and the passive, but nonetheless felt there were common features. His
description is succinct and accurate and he lists five elements
most commonly seen:

A state of dissatisfaction and a disinclination to action; a state of
longing and an inability to designate what is longed for; a sense of
emptiness; a passive expectant attitude with the hope that the external
world will supply the satisfaction; a distorted sense of time in which
time seems to stand still.*

Obviously, this definition attempts to span both boredom
and ennui. It explicitly describes the passivity and inability
to move against the mood and implies the edginess of the more
typical boredom that most of us experience. It is my contention
that the feelings are different, because their mechanisms are
different. Boredom moves to defeat that which ennui accepts.
Boredom is a call to action; ennui is resignation. In that sense
they act in an analogous way to fear and depression.

Fear and depression are traditionally seen as alternative
mechanisms, if not quite opposites. Fear is an alerting mechanism. It is not merely a signal of some danger to our survival
or well-being, but a mobilizer that gets us going. In that sense
fear and anger share at least the same purposes, although they
get us going in opposite directions: one running from and the
other running toward. Depression, on the other hand, is essentially seen as the acceptance of our own destruction.

The difference between boredom and ennui can be understood in similar terms as reactions leading either to defense
against the conditions producing boredom or to a resigned
acceptance. "I'm *so* bored!" is not a passive statement. It is
an irritated, jumpy, nagging call to action. It is a feelable feeling, whereas ennui seems almost the absence of any feeling—

---

* R. Greenson, "On Boredom," *Journal of the American Psychoanalytic Association,* 1 (1953): 7–21.

as does depression. Of course the two can occur at the same time in overlapping or alternating patterns. It is part of the delight and difficulty of dealing with feelings that they often occur as a mélange in which the fused elements are recognized with difficulty.

The close relationship between ennui and depression can be seen in two poems by C. P. Cavafy. The first is called "Monotony," and presumes to describe this feeling.

> One monotonous day follows another
> identically monotonous. The same things
> will happen to us again and again,
> the same moments come and go.
>
> A month passes by, brings another month.
> Easy to guess what lies ahead:
> all of yesterday's boredom.
> And tomorrow ends up no longer like tomorrow.*

In the poem "The City," Cavafy gives an extraordinarily accurate literary representation of the despair and hopelessness which are the key elements of depression. Yet the mood of this poem is a direct extension and intensification of the feelings of the first.

> You won't find a new country, won't find another shore.
> This city will always pursue you
> You'll walk the same streets, grow old
> in the same neighborhoods, turn gray in these same houses.
> You'll always end up in this city. Don't hope for things elsewhere:
> there's no ship for you, there's no road.
> Now that you've wasted your life here, in this small corner,
> you've destroyed it everywhere in the world.†

There is no mobilization in either, there is no plea for change. There is the passive acceptance of the fate. The first quotation

---

* C. P. Cavafy, *Collected Poems,* ed. George Savidis (Princeton: Princeton University Press, 1975), p. 45.

† Ibid., p. 51.

expresses what I call ennui (*not* boredom) and which I see as a direct antecedent to despair or depression.

The more typical boredom is so clearly a call to action that it is often said out loud even when, as is more likely in boredom, we are alone. If not actually articulated, I have heard myself saying in my inner mind, "I am *so* bored!" And *always* as an exclamation. The emotions of ennui are as alien to me (and I can only hope will always be) as the nineteenth-century world with which I, at least, tend to identify it. The boredom I am now describing is an old antagonist and familiar feeling. It is not a passive state, nor is it the absence of feeling, as is this deadness of ennui. It is an impatient, almost resentful feeling; it is sharp, motivating, and, at base, very close to the anxiety from which it is derived. It is not surprising therefore that the defenses against boredom are often identical to the defenses against anxiety.

Defenses against what, however? What does boredom signal? What is its warning? Fear is a defense against perceived threat. The threat may be real or imagined but it signals something dangerous about to happen. Boredom obviously does not serve this purpose. When we feel bored, it is not in response to a threat to survival—but rather to the *value* of survival. Life is presumed to supply pleasure and have worth. For the most part, we do not acknowledge or question that premise. It is when we begin to be unsure of our capacity to "enjoy" life that most of us come closest to the rather theoretical concept of existential anxiety, so popular in the post-World War II era.

With existential anxiety, what is frightening us is not a direct threat to our life, but a threat to the meaning of life or, more accurately, an awareness of the absence of meaning in our life. If we detach ourselves too much from our daily existence, it is possible to get into the mood of visualizing human life like the life of an ant, a meaningless round of diversionary activities where ultimate purpose is belied by the fact that all life ends in the identical and unavoidable terminus of death. That being the case, the meaning of life must be not in its end but in its means. Like the trip around the world, the final destination is not the point. It is not where you are going that counts. You are going nowhere, and therefore you had better enjoy the trip. It is only the trip that counts. The "I can't wait till I get there" phenomenon has no meaning when applied to life.

In periods of real and immediate threats to survival, one has little time for existential anxiety—or, for that matter, for neurosis altogether. The struggle for existence, for labor to earn food, shelter, comfort, and survival, allows no time for preoccupation with self, or for philosophical speculations on the meaning of life. In a middle-class society, however, few of us are still struggling for basic survival. Here the ground is ripe for that form of alienation which presages ennui. The emotions against which we are defending in boredom and ennui involve the emergence of a sense of meaninglessness to life or an emptiness of our own resources—an impending lack of confidence in ourself, not as an instrument of survival but as an instrument of pleasure and pride. When we begin to get anxious about the potential for survival, we feel depressed. But survival without emotional meaning is its own form of horror. When we begin to become anxious about our potential for a pleasure or purpose in survival, we become bored. Boredom, then, is a mobilization for action against the absence of pleasure; ennui is the resigned acceptance of a pleasureless and meaningless existence—the ultimate giving up on ourselves as a source of pleasure. The defense against existential despair is in the actions of living: in the accretion of experiences, achievements, sensations, and pleasures.

In one short essay, Albert Camus shows the relationship between boredom and ennui and impending depression as well

as anywhere I am aware of in literature. "Death in the Soul"
was written when Camus was only twenty-one. It describes
the young Camus's visit to Prague.

Around me were a million human beings who have been alive all
this time whose existences have never concerned me. They're alive.
I was thousands of kilometers from home. I could not understand
their language. They walked quickly, all of them. And as they overtook
and passed me they cut themselves off from me. I felt lost.

Broke, friendless, and insecure, with the self-pity and self-dram-
atization of the young, Camus decides to wallow in his isolation,
a decision, however, which is dangerous even despite the self-
inflicted aspects. The streets frighten and depress him with
the alienation of language and the lack of communication.

Still more afraid of being alone in my hotel room, without money
or enthusiasm, reduced to myself and my miserable thoughts. . . . I
ran all the way to my hotel, I went to bed, and waited for sleep
which came almost at once.

He tried to cheer himself up by intellectualizations.

"Any country where I am not bored is a country that teaches me
nothing."*

Nothing seems to work.

Anguish was gaining ground. I paid too much attention to that
sharp twinge of pain in my head. I decided to organize my days, to
cover them with points of reference. I stayed in bed as late as possible
and the days were consummately shorter. I washed, shaved, and me-
thodically explored the town.
I lost myself in the sumptuous baroque churches, looking for a home-
land in them, emerging emptier and more depressed after a disap-
pointing confrontation with myself. . . . I wanted my rebellion to
melt into melancholy. But in vain. As soon as I came out I was a
stranger again.†

---

* Albert Camus, "Death in the Soul," *Lyrical and Critical Essays* (New York:
Alfred A. Knopf, 1968), pp. 40–41.
  † Ibid., p. 42.

Here is a young man who—despite all pretenses—desperately needs companionship. The isolation is threatening to him. He is forced to confront himself alone with no stimulation from the outside world and he is unprepared for it. He is at a stage in life where his need for communication is particularly urgent. He needs the sense of other to appreciate his sense of self. It is this isolation which feeds his boredom, melancholy, ennui, and impending depression. He looks into himself and at this point of his life finds little comfort and little respect for the self as the source of pleasure.

Here I am stripped bare in a town where the signs are strange, unfamiliar hieroglyphics, with no friends to talk to, in short without any distraction. I know very well that nothing will deliver me from this room filled with the noises of a foreign town, to lead me to the more tender glow of a fire. . . . Man is face to face with himself: I defy him to be happy.*

In the midst of this rather florid philosophizing, so atypical of the more mature Camus with whom we are familiar, comes a description of devices to counter boredom with which every reader must be familiar.

Without paying attention to what I was doing, my mind empty, I wasted a few moments reading the instructions for a shaving cream that I had already been using for a month. The day was heavy . . . I spent the afternoon in a state that would be hard to describe. I lay on my bed, thinking of nothing, with a strange heaviness in my heart. I cut my nails. I counted the cracks in the floorboard. "If I can count up to a thousand. . ." At fifty or sixty I gave up.

Toward the end of the afternoon, broken with weariness, I stared madly at the door handle, endlessly repeating a popular accordion tune in my empty head. At that moment I had gone as far as I could. I had no more country, city, hotel room, or name. . . . There was a knock at the door and my friends came in. I was saved.

Camus then leaves with his friends and finds his agitated mood gradually easing:

---

* Ibid., p. 44.

Life was about to break through. I know now what it was: I was ready to be happy. . . . I had not changed, of course. It was simply that I was no longer alone. In Prague, I was suffocating surrounded by walls. Here, I was face to face with the world, and liberated from myself.*

The liberation from self was the key element of relief. It was a relief to Camus because the self was failing to supply him with the sources of pleasure and, in so failing, had begun to suggest that life itself was pleasureless. When the self is an adequate source of pleasure, we do not have to escape. When it fails to serve us, we suffer not just the absence of pleasure but the fear that there may be no such thing as pleasure. It is then we are often frantic in seeking distraction, entertainment, reassurance that there are external sources to feed our hunger for pleasure.

It is writing such as this which explains why most people tend to link Camus (despite all of his protestations) with his contemporary Sartre as an existentialist. Existentialism, like most things, can be the source of either despair or joy. The fact that there is no "meaning to life outside of the living" can create a sense of purposelessness or can direct one to attend seriously to the living. If there is no end, only means, then the means must be an end in itself and the means must be a source of joy. If living is all, then living should be rich, full, devoured greedily and lustily. But if living is all and living is boring, then there might as well be nothing.

There is too much action, too much self-pity, too much rebellion, too much irritation, too much youth in this essay to be classifiable as ennui. Ennui is resigned; boredom is restless. This to me is boredom. And it is, as the author clearly states, a defense against our own emptiness. We have numerous defenses against the feeling. Obviously, the chief defense is a joy in our own existence, a sense of ourselves as creators of our own pleasure. Our very emotions are often a defense—

---

* Ibid., pp. 45, 46, 47, 49.

and not just the salutary ones. Pain, as well as pleasure, creates a sense of aliveness and participation. The defenses that serve us well in protecting against anxiety can be mobilized by boredom. Action is a defense, for it defines the self as actor. We feel ourselves in our actions and, as will later be seen, we feel good through our action.

We can and do, when we are bored, resort to the regressive defenses represented by orality and dependency. One of the first things that most of us do when we are bored is find some way of putting something in our mouths. The refrigerator is, generally (with the possible exception of the television set—a whole other story), the first line of defense against boredom. Boredom, then, is the opposite of interest, the opposite of involvement, the opposite of engagement.

One of the traditional defenses against boredom is fantasy. Since part of the problem of much of our life today is that it is stripped of the mechanisms which made us feel worthwhile and the devices which gave us a sense of pride and creativity through work, fantasy becomes a substitute.

In relation to the need and usefulness of fantasy, work can be divided into three crude categories. In one category, the work itself is intrinsically rewarding, and one does not need fantasy. This is becoming an increasingly smaller division of the working population. The reduction of crafts to an industrialized process of small incomplete parts has made the assembly line a mechanical, unremitting bore.

But beyond the assembly line, even the more glamorous fields of the professions can be reduced to boredom with the increasing specialization which demands mastery, and in demanding mastery demands limitation. To a specialist surgeon, the perfection of an operative procedure may have in itself a great measure of excitement and challenge, but he may then be reduced to spending his life doing the same few operative procedures which must inevitably become a bore. That it is not inevitably so is because of the inbuilt complexities of the human being and the fact that the "same" procedure can often have multiple variations. But the fact of boredom within the professions is recognizable to any psychiatrist who finds a large percentage of his patients drawn from those professions. The work here, however, commands attention—if not interest—and precludes the relief of fantasy.

At the other end of the scale is a kind of work which is so mechanical that it need not be boring. I can recall working as a boy at a drill press where my entire job was taking small ball-bearing casings from a huge barrel, holding them for a moment under a reamer to take off the rough edge, then dropping them into another huge barrel. I did this eight hours a day for a few weeks in the summer to earn money for college. It was, surprisingly, not a boring job. It was purely mechanical and therefore did not involve utilization of anything remotely approaching mental functioning. It was a musculoskeletal operation. Since it required no thinking at all, I was then free to think about anything I wished and here had the recourse to that great defense against boredom—fantasy. I was rarely inside that factory. *Where* I was is best reserved for private memory, but, being an adolescent, the power of fantasy was still great within me. Life for an adolescent, after all, is still more potential than realized, and fantasy intrudes readily on reality. With age we lose the power to transport ourselves with fantasy. Reminiscence is the old man's alternative.

I suspect I could have sustained that job through the entire summer were it not for a chance accident. The ball-bearing casings from which I worked seemed an inexhaustible supply. But it was not. I began to notice that slowly over the days I was getting closer and closer to the bottom of the barrel. I therefore unconsciously instituted a purpose to the job. I was not aware that this had happened until one day the supplier in the factory, evidently noticing the casings diminishing, came with an even larger barrel and filled mine once again to the top. That was it. What had been added was a sense of the hopelessness of the task. Had I been allowed to complete my barrel, I suspect I could have gone on to the next and the next, but being deprived of even this small example of closure, of termination, of achievement—of creativity, if you will—I could not bear it. I quit at the end of that week.

When fantasy fails and when we feel stripped of stimuli, we begin to feel that special kind of restless anxiety that constitutes boredom. Predictability and routine are the allies of boredom. Therefore the unpredictable and the new are defenses against it. I suppose this explains the popularity of fashion in all of its broad manifestations. We are ready for change in the form, if not the substance, of life. Surely it explains the depressiveness of a constant environment. Seasons are renewing. As much as I may hate the cold, oppressive, and constricting winter—with short days and long nights, with its limits on my actions and activities—if it allows for the emergence of spring, it is worth enduring. We may be the most avid of gardeners, but by the end of August most of us are ready to close shop. I cannot imagine enjoying gardening as much as I do were I to live in a tropical climate. I need the termination in fall, the absence in winter, and the anticipation in spring to sharpen and complement the three months in which gardening supports my restless attention.

Change and alternation—even pretended change, even artificial change—supply a kind of renewal that denies that all is predictable, that all has been experienced, and that there is nothing new under the sun.

Nietzsche has said that "against boredom even the gods themselves struggle in vain." Even the gods? Especially the gods! To know all, to have done all, to have seen all, to predict all—in an unending immortality through an endless infinity of time—would lead quickly from boredom to ennui to despair. Man is the savior of the gods. By endowing *Homo sapiens* with free will, the gods have created the ultimate, unpredictable toy. They have introduced chance and variation, danger and delight, into the eternal design.

But predictability is one of the prices of security, and we human beings must insure our own security. We are not free to change jobs every fifteen years—except an extraordinarily indulged minority of us—because survival must come first, and only then the pleasure of survival. If pleasure cannot come from true creativity and true pride, we can turn to other sources. This brings us to the field of entertainment.

Very young children are presumed not to experience boredom. As they get older, one begins to find the signs when they articulate "What shall I do now, Mommy?" But even then it is incredible how simple-minded a suggestion can involve the three- or four-year-old for considerable periods of time. He is at the height of his intellectual curiosity. This curiosity is an instinctive phenomenon present in all children which drives them into the environment and away from clinging to the parent. It is a necessary step in the whole process of individuation whereby we move from dependency to autonomy. Ironically, we first require attachment—before we are capable of separation. We require the safety of a caretaker to allow us the peace of mind and confidence to move around in our world. As long as he is in the reassuring presence of the parent, the child can begin to separate himself from that parent and explore the environment.

It may be that premature boredom in adolescence and young adulthood is a sign of the early death of curiosity. When there are new worlds to explore simply within our fingers and toes, or the pots and pans of a kitchen cupboard, there can be no boredom. When we have exhausted the resources of ourselves and our immediate environment—or, worse, before we really have but only think that we have exhausted those resources— we turn to other forms of entertainment.

Play is the primary form of physical entertainment and it

is creative. We enjoy the sense of self through body movement and interaction with others. There is of course a form of intellectual play, and reading for pleasure is a major part of it. Those who are blessed with the joy of reading have an almost infinite capacity for protection against boredom. With fiction and biography, we can play at being others in other times. It is an extension of identification which allows us, beyond the people we know and love, to live with, share with, suffer with, experience and thrill with a whole gamut of real and imagined people. We can transcend our time, our space, our age, our sex. We can share Elizabeth's anguish as she watches the building of the Spanish Armada; we can raft down a Mississippi that no longer exists with Huck and Jim; we can share the laboratory with the distinguished scientist; we can relive an adolescence similar to, different from, more painful, or less painful than our own. All of which by expanding our sense of self is a kind of entertainment.

Through literature and the arts, we can enlarge our intellectual horizons and our emotional depths. Learning, with its implication of newness, open-endedness, self-achievement, and pride—with its promise of mastery—is the greatest antidote to boredom. Unfortunately, even here, the twentieth century seems to have conspired against modern man. We have reduced most of our entertainments to diversions. The distinction here is the degree of involvement. As I see an entertainment, it uses us, even if we seem only to be sitting in an armchair. Diversion simply distracts us as we continue a kind of intellectual passivity and emotional numbness. It is one of the most distressing things about the conversion of much of our playtime into a watching of play. There is a difference between playing football and watching it played. The increasing tendency to be passive participants is dangerous because of the ultimate inadequacy of the passive role as a builder of self-confidence. It is true that spectator sports allow us to identify, and in that sense to expand ourselves. We can take joy in "our" team, and take pride in it. In the moments we are watching the professional, we become that pro, and by identifying with him, achieve a level of mastery and accomplishment we could not attain by ourselves. But it does not help our sticking power, it does not nourish, like actual involvement. With televised sports a decent percentage of interest is augmented by gambling. The estimated amount of gambling on games is enormous. This would represent true involvement—but on the most elemental and magical level. Gambling is a peculiar counterphobic (and masochistic) mechanism for proving "luckiness" (i.e., lovability) or its opposite. It produces excitement and danger and promise and fear.

Television, that immensely powerful and potential medium of the arts, nonetheless still primarily serves the role of diversion rather than true entertainment. With rare exceptions, watching television is not the equivalent of the music lover's listening to music or an art lover's viewing of paintings. It is much closer to the experience of being massaged. One sits there facing the set and allows the diffusion of the non-stimulating and bland stuff of the set into, over, and around oneself, like busy little fingers kneading one's muscles. It relaxes without provoking, it diverts without stimulating. It requires little from you, but of course gives little to you. Since it requires little from you—in the energyless state of many adults at the end of a dry working day—it is all for which you are prepared. Distractions are not entertainments. The peculiar phenomenon of television is our bridge from boredom to ennui. This institutionalized form of literally staring into space is making Oblomovs of us all. Television is abrogating the energizing role of boredom.

To repeat, then, boredom is not ennui! Ennui is a *settling* for an unsatisfactory state; boredom serves a purpose. It is indeed a cautionary signal. In that sense, it is a "good" emotion. It is useful. Its very unpleasantness drives us out of our lassitude and, if not into something worthwhile, at least into an awareness that we hunger for what we do not possess. With boredom we are directed toward the recognition of a deficit which could be dangerous. Boredom, like the emotion from which it derives, anxiety, is an alerting phenomenon that all is not well and something must be done. It cries out to us that "attention must be paid" to the quality of our lives.

⇜§ 8

Feeling Envious

THE CONCERN OF THIS CHAPTER is not with envy in its sense as a synonym for "admire," as in "I envy you your musical ability." Envy, as discussed here, is the bitter, resentful feeling that one has in the presence of and toward the person who is superior, in possessions, traits, or what have you, to ourselves.

Envy is perhaps the most tortuous and tormenting of emotions. It feeds on itself and ultimately humiliates the experiencer. Milton was right in making it the Devil's own emotion. In *Paradise Lost*, Satan, seeing Adam and Eve in love in Paradise, envies them and plots their fall.

> . . . aside the Devil turn'd
> For envy, yet with jealous leer malign
> Ey'd them askance, and to himself thus plain'd.

Sight hateful, sight tormenting! thus these two
Imparadis't in one another's arms
The happier *Eden*, shall enjoy their fill
Of bliss on bliss, while I to Hell am thrust,
Where neither joy nor love, but fierce desire,
Among our other torments not the least,
Still unfulfill'd with pain of longing pines . . .*

It is a peculiar combination of both desire and resentment fused in bitterness. It is a mean emotion. Unredeeming and unredeemable, it seems to serve none of the purposes of so many other emotions. It does not alert us; it does not motivate us, liberate us, or improve us. Envy represents the degradation of the emotion of jealousy. Jealousy is no great joy either, but in its earliest origins in childhood competitiveness, it probably serves an adaptive purpose. Certainly in a more primitive time it could have contributed to a survival of the fittest.

The roots of competition, like so many other things, arise in the dependent and vulnerable position of early childhood. Psychoanalysis had traditionally cast competition in the Oedipal model. The paradigm was the son competing for the love and affection of the mother against the father. The Oedipal conflict, of course, is never won by the child, and the good parent must struggle to protect his child by reducing the competition, by avoiding the power struggle.

If this competition is allowed to develop, it can only destroy the confidence of the child. Inevitably he is destined to lose. First, he is in a weak position relative to the adult and cannot hope to compete successfully. But in such areas where he does compete successfully the loss is even greater. The destruction of the parent is a Pyrrhic victory, indeed. As children, we must ultimately recognize our own vulnerability, our own helplessness, and see the strong parents as the real guardians of our future. To destroy the parent is to be stripped of our chief

---

* John Milton, *Paradise Lost*, ed. Merritt Y. Hughes (New York, Odyssey Press, 1935), Book IV, p. 128.

protector during our period of dependency. We will have proved that one of the two people with whom we invest our security is inadequate.

By destroying the parent of the same sex, we are in addition destroying a model on whom much of ourselves has been constructed. In proving him weak, we weaken our self-image. And, finally, if we do win the victory with the parent, the overwhelming guilt will lead us to expiatory, self-destructive pieces of behavior.

With the developing interest in child psychiatry, a new model for competition emerged which was given the title "sibling rivalry." Here the rules are changed. To have a brother competing for the affections of the mother is not the same as competing with the father. Here the rivalry *can* be won or lost, and here, at least in the child's perception, the "stew pot" is in operation. The mother has a limited amount of time and a limited amount of energy, and this may be translated by the child into meaning a limited amount of love. Obviously, the child is not sufficiently sophisticated to recognize that generally speaking the more love the mother gives to a sibling, the more evidence of her loving nature exists, and therefore the more love is probably being given to him. It is rarely recognized as a general principle, and in specific cases it is often not true. There are some parents who possess marked variability in their capacity to love all of their children. In their cases, there is indeed a particularly favored or disfavored child.

As with so many neurotic anxieties, whether the fear is initially true or not can become irrelevant. Psychological definitions are self-fulfilling prophecies—they convert our fantasy fears into realities. A strong sense of rivalry, involving the terror of the loss of the mother's love, may drive the child to a kind of angry and resentful life style. The competitive and anxious child does often become an essentially unlovable creature. He can drive the parents further and further away until he precipitates the bias he fancied. He creates out of his own fear the very thing he dreads.

Nonetheless, sibling rivalry does operate in a field in which there can be true victory and true defeat. If one could indeed destroy the sibling, one could eliminate the competition. To impugn a brother, to see him in disgrace, is to sense victory. The least charming aspect of childhood is exemplified by the smirky, ingratiating denial of culpability by one sibling on seeing another punished. "I didn't dump my cereal [crayon the wall, eat the cookies, tease the cat] like Charley, did I, Mommy?" is an infuriating statement recalled by all the Charleys of the world.

It is likely that the exclusive possession of the mother is the primary goal of all children, that competition is normal, and that sharing must be learned. Certainly the complicated concept of the expandability of love must await a certain maturity. Out of the same sibling rivalry emerges the incipient emotion of jealousy. It is with trepidation that I introduce this emotion so closely allied to envy. Jealousy itself has two separate meanings, and in at least one of those meanings it is so confused with envy as to be used almost interchangeably. Perhaps it is an arrogance to say "confused." No one, after all, is the final authority on what precisely defines a feeling. All an individual is expert on is his own feelings. The primary purpose, however, in my demanding distinctions between closely allied feelings is not simply in the proper labeling for communication, but in the recognition and individuation of separate emotions. Whether what I call jealousy is what you call envy, or vice versa, it is important—if they are two separate emotions—at least to distinguish between them and establish the fact that these are separate individual phenomena. We can then proceed to argue as to which we prefer calling what.

Jealousy is an emotion with dual meaning. One aspect of jealousy is suspicious jealousy. That is the jealousy specifically associated with sexual and romantic relationships. It involves the fear of loss of a loved object to another one. This suspicious jealousy is a problem of its own, and for this chapter not our primary concern.

The jealousy that has importance to us is the form that is confused with envy; i.e., it relates to what others already have, not what they might take from us. Historically, it is the primary phenomenon, and envy is its derivative. It is easy to see jealousy in the small child, whereas generally we cannot conceive of the three- to five-year-old as being envious. Jealousy is rooted in the same sibling rivalry that was previously described, and is first felt in relation to brothers and sisters, or the parent of the opposite sex.

Jealousy is the feeling that the rival is getting more of the parental affection than you are. It was jealousy that Cain felt for Abel, albeit a jealousy of a savage degree. Still, it is unlikely that we would use the word "envy" in this case. Jealousy is a personal emotion directed to people about people. The envy sense of jealousy, like the sexual sense, evokes the image of a triangle rather than a duality (like the teeter-totter) of envy. It is something we tend to feel about someone in terms of our relative position to a third party. Most often we are jealous in relation to affection, credit, or approval that the rival has received from someone from whom we would have liked to have received it. In this sense the mother-father-child triad— the Oedipal conflict of traditional psychoanalysis—is a proto- type. The little boy is often envious even of the mother's affec- tion for the father. He wants to displace the father. "When I grow up," the little boy says, "I want to marry you, Mommy." There is no direct reference as to where Daddy will be in this whole picture. It is here that we begin to see the relation- ship between envious jealousy and suspicious jealousy.

Jealousy, which leads to such difficulty in our culture, may have originally stirred competition to serve survival needs. In a more primitive society, it may have assured the ascending of the most fit. Certainly in childhood, competition can serve to extend the efforts of the child and can drive him to fulfill more of his potential. The fact that in our paranoid society we need no spur for competition to develop does not belie the original useful purpose of the emotion. The feeling of jealousy supplies a painful stimulus to achieve. Since the original jealousy is in terms of parental love and approval, it can reinforce the behavioral standards of the parents. In this sense, this peculiarly combative feeling can serve a cohesive communal purpose. With parents who value service, giving, sharing, and loving, it is possible that jealousy—the very emotion born in competitive struggle—can be directed to *limit* competitive drives.

Envy is a generalization from and extension of jealousy. The individual giver and receiver are less important. The envious person often feels the same quality of pain in the same way that the suspicious-jealous person does, but not necessarily in relationship to someone who is about to be lost, or someone whose affections are about to be stolen. We carry our envy into all situations of life. Envy represents a niggling resentment of other people independent of their relationship to us. We will envy them their comfort, their possessions, and, beyond that, their existence.

Envy is a complex amalgam of at least four conditions—all necessary for its full and true development. The first is a feeling of deprivation. Deprivation is not one of privation; that is, not merely the sense that we are missing something we need or want. The mere absence of money, position, or pleasure does not in itself give one a feeling of deprivation. We must go beyond the feeling of the absence, and feel that somehow or other the deprivation was imposed. To feel deprived, we must feel that we have been *denied* the thing we want. It is not essential that we even visualize a denying individual. That may be vague and unarticulated. We may have only the sense that it was life, fate, chance, or destiny rather than an individual that has denied us our just share. Envy begins and ends with the feeling of deprivation.

The second essential ingredient of envy is the sense that others have what we have been denied. Crucial to envy is the comparative point of view. It is not necessary that this be visualized in what seems the logical order: I do not have X; he does have X; I feel deprived and envious of him. If anything, once the process of envy starts, it more often than not works in the opposite direction; that is, we do not necessarily desire something until we have seen that the other has it. It is the presence in, or possession by, the other that may generate the desire in us and thus the feeling of deprivation. This is a particularly malicious component of envy, because in the individual in whom it is operating, the desirable will only be defined as that which the other has, or similarly as that which he does not have. By this process, the feeling of envy is not only caused by deprivation, but will generate a sense of deprivation.

A feeling of deprivation and the *comparative* mode of thinking which underlies deprivation are still short of the feeling of envy. I think particularly of the case of a good friend of mine who clearly had both of the two aspects, yet by no definition was an envious person. He suffered from a sense of deprivation obviously stemming from his early childhood, but it neither embittered him nor prevented his pleasure in the pleasures and successes of his friends. I recall specifically my discovery of these qualities in him when we were both students. We used to share a quick lunch at a typical greasy-spoon counter restaurant—one of those hole-in-the-wall niches that seem a standard part of every academic community. The two of us would sit side by side along the counter and give our identical orders to the counterman, who then prepared them in our presence. For months we each had the same meat-loaf sandwich on a hard roll with a cup of coffee. After a while I became aware of the fact that during the period the counterman was preparing the sandwiches, my colleague was so obsessed with the process that he was literally tuned out of our conversation.

Once alerted, I began to study his behavior and it became obvious that he was intensely occupied with the amount of meat loaf that went into his sandwich versus the amount that went into mine. It became absolutely clear that he was convinced that I always got the bigger sandwich. I observed this behavior for a few weeks, without saying anything, until I was positive that my assumptions were correct. The inevitable frown when the two sandwiches were positioned indicated his fatalistic acceptance of perpetual deprivation. One day when the counterman plunked the two sandwiches down in front of us, I reversed the two. He was somewhat startled and said, "Why did you do that?" I answered with a straight face, "He made a mistake today. He gave you the bigger sandwich." My friend, to his credit, blushed and started laughing.

Obviously, students though we were, neither of us was in the habit of going hungry, and either of us could have afforded two, three, or four sandwiches. This profound sense of deprivation was irrational and he knew it. Nonetheless it possessed him with a reality beyond his perceptions. Somehow, in a comparative sense, he would always assume that he got the smaller serving and therefore in "his" world of perception he *would* always get the smaller serving. But this is not envy.

The forced comparison between the treatment of the other and the treatment of the self is the foundation on which the feelings of envy will be built. The roots of envy are traditionally traced to an early and true privation in the face of privilege (although it will be seen later that it is the symbolic sense of deprivation that is more often crucial). The simple paradigm of childhood envy is expressed by Becky Sharp, a charity pupil at a select seminary for young women.

The happiness, the superior advantages of the young women round about her, gave Rebecca inexpressible pangs of envy. "What airs that girl gives herself, because she is an earl's granddaughter," she said of one. "How they cringe and bow to that Creole, because of her hundred thousand pounds!" I am a thousand times cleverer and more charming than that creature, for all her wealth. I am as well-bred as the earl's granddaughter, for all her fine pedigree; and yet every one passes me by here. And yet, when I was at my father's, did not the men give up their gayest balls and parties in order to pass the evening with me?*

Becky continued her competition and her acquisitive nature into maturity, and eventually it was to destroy her. Yet I, as one reader, felt no sense of joy or triumph in her downfall. For me, she was never completely the villain. Driving, ambitious, competitive, yes; capable of *feeling envy,* yes; but the embittered, envious anti-hero, she was not. At least not in my eyes. I suspect most readers of Thackeray's *Vanity Fair* have a certain fondness for Becky and a certain chagrin at her defeat.

Compare her with her sister under the skin Lisbeth Fischer, in Balzac's *La Cousine Bette.* The French have always had a way with *ressentiment.* The very word is heirs and they understand the envy that is at its core. *La Cousine Bette* is the true anti-hero, and we sense that from her very beginnings.

The family, who lived as one household, had sacrificed the plebeian daughter to the pretty one, the astringent fruit to the brilliant flower. Lisbeth worked in the fields while her cousin was cosseted, and so it had happened one day that Lisbeth, finding Adeline alone, had done her best to pull Adeline's nose off, a true Grecian nose, much admired by all the old women. Although she was beaten for this misdeed, that did not prevent her from continuing to tear her favoured cousin's dresses and crumple her collars. . . .

The family misfortunes, the knowledge borne in upon her that she counted for little in the immense turmoil of contending people, ambitions, and enterprises that makes Paris both a heaven and an inferno, intimidated Bette. The young woman at that time gave up all idea of competing with or rivalling her cousin, whose many and various points of superiority she had realized; but envy remained hidden in her heart, like a plague germ which may come to life and devastate a city if the fatal bale of wool in which it lies hidden is ever opened.†

---

* William Makepeace Thackeray, *Vanity Fair* (New York: Simon & Schuster, Pocket Books, 1972), p. 13.

† Honoré de Balzac, *La Cousine Bette* (Baltimore: Penguin Books, 1965), p. 39.

Bette and Becky are different people. Becky envies what others have; Bette goes beyond that. She envies what others are. Becky is greedy for life. She wants anything that anyone has which she does not. Bette wants no one to have more than she, and she in her mind has nothing. Becky wants more for herself; Bette wants less for others.

In addition, Becky's sense of her own superiority pervades her quotation. It is precisely because she is as good as the others that she ought to have as much. And, indeed, the quotation continues with her resolve:

> She determined at any rate to get free from the prison in which she found herself, and now began to act for herself, and for the first time make connected plans for the future.*

Bette can never rectify the disparities and inequities she perceives, for the inadequacy extends beyond privilege and involves endowment. Her life is directed to redressing the imbalance—not, as with Becky, by getting more of her own, but by depriving the other.

> By the end of nearly three years Lisbeth was beginning to see some progress in the undermining tunnel, in the driving of which her whole existence was consumed and the energies of her mind absorbed.†

And when she was able to bring tears to her hated cousin's eyes, "Bette watched them with greedy absorption, like a cat lapping milk."‡

In *La Cousine Bette* we saw that third factor essential to the development of envy. That is the feeling of impotence in the face of disparity. The impotence may develop either because of the powerlessness to change the circumstances of life or because disparity is felt in such basic natural attributes

---

* Thackeray, *Vanity Fair*, p. 13.
† Balzac, *La Cousine Bette*, p. 170.
‡ Ibid, p. 214.

that there is no redress. It is the impotence that adds the resentful quality to envy. Frustrated rage and helplessness are key ingredients in the building of envy.

The final element that completes the portrait of envy involves the slippage from a comparative to a competitive mechanism—the envious person begins to ascribe a causal relationship between his own deprivation and the abundance of the others. It is not just that he does not have what they have; it is that he does not have it *because* they have it.

It is this imposition of a false competition on non-competitive events that links envy to paranoid feelings. In both there is the assumption of a limited quantity to things which in actuality are unlimited. It is the stew-pot mentality of children, which assumes that the more others have of wealth, pleasure, love, the less there is that remains for us.

The other dominant image that envy shares with paranoia is the teeter-totter phenomenon where every elevation of the other is seen as a lowering of ourselves. This paranoid envy, at its most extreme, can decimate an individual. One of my first exposures to this occurred early in my practice in relation to a young actress. Highly competitive, and narcissistic, she had come to me in a state of mild depression. One day she arrived in a mood of euphoria. She had just been offered a significant part in a play which could with luck (and, indeed, did) launch her career. While I was not so naïve as to assume that this would cause a reversal in her depression, I was still not quite prepared for the despondency in the very next session. The pride, the euphoria, the elation, the joy, the promise were all gone in twenty-four hours, and she was again despondent. Her explanation of the turnabout was that she had read in the morning's paper the announcement that a friend of hers had just been awarded a major part in an important movie. When I questioned why this produced such a reaction in her, she announced, "Don't you understand? In order for me to be happy it is not enough that I succeed. My friends have to fail." This is a feeling, at a level of intensity, that most of us fortunately do not share; nonetheless, I suspect most of us can relate this to the ambivalence with which we often greet a colleague's success—even though that success was in no way at our own expense, or in no way diminished our own opportunity for success.

This false sense of competition exists with such intensity in certain people that they have difficulty accepting the patent falseness of its basic premise. They deny any attempt to expose the illusory competition. They will seek all forms of rationalization to prove its true existence. Obviously, we live in a competitive world and there are areas in which another's failure is the equivalent of our success. If I am running a race, the slowness of my opponent is the direct equivalent of my own speed. They are alternative methods of winning. If two men are competing for public office or a job, the failure of one contributes to the success of the other. This does not explain, however, the competitive feelings that one might feel when, as a lawyer, one reads of the early success of a classmate in science or business. It does not explain the emotion of competition that the divorced feel for the happily married friends, or the lonely for the popular. These are noncompetitive situations, but in the crabbed world of the envious all prizes are seen as stolen from them, the deprived. Of course, the tendency to cast noncompetitive phenomena into competitive molds is compounded in a society where competition is emphasized and disparity exists.

One sees the conversion of noncompetitive aspects of life into false competitions in the most peculiar places. At its most dangerous it is seen on the roadways of any major city. There is something about an automobile that brings out the paranoid in the least paranoid of individuals. When I commuted to New York City by car, not a day would pass where I could not observe the following scene. One car is going up the highway. Another car, either out of inadvertence or rudeness, will cut

off the first car. The driver of the first car is frightened by
the near miss, and in a rage. Logic would dictate that he avoid
the careless or aggressive driver who cut him off. But logic
has no place on the streets of New York City. He handles this
assault on his safety by himself doing precisely the same thing
to the other, thus putting himself in jeopardy again and compounding his own danger. Somehow or other, the situation
has been converted into a test to determine who exploits and
who is exploitable. An injury has been done to his dignity,
his manhood; a challenge has been offered—and accepted.

Everything is in short supply in the city: pride, privacy, and
space. One cabdriver was quoted, in defense of tailgating: "Lis-
ten, mister, in this town if you leave space you lose it." The
concept of space on a highway as a possession from which
one can be deprived is a strange one indeed.

This readiness to interpret a chance event as an attack on
self is a model of the establishment of false causal relationships
characteristic of envy. It is that attribution of purpose where
purpose may not exist. Fabrications of such "true" connections
are facilitated by the psychological concept of projection. Projection refers to the process whereby we handle unacceptable
ideas within ourselves by attributing them to others. A child
who comes out of early life feeling deprived may carry with
him into adulthood a desire to take from others what he feels
has been taken from him. The projection of that desire operates
to allow him to assume that the very feelings rising within
him are actually arising in others and directed toward him.

Jealousy at least pretends to be directed to what others have.
Envy is concerned about what we already feel deprived of.
The jealous person is anticipatory; he is afraid of something
that is happening or about to happen. The envious person is
convinced that it has already happened. Where the jealous
person is worried that someone else might take his share of
love and approval, the envious person feels the emptiness already with him. It is that emptiness which drives the envious

person to look for justifications, to rationalize his constantly felt deprivation, and may drive him to projection.

Whereas jealousy almost inevitably is tied to a personal quality involving approval or recognition, envy can be generated by the most trivial, the meanest, and the least worthwhile possessions of life.

The envious person can be miserable over a larger serving of ice cream. It is almost impossible to conceive of feeling jealous over this, except as a child—and even then what the child is experiencing with jealousy is the symbolic meaning of the ice cream. If I envy you your ice cream, it is the ice cream that is the center of focus. If I am jealous of the fact that Mom gave you a larger serving, it is because I am afraid that more ice cream implies more affection. It is Mom's affection that is being competed for—surely a more sympathetic and understandable emotion.

One has to assume that the normal jealousy emerging from sibling rivalry is something present in all of us. We can all conceive of feeling jealous of the attention paid to a good friend for the success of his achievements while still glorying in them.

In the specific emotion of envy, the bitterness is always present, because in the forefront is always not just what others have but what has been taken away from us. I recognize that others will use jealousy in this sense and see jealousy as having an embittered quality. I cannot argue the rightness of one or the other, but if the individual reader identifies for himself the two distinct emotions and recognizes the separate "feelings" generated by each, he will see that there is a subdivision whose separation warrants maintenance.

Most of us, however, will agree that jealousy is more tied to the specific person—and the specific feelings of attention, love, and recognition. In that sense most will also agree that jealousy is much more primarily bound to the family structure and the early-childhood experience.

While many people can be reduced to envy in certain situations that impinge on their special sensitivities, there are those poor creatures who live with chronic envy. To be consumed by envy is a uniquely apt metaphor. It is true that we are consumed by other emotions but interestingly related ones. We talk about being consumed by jealousy, but then jealousy and envy are often confused. We also talk about being consumed by rage (most often frustrated rage), but here we visualize the act of being consumed differently—rather as in a conflagration. With envy it is a slower process and what is being consumed is our pride, self-confidence, and joy. Chronic envy is an erosive, self-destroying disease. Like the old consumption (tuberculosis) in the years before modern treatment, it eats away at the vitals of those who must live with it daily. And once again—as is typical of neurosis—it feeds upon itself. When envy is a way of life, it converts the envious person into a grievance collector who masochistically embraces situations that confirm his deprivation and exploitation. And of course, if necessary, he creates the situations. Every road taken will be the wrong one. It is always his lane that is the slowest to move, his seat the worst in the house. Every ambiguous situation will be interpreted by him as a decision against him.

To a certain degree, we can identify with the feelings of a chronic envier by comparing it to our own milder forms of competitive insecurity that result from the bruising crowded urban life many of us choose to live. Being an early diner, it is not unusual for me to be with my family in a large restaurant almost alone. At that point one can watch the headwaiter ushering in new arrivals to a nearly deserted restaurant. Almost arbitrarily he will guide them from right to left, from left to right, from back to front; and almost inevitably at least half of the customers will refuse the initial table offered and choose one in an opposite locale. Individual taste? I doubt it. The sense of competitive anxiety in a society where glory and deference are in short supply creates a wariness, a readiness to feel denigrated and exploited, and a determination to guard against potential slights even where they do not exist.

The grievance collector of course goes beyond this, and at his most paranoid he becomes a litigious creature, suing at slights or threatening to do so. Since, with the envious individual, well-being is always judged on a comparative basis, it becomes apparent that an alternative for benefiting his own position exists in the undermining of others. A particularly offensive characteristic of the envious person is his love for faultfinding. He is the born iconoclast who thrives on the exposure of the defects of heroes. While all of us may get some pleasure at some time in the fall of *some* mighty (i.e., the wicked), he takes pleasure in the bringing down of all. Indeed to the envious the greatest pleasure is in the fall of angels. He is a clay-foot fetishist, and a sour-grape addict.

And it need not be the mighty who fall—although there is always special joy in that. He is equally ready to find defects in those around him. He is always happier with the frustrating failures of his colleagues than with their successes, and he is pained by a compliment to anyone, which is particularly interpreted as a grievous injury if, indeed, the person complimented happens to be in a comparative (which by his definition will always be seen as competitive) situation with himself. He is the physician who never has a good word for another physician, the attorney who acknowledges no competence beyond his own, the new dentist who frowns as he examines your teeth and politely restrains himself from the verbal criticism of the previous dentist that he eloquently portrays in his expression.

Closely related to envy but differing in key and significant factors is the emotion of resentment. Where envy tends to be individual-oriented, resentment is often felt as a group phenomenon. It is a class-action feeling. Where envy is directed at the person of another, resentment may be aimed at the state of affairs, conditions, classes of others.

Resentment has a legitimacy that envy does not. It most often stems from a feeling of deprivation in the presence of privilege; it is founded in a sense of true injustice; and because of its group identity, it has a less selfish and narrow focus. Resentment, particularly political and social resentment, can mobilize an oppressed minority and forewarn an oppressor group.

Max Scheler in his masterful essay on *ressentiment,* which in his terms is a pathological and destructive condition, nonetheless says a great deal about normal resentment. He describes the emotions of *ressentiment,* including revenge, envy, spite, rage, and then says:

> *Ressentiment* can only arise if these emotions are particularly powerful and yet must be suppressed because they are coupled with the feeling that one is unable to act them out—either because of weakness, physical or mental, or because of fear. . . .
>
> There follows the important sociological law that this psychological dynamite will spread with the *discrepancy* between the political, constitutional or traditional status of the group and its *factual* power. It is the difference between these two factors which is decisive, not one of them alone. Social *ressentiment,* at least, would be slight in a democracy which is not only political, but also social and tends towards equality of property. . . . *Ressentiment* must therefore be strongest in a society like ours, where approximately equal rights (political and otherwise) go hand in hand with wide factual differences in power, property, and education.*

The "society like ours" which Scheler is describing is not, as one could assume from the description, modern America, but rather, to be sure, Germany in 1912. Where resentment has a political orientation and a group identity, it departs in intention and effect from the individual envy which it so closely resembles in structure. Individual envy is rarely based on reality. It is a self-created emotion based on self-fulfilling prophecies. I is the imposition on the present of vividly felt injuries of the past which may or may not have a foundation in reality.

Scheler quotes the marvelous Goethe statement "Against another's great merits, there is no remedy but love." Short of love, identification will serve the purpose. Identification is

---

* Max Scheler, *Ressentiment* (New York: Schocken Books, 1972), pp. 48, 50.

the process by which we fuse our sense of self with those we admire and envy—but particularly with those we love. The highest form of identification can be seen in the love of a parent for her child. Here, in all her reactions, it is difficult for the identifying person (the mother) to know where herself ends and the other (the child) begins. To hurt her child is indistinguishable from hurting her. Indeed, it may be the most intense form of pain you can inflict on her. To praise her child is to serve her vanities.

Envy implies a relationship with an individual the opposite of identification. The only true antagonist of envy, therefore, is that identification. Identification involves fusion of fate and feeling. As envy separates us from our fellows, identification joins them to us. Identification permits for the expansion of our achievements, our pleasures, and, unfortunately, our pains. It is not necessary for us to have experienced every joy; we can share that with those we love. My friends' victories are my victories, as are his joys and sadnesses.

Identification binds us to others in a common fate. It permits for compassion, sympathy, and empathy. When the forces of society isolate us as individuals or reduce us into separate minority groups who cannot identify with the common purpose and the common cause, the stability of that society is endangered. Those forces which encourage the sense of an alienated self will drive us to envy our neighbor and resent the members of the majority. Since we are all part of the social unit, since no individual can survive without the nourishment of the group, we must be generous in sharing the common goods. Each man's survival demands a readiness to include every other individual to full membership in the community. Envy is the divisive result of competition gone wrong. It will always be present in some individuals within every society. When it becomes generalized to the group, when envy becomes *ressentiment,* we must look not at the individual but at the society. It is the society which is at fault; it is the society which is at risk.

⋖§ 9

Feeling Used

O NE OF THE MORE painful of the small emotions is the feeling of being used. It is significant to compare the distinction in our reactions between the humiliation of feeling used and the pleasure of feeling useful or "of use."

Why should we not want to be used? Why should we not want to be taken advantage of? If I have a sailboat, summer house, garden, or any possession of value, the more I value it the more I want it to be used. Particularly if it is a luxury, it is important that it be used; otherwise I run the risk of feeling guilty for having indulged myself. The unused expensive item is the pointing finger shaming us with our extravagance. But beyond guilt—or luxury—we are flattered when people want to borrow our things, although we may not wish (for a variety of reasons) to lend them. Why, then, with the most valuable of things, our very selves, our minds, our bodies, our utility, do we so often resent being used? And here I am not alluding only to the chronic use which becomes an exploitation. Why, even in the isolated situation, do we take umbrage when we know someone wants only the use, not the company, of ourselves?

The utilization of ourselves, the feeling of usefulness, provides a great joy and pleasure. To feel of use is one of the fundamental ingredients of pride. We pride ourselves by our uses. We even sense or acknowledge ourselves through our uses. We exist in our own mind's eye through the exploitation and expenditure of all of our personal resources. When we use ourselves, in almost any sense of the word, we are building a sense of our own worth.

When it is *we* who are using ourselves to benefit others, there is an added implication: it is not just that there is something worth using, but it indicates that the person, the self, is generous in the sharing of that self. And generosity is also an expansive and prideful action. But even when others find use in us it enhances our self-esteem. How, then, do we explain the almost universal feelings of outrage, shame, hurt, and resentment that combine in that most humiliating feeling of "being used?"

Obviously, that which when given freely provides pleasure is a source of pain when taken away. To feel used is to have a sense of something of ours being taken away. But it is more than that. To feel used is to feel that our services have been separated from ourselves. It is a sense of the violation of our central worth, as though we ourselves are important to the other individual only because we are a vehicle for supplying the stuff that he desires. It may be most graphic and evident when what he desires is a material or physical thing—our money or our possessions—but we are equally offended when what is taken or used is our intelligence, our creativity, our companionship, or our love.

There are two separate sets of conditions which, while differing in circumstances, inevitably lead to almost the same sense of injury, to the sense of being used. The first is where we have been deceived; where someone has lied to us or at least has concealed his purposes. The second is where, with no apparent sense of deception, we are still aware that the person is primarily interested in what we see as our services rather than ourselves. Here the feeling of being used is even more painful, because it is not mitigated by the righteous indignation of the first example. Part of the problem here is in determining what distinguishes the esential "us" from our services. What we have and what we give are both significant components, after all, of what we are.

The sense of use and abuse is nowhere more poignantly told than in Sophocles' play *Philoctetes*. The play is a masterpiece of moral dilemmas in its concern for the ethics involved in interrelationships between people: the role of truth versus larger purpose; and individual honor versus obligation to the state. Before the action of the play, we know that Philoctetes has been badly used by the Greek leadership. As a young man, he joined the army of Agamemnon to serve in the Trojan expedition. In the course of this he was instrumental in guiding the Greeks to the island of Chrysa's shrine, where it was essential that a religious sacrifice be made. In the process he was bitten by a snake, producing a horrible, foul-smelling wound. With a shocking lack of gratitude, Ulysses maroons him on the uninhabited island. Here, alone, abandoned, suffering terribly from his wound, he barely manages to survive. But with him he has the bow of Hercules, a gift given to him in his childhood. And the gods have now informed the Greek leadership that the ultimate victory over Troy demands possession of the bow and arrows of Hercules. To that end Ulysses convinces Neoptolemus, an honorable youth, that it is his duty to lie to Philoctetes to gain the bow. When the deception is revealed, Philoctetes, in absolute despair, addresses his nemesis Ulysses:

> Thou abandoned,
> Thou shameless wretch! from whom nor truth nor justice,
> Naught that becomes the generous mind, can flow,
> How hast thou used me! how betrayed! Suborned
> This stranger, this poor youth, who, worthier far
> To be my friend than thine, was only here
> Thy instrument; he new not what he did,
> And now, thou seest, repents him of the crime
> Which brought such guilt on him, such woes on me.
> But thy foul soul, which from its dark recess
> Trembling looks forth, beheld him void of art,
> Unwilling as he was, instructed him,
> And made him soon a master in deceit.*

The accusation involves both forms of being used. Philoctetes has been deceived and lied to, but in addition, he accuses Ulysses of manipulating and using Neoptolemus also, for he was "only here thy instrument." It did not matter that Ulysses shared his purposes and his intentions with Neoptolemus—that he was honest with him. Neoptolemus was being used by the older man and, as such, dishonored, just as was Philoctetes.

To be exploited, to be seen as a vehicle, a machine for the intentions of others, is to be seen as less than a person. The right to use us as instruments of selfish design is a right reserved for the benevolent gods. Philoctees is outraged when he realizes he is being used to serve the purposes of Ulysses. Nor is he comforted when it is argued that it is for the purpose of the state itself. The state that uses its citizens beyond the limits demanded by their rights as people may not be worthy of survival. Only with the gods—in whom we vest the very concept of justice—are we honored when they use us. To be the "instrument of the Lord" is to be used nobly. "Lay me on an

---

* Sophocles, *Philoctetes*, in *The Complete Greek Drama*, ed. Whitney J. Oates and Eugene O'Neill, Jr. (New York: Random House, 1938), 1:590.

anvil, O God. Beat me and hammer me into a crowbar," Carl Sandburg entreats—echoing Edward Taylor's readiness three hundred years before to serve the Lord: "Make me, O Lord, Thy spinning wheel, complete."

And so it was two thousand years earlier; only when the immortal Hercules revealed himself as the designer of Philoctetes' despair was he comforted. Philoctetes' humiliations are seen as serving the immortal purpose, and Ulysses himself is also merely an instrument of these same Gods. Hercules reminds him that he, too, in his time, labored and suffered in the mysterious service of the immortals:

> Therefore attend.
> Thou knowst what toils, what labours I endured,
> Ere I by virtue gained immortal fame;
> Thou too like me by toils must rise to glory—
> Thou too must suffer, ere thou canst be happy.*

Unfortunately, these days when we feel used and abused, impotent in the fact of the alternatives offered us, the gods are unlikely to intervene. When we do feel the direct intervention of God, we are in all probability suffering from an acute paranoid psychosis. The paranoid delusion has replaced the *deus ex machina.*

An extraordinarily beautiful account of this occurs in Freud's discussion of the case of Justice Schreber, one of the five clinical cases on which all modern psychoanalysis is founded.

Justice Schreber had published an autobiographical account of his paranoid illness. Freud, in one of his most brilliant conceptions, analyzed this literary fragment and built the theory of paranoia on this brief evidence. For our purposes here, the importance of the case, beyond the specific disease, is in the light it sheds on the relationship between self-pride, social humiliation, and being used.

Most readers will not be able to identify with the delusional

---

* Ibid., p. 606.

system of Justice Schreber. Nonetheless, a psychotic example is useful in the sense that it offers a magnifying glass to the smaller emotions that most of us feel. Paranoia is closely related to the fear of social humiliation. The delusional systems of paranoia therefore express our worst fears, and the protective devices we mobilize against them. Not surprisingly, the vast preponderance of paranoid delusions in psychotic men in our male-oriented culture involves being accused of being a homosexual, and of being used as such.

The homosexual image is an image of being used that dominates our modern culture. The street language for being taken advantage of, particularly in a humiliating way, for being used as an instrument for someone else's purposes, abounds in homosexual images. "Did he screw you!" "You really got the shaft!" "If you're not careful, you're going to get it in the ass." "Boy, did he stick it to you." These are not expressions of sexual endearment; nor are they reflections of an unconscious desire for anal stimulation. They are a borrowing of homosexual imagery as the most graphic metaphor for degradation, social humiliation, and the feeling of being used, one man to another. The loss of one's sexual identity as a man is seen as the loss of one's power and potency—as being used at its ultimate.

In early psychoanalytic theory this was invariably interpreted as protection against actual homosexual desires arising from within the individual himself. They are unbearable, and the individual handles the impulse by projecting it onto someone else in the environment. The fear, anxiety, and social humiliation implicit in the homosexuality becomes relieved by saying it is what others are doing to us.

Justice Schreber had just such delusions. He felt that people were calling him a homosexual and he felt that homosexual advances were being made toward him. The Schreber case shows how the paranoid, in his delusions, works out an individual solution not unlike the solution of Sophocles for Philoctetes. It goes without saying that the modern psychoanalyst would "recognize" the injured Philoctetes, and see his symbolic "castration" as akin to the illusory castration of Schreber.

Schreber's guilt over his homosexual desires and his anxiety about this humiliation are handled by the paranoid mechanism of projection. It is not he who wishes this, but others who are imposing it on him. Nonetheless, it is still a humiliating—if not guilt-provoking—experience, and it is frightening. Someone is trying to use him and exploit him. He seems helpless to defend himself. The answer is to convert the persecutory delusion into a grandiose one. This delusional system is the final effort to salvage pride and self-respect out of the sense of one's own weakness. Schreber forms the delusion that it is not his doctor who is trying to homosexually reduce and humiliate him, but indeed it is God himself. He builds a fantasy world in which he anticipates the destruction of the world because of its inadequacies and wickedness. Then God will create a new world, and a new breed of better beings. God has chosen him. He will be the central figure in this redemption scheme, but to do so he must sacrifice his manhood and "endure" the experience of intercourse as a woman. It is God's rays which will impregnate him and through him create a new race of worthier human beings.

The delusion solves all aspects of his conflict. It allows Schreber to have the sexual gratification he desires without the humiliation he fears. Quite the contrary. Instead of the homosexuality being a stigma and disgrace, it is a sign of a superiority and moral worth. To be penetrated by God's rays is a religious and not sexual experience, and therefore no disgrace for those to whom sexual desire is—for one reason or another—unacceptable. One may, I hope, be forgiven for finding in the ecstasy of St. Teresa of Avila some suggestion of sexuality.

In his hands I saw a great golden spear, and at the iron tip there appeared to be a point of fire. This he plunged into my heart several times so that it penetrated to my entrails. When he pulled it out, I felt that he took them with it, and left me utterly consumed by the great love of God. The pain was so severe that it made me utter several moans. The sweetness caused by this intense pain is so extreme that one cannot possibly wish it to cease, nor is one's soul then content with anything but God. This is not a physical, but a spiritual pain, though the body has some share in it—even a considerable share.*

Once again, we see that to be used by God is a form of elevation, whereas to be used by man is a reduction. In the former, the use implies our selection as the highest of our kind. Like Abraham, Moses, and the heroes of the Bible, we have been chosen amongst all men. To be used by our fellows, however, is to be reduced to the level of an instrument or a commodity, and to be less than human.

To be used in any sense is to violate that basic imperative of Kant, that in dealing with people we must never consider them only as means. To use someone as a means to a specific end is then to treat him as a thing and to dehumanize him.

Deceit and lying make particularly evident that there are hidden purposes in an enterprise between people. So when we discover that we have been deceived, or lied to, it prevents our even taking comfort in denial, or in the ambiguity that exists in most interactions among people. We cannot always be sure when we are viewed as means or end, but the use of deceit clearly enunciates the intention of its author. It gives us the feeling not just of having been used but of having been taken advantage of—of having been put upon in a special way. Compounding all of that, we feel humiliated by the awareness of our capability of being deceived. Deception, after all, represents a kind of victory over our judgment and intelligence. It is humiliating in the sense that in addition to having been used, we have been duped.

We tend to use the word "put-down" to mean humiliated, just as we often use the words "put upon" to mean used or taken advantage of. The using of the word "put" links both

---

* J. M. Cohen, trans., *Life of St. Teresa,* cited in *Bernini,* by Howard Hibbard (New York: Penguin Books, 1965), p. 137.

of these to our sense of ourselves as having been used as an object. We put a thing on a shelf. We do not "put" people anywhere.

The "put-down" has become a form of low-grade humor; it is often experienced by the individual involved with a particular humiliation. The individual senses he is being used as a prop for the humorous effect of a put-down purveyor. It is again a double humiliation. When we are made the source of ridicule, two things happen: we are reduced in relationship to the other person—we are indeed put down as he is elevated; in addition, we are put down in the sense that we, like the banana skin, the false nose, the lampshade on the head, are merely props, objects to be exploited for purposes of humor.

The "put-on" is another form of humor which utilizes the word "put" and equally manages to make a person feel embarrassed or publicly humiliated. It is a gentler form of embarrassment, since it uses us as both victim and audience. It is probably related to the teasing of the young. This humor depends on a certain amount of naïveté on the part of the individual who is its object. The put-on is ultimately a form of leading down the garden path. It draws on the individual's trust; he accepts the literalness of what you say until the moment in which you expose his gullibility.

People who are capable of being put on are usually enormously attractive—generally more so than the put-on perpetrator. They are sincere, trusting, and ingenuous; they are often more literal than the rest of us and almost always honest. The essential expectation of treatment from others as you treat them is what leads these people to special vulnerability.

People who put on, nevertheless, are kinder than people who put down. There is an affectionate quality about the put-on, suggesting a friendly relationship between the putter-on and the person put on. The put-down is not so. It is part of that competitive, comparative, verging-on-paranoid struggling for position and status that is so unattractive a part of our culture.

The rise in popularity of this kind of humor may indeed be a reflection of just that culture. It is so difficult to have a sense of achievement and real pride in our current society. The very open-ended quality of it, which has been so admired, is, first of all, not as open-ended as it had seemed, and, secondly, suggests a potential for unlimited upward movement which by definition reflects adversely on the position in which one has settled. If this far, why not farther? Such a society operates like passengers on a forward-facing, upgoing escalator, in which one only sees the man ahead, and feels inadequate in relationship to him. It is this aspect of competition which relates envy to the exploitation of the put-down. In both, lowering the other is a way of raising yourself. It is our unconscious recognition of the inherent hostility in the put-down that is so upsetting to us.

The sense of being used, therefore, arises from the fear that the person dealing with us is not involved with us in emotional ties and affection—where there may be mutual use—but is simply using us as an instrument, a vehicle of his own purposes. We then are equated with the *things* in his life. We are signs of his needs, not of his affections.

Anything which makes us feel used as a thing is uncomfortable. It explains our anger and anxiety in the face of all sorts of forms of manipulation—manipulation here being defined as controlling and influencing behavior, actions, or attitudes while bypassing the sense of reason. Everyone resents being conned. Beyond that, we resent even legitimate devices for influencing our behavior *too* directly. It underlies our wide distrust of respectable behavior-modifying methods, particularly high technology methods. Technology compounds our feeling that we may be related to the laboratory animal. We are worried about electrode implantation, drugs, and psycho-

surgery as means of modifying behavior, even beyond the specific abuse to which those could be or have been used. We
are worried about them beyond and above the anxiety generated by less technical but often more effective methods of
changing behavior which do not have the image of high
technology.

Behavior modification, reward systems, and operant conditioning surely bypass reason as much as electrode implantation,
but somehow or other they seem to have the form of direct
communication that we associate with persuasion and education. In actuality, the low technology methods offer much
greater potential for abusing the individual. It is unlikely that
some Fascist dictator is going to control large populations by
planting electrodes in their heads, or by performing psychosur-
gery on them—popular Hollywood entertainment to the contrary. But behavior manipulation and modification through
preschool training, particularly through the exploitation of the
extraordinary medium of television, has a significant potential
for manipulation for good or bad. It allows the educators, the
entrepreneurs, the potential manipulators, to enter directly
into the home and beguile the child for the forty to sixty hours
a week that television is watched by the average preschool
child these days.

The fear of being reduced to a thing, of being used as an
item, also explains much of our frustrations and resentment
with computers, forms, and labels. We do not like to be classified. We do not want to be part of a group of things. We do
not even particularly like being seen as part of a group of
people. Codification threatens our sense of individuality and
dignity. It challenges that sense of unique worth and lovability
which we like to attribute to ourselves.

So we will always feel hurt, humiliated, threatened, and angry—when we feel used. To be used by a casual acquaintance
rarely results in serious injury; to feel used by one we love
can cause considerable harm. When we sense that we are being

viewed as a means, not an end, by our loved ones, it threatens a valuable aspect of our lives.

But what does it mean to be used as a means, not an end? And is it always that easy to distinguish between means and ends? Some of the greatest self-manufactured difficulties arise when we define "end" too exclusively and purely. I recall one particularly poignant case involving confusions about being used. An attractive young woman, gentle and somewhat intimidated, had been married for fifteen years to an impotent man. Her general sense of duty and responsibility and her low self-esteem allowed her to endure the situation until she discovered that she had developed a condition in her late thirties which required a hysterectomy. Despairing over this, she sought treatment, during the course of which she separated from her husband.

Shortly after that, she became involved with a loving, gentle man and established a sexual relationship. She was not in the beginning of this relationship orgastic, although receiving her partner with great joy and great pleasure. He was concerned, however, about her failure to have orgasms and told her that it made him feel guilty, that he loved her and did not want to be in a position of using her.

In the course of her treatment she expressed bewilderment about his guilt. To her, the fact that someone took pleasure from her was sheer joy. "What a wonderful feeling, to be used," she said. "To find that this body which I despised, and my person, my self—which I assumed inadequate to giving *or* receiving pleasure—could be a source of joy, pride, and passion. What a glorious feeling!"

Her partner had mistaken her lack of orgasm for a lack of pleasure in the activity. Besides that, there was a natural confusion. Even simply being a source of pleasure did not imply to her that she was being used. For her to give pleasure was, at that time, pleasure enough. Her lover, on the other hand, may have wanted to reassure her that he loved her for herself.

And here we enter an area of difficulty. What is the essential person?

> "Never shall a young man,
> Thrown into despair
> By those great honey-coloured
> Ramparts at your ear,
> Love you for yourself alone
> And not your yellow hair."

> "But I can get a hair-dye
> And set such colour there,
> Brown, or black, or carrot,
> That young men in despair
> May love me for myself alone
> And not my yellow hair."

> "I heard an old religious man
> But yesternight declare
> That he had found a text to prove
> That only God, my dear,
> Could love you for yourself alone
> And not your yellow hair."*

To say that I want you to love me not for what I do for you but for what I am; to love me not for my body but for the essential me; to love me not for my mind, my achievements, my humor but for myself represents a silly set of non sequiturs only made possible by the confusion in some people's minds about the lessons of psychoanalysis.

There is an unfortunate prevalent tendency to think of the inner person as the real person and the outer as an illusion or pretender. Psychoanalytic data, which should never be viewed as other than supplementary information, have unfortunately come to be seen as an alternative (and superior!) view of human behavior. While psychoanalysis supplies us with an incredibly useful tool for explaining motives, purposes underly-

---

* W. B. Yeats, "For Anne Gregory," *The Collected Poems* (New York: Macmillan Co., 1956), p. 240.

ing human behavior, most of this has little bearing on the moral nature of that behavior and therefore has little to say about the essential judgments of a human individual. Like X-rays, psychoanalysis is a fascinating but relatively new technical tool in helping to illuminate certain aspects of the person. Few of us would want to enclose the X-rays of the principal parties with the photos in their wedding albums.

The inside of a man represents another view, not a truer one. A person may not always be what he appears to be, but what he appears to be is always a significant part of what he is. A man is the sum total of all of his behavior. To probe for the unconscious nature of an individual and to think that that defines the person exclusively, ignoring overt behavior, leads to a greater distortion than would ignoring the unconscious completely. You are for the most part what you seem to be, not what you would wish to be, or indeed what you believe yourself to be. Part of this feeling has been compounded by the current tendency toward psychohistory, which, by exposing the goodness inside the bad man and the evil in the good, invariably establishes a vulgar perverse egalitarianism. As if the arrangement of what is outside and what is inside makes no moral difference. I am not relieved to learn that Hitler's heart was in the right place! It is of no importance. A knowledge of the unconscious life is an adjunct to understanding behavior, *not* a substitute for the behavior in describing a person.*

In Murray Schisgal's play *Luv* there is an informative and funny scene in which two lovers are testing whether they really love each other for "themselves" or for their behavior. They proceed to act miserably and provocatively toward each other. After each assault, insult, or humiliation, one screams to the other, "Do you still love me?" And by the time the mink coat is thrown over the bridge, one does not know any more.

There is no "you" independent of your behavior, and so,

---

* See Willard Gaylin, "Will the Real Adolf Hitler Please Stand Up?" *The Hastings Center Report*, Vol. 7, No 5 (October, 1977), p. 10.

of course, we love you at least in part for your behavior. This is also true of the nature and supply of services. To see only the services would be an absence of love, but I am not sure that one can ever completely separate the services from the person. The kindnesses, attentions, comforts, affections, support, and nourishment establish the nature of the one in relation to the other.

How, then, do we get this idea of an essential love which one can somehow or other separate from other forms—love for ourselves rather than our uses or services? I suspect it is from the one time in life when we are truly loved "for ourselves," independent of anything we do. It is present at the one time of life in which we do nothing—infancy. The infant is universally adored by the typical parent, even though it is a totally narcissistic, self-involved, demanding, parasitic, and uncharming (except in the eyes of those who love him) individual. That we do tend to find our infants charming is an expression of an instinctive behavior bred into us that goes beyond rationality; parental instinct, if you will, forces us to respond to the infantile of our kind with love, adoration, and protectiveness. This is the only mechanism capable of insuring the survival through that prolonged dependency period that we previously discussed. Love is showered on the infant, even though he does the kinds of things which normally only offend us. He urinates on us, passes gas and more in public, drools on us, disturbs our sleep, interrupts our meals, breaks our valued possessions, and upsets the tranquility of our lives—and we adore him for it.

This concept of early love—total, pure, and unselfish—may be the basis for our striving to replicate the love of "self" beyond action. The problem is that the self of the infant is just a reflexive blob; the self of the adult that must be loved is a behaving, thinking, interrelating individual. To love the infant only for himself is to love a passive creature with few attributes other than the physical ones. You have to love him for what he is—not what he does, since he does little that is lovable. To love the adult for himself is to love him for his generosity, kindness, sensitivity, humor, dimples, life style, or you name it—all parts of himself. I am not here implying that the self is merely a sum of these parts, or that love can ever be rationally or objectively reduced to elements of behavior. I am merely stating that one cannot exclude these from their contribution to the self. We are partly our "parts" but more than our parts.

The concept of unearned love as being better than earned loved is a common one in our society. It is related to the adolescent quality of denying having studied for an exam, so that when the A is received it will seem a reflection of natural superiority. Somehow or other, to work for something and to get it demeans it for some people. If we are the beloved of the gods, it will come to us without our lifting a finger. This can be one of the most destructive vestiges of infancy extended into adult life. It is a trait which ties the closet grind to the psychopath who only values what he does not earn, therefore refuses to earn anything.

It is all right to be loved for our achievements and our kindnesses if not *only* for them. They are not alternatives to ourselves. They are part of that which defines ourselves. We must be very careful, then, when we indulge in feelings of being used. We must, before taking umbrage, understand the context of the use. When there is an exploitative element, when we are, in addition, manipulated; and when we have the feeling that our only value to the other individual is in the non-reciprocal comfort or end that he is capable of achieving through us, then we are entitled to feel used. But in a loving relationship, generally, there ought be using and being used. To be of use to someone you love should be a prideful experience. But even being "used" in the context of love is appropriate. When we can be of service to our children, we almost invariably respond with pleasure. When they ask us for our help or when they use our knowledge, our ability, our persona, it is a compliment, and we respond that way. Only when such use is the exclusive aspect of the relationship, when we begin to suspect that beyond such use there is no esteem, do we begin rightfully to resent being used. And even then, with a bounty of self-esteem, a generosity of spirit is available which allows our being used without feeling spent.

It is not the worst thing occasionally to be used even in the worst sense—not nearly so debilitating as to feel used by each request for favor; to view each approach as potential exploitation; to measure meanly the give-and-take of relationships; or to withdraw into the private and paranoid agony of the ever-vigilant.

PART III

Signals of Success

Reaching Out
and Moving Up

✌§ 10

Feeling Touched (and Hurt)

F OR A MOMENT, pause and think how "touched you were when . . ."

It is of course impossible for any other individual to identify the specific context in which this emotion last occurred for you. The emotion can be elicited in a limitless number of situations—but the feeling engendered is so specific that it can be identified across the variables.

It is not a grand emotion and yet it constitutes one of the great joys of life. It is a specifically human emotion that involves sharing: it demands person-to-person "contact." The multiple meanings of that word show the intimate relationships between touching and communication. The word is derived from the Latin *contactus* (touching), and has come to mean coming together and communicating—"Keep in touch!"

We can be moved by a piece of music, angered at events, disappointed in ourselves, but we are touched by something that passes between us and others. Of course, again it must be remembered that with our powers of identification, recall, and imagination we can expand our personal experiences to include those of others. By these processes of identification we may be touched by what we see around us, by what we may have imagined happening to others, or by what we recapture from our own experience, or even from a past that exists only in our imaginations.

One particularly delightful aspect of being touched is that almost invariably it carries with it an element of surprise. We are touched by the thoughtfulness of a friend, by an unexpected courtesy, the unusual service, an unaccustomed act of kindness or charity—or by the observation of these. In summary, the caring and loving of others touch us whether we experience them directly or in some abstraction. And, always, being touched is enhanced by the delight of surprise. It is the unexpected kindness from the unexpected source at the unexpected moment that catches us up with emotion and "touches" us. It is for this reason that we are more likely to use the term in a relationship to the distant person rather than the close. We are more apt to be touched by the expression of caring from the near stranger, or stranger, or in a context normally devoid of such human emotion.

The feeling of being touched is captured in a small scene from *The Red and the Black*. The Abbé Pirard is about to leave the directorship of the seminary at which Julien Sorel has been a student. He calls him into his office and takes leave of him:

"After fifteen years of labor, I am on the point of quitting this house. . . . Before I go, I want to do something for you; I am making you assistant master of the New and the Old Testament." Carried away with gratitude, Julien seriously considered going down on his knees and thanking God; but he gave in to a more genuine impulse.

He walked over to the Abbé Pirard and took his hand, which he raised to his lips.

"What's this?" exclaimed the director, looking very cross, but Julien's eyes spoke louder than his action.

The Abbé Pirard gazed at him in astonishment, like a man who, for years, has been unaccustomed to dealing with delicate emotions. This gesture had caught the director off guard; his voice faltered. "Very well, then! Yes, my child, I am fond of you. . . ."

It had been so long since Julien had heard a friendly voice that we ought to pardon him for his weakness; he burst into tears. The Abbé Pirard opened his arms to him; this moment was very sweet for both of them.*

The lonely Julien, grown unaccustomed to gentleness and love, starving for it, was touched by the recognition of the Abbé's concern. What is delightful in this particular passage is to see how the emotion of being touched is transmitted from Julien to the Abbé. Here we see one of the important effects of emotion: it not only serves our individual purposes—it not only communicates to us the situations to be acted upon—but it serves a social function by transferring emotion from one member to the other. Here we see, then, the contagion of emotion. It is the awareness of Julien's emotion that in turn touches his Abbé.

The surprise element in the emotion of being touched accounts for the fact that very small gestures are capable of precipitating major changes in relationships and feelings. This is particularly true when the feeling is compounded by the hunger for affection that exists in so many lives, or when it arises in specific relationships where affectionate approval is traditionally absent. Witness this combination in a scene from Flaubert:

They found a little chestnut-coloured hat, made of plush with a long nap; but the moths had ruined it. Félicité asked if she might have it. The two women looked at each other and their eyes filled

---

* H. Stendhal, *The Red and the Black* (New York: New American Library, Signet Classics, 1970), p. 203.

with tears. Then the mistress opened her arms, the maid threw herself into them, and they clasped each other in a warm embrace, satisfying their grief in a kiss which made them equal. It was the first time that such a thing had happened, for Mme. Aubain was not of a demonstrative nature. Félicité was as grateful as if she had received a great favour, and henceforth loved her mistress with dog-like devotion and religious veneration.*

The unexpectedness of the kindness—so essential an ingredient of being touched—explains why the term is more often used in the context of our casual relationships. If a stranger offers us a part of his lunch when food is scarce, a lift when needed, we are touched. When a mother does these things, it is an unnoticed part of the tacit loving arrangement. After all, isn't that what mothers are for? We generally are not "touched" to arrive at the breakfast table in the morning and find food presented to us—unless "we" are the mother.

In those cases where we are touched by those we love, it is likely to be in an unlikely or unexpected situation. Here the feeling initiates—and quickly dissolves into—the deeper emotion of love. Love can remain silent and often unfelt, part of the conditions of a contract long ago made and therefore almost forgotten. When we are reminded of its presence—when it comes anew, almost as from a stranger—the feeling of being touched then precipitates an overwhelming and sometimes unbearable flood of the more profound emotions which had existed dormant and unappreciated.

The following birthday scene between mother and son starts with what might be called the feeling of being touched but then rapidly moves in intensity into something too profound for that gentle and delicate emotion:

She turned away, passing one damp hand across her forehead, and went to the cupboard. Her back was to him, and he watched her while she took down a bright, figured vase, filled with flowers only

---

* Gustave Flaubert, "A Simple Heart" in *Three Tales* (New York: Penguin Books, 1961), p. 42.

on the most special occasion, and emptied the contents into her palm. He heard the chink of money, which meant that she was going to send him to the store. She put the vase back and turned to face him, her palm loosely folded before her.

"I didn't never ask you," she said, "what you wanted for your birthday. But you take this, son, and go out and get yourself something you think you want." And she opened his palm and put the money into it, warm and wet from her hand. In the moment that he felt the warm, smooth coins and her hand in his, John stared blindly at her face, so far above him. His heart broke and he wanted to put his head on her belly where the wet spot was, and cry. But he dropped his eyes and looked at his palm, at the small pile of coins.*

Since surprise is an essential element in being touched, what is necessary to precipitate the emotion will depend on what we are used to, and will, therefore, vary with our personal experience. To those who are used to gentleness and concern, a form of casual and cocky entitlement may develop which makes them immune to even rather significant gestures of consideration and kindness in their lives. In contrast, there are those whose lives are so deprived of affection, where caring is so alien to their experience, that any evidence of it is likely to touch and unsettle them.

With this particular emotion so bound to care, concern, and love, a question remains as to why we use a word like "touching," with its implication of tactile contact. Why is the skin seen as the source of this emotion? In one sense it should not be surprising. The skin has semantically, at least, always been bound to all of the subjective emotions through the dual and quite different meanings of the word "feeling." These two separate meanings indicate the primordial fusion that binds the skin to our entire emotional life.

The importance of touching and tactile stimulation in the early life of young mammals has long been observed by zoologists. The amount of actual skin contact given by the mother

---

* James Baldwin, *Go Tell It on the Mountain* (New York: Dell Publishing Co., 1953), p. 31.

to her young is surprising. Still more surprising, however, has been the growing recognition of how important that tactile stimulation is physiologically, how vital an element it is in the developmental chemistry of the newborn. What had been viewed as essentially a grooming procedure—perhaps related to affection, or some peculiar need of the mother, something akin to the nuzzling and stroking of the human infant by its mother—proved on careful and rigorous examination to have a more substantial and basic physiological significance in lower mammals. Life-sustaining processes are often dependent on these very actions for their initiation.

Close observation in the animal kingdom demonstrated that the grooming contact that had formerly been interpreted as indiscriminate poking, nuzzling, or licking served specific biological purposes. It was not purely a matter of affection. Even if the sole conscious purpose of the mother was the pleasure it gave her, she was, unwittingly, serving the biological needs of the infant. One example is particularly dramatic. It was discovered that when deprived of the perianal licking of the parent, it is quite impossible for certain young mammals (a dog or cat, for example) to initiate the essential function of urination. If the animal is incapable of urinating, such retention will lead to its death. The licking contact and stimulation are essential triggering mechanisms that initiate the complex processes of evacuation. Skin contact—nuzzling, proprioceptive contact, touching in the physical sense—may serve multiple purposes still unknown and may represent as crucial a part of the nourishing role of the mother to the child as the supply of food.

It may be that food was the culprit; so much attention was paid to feeding that there was little recognition of anything else in the early interactions of life. One of the significant discoveries of early psychoanalysis which most influenced developmental child psychiatry was the crucial link between food, love, and security. Freud's case for "orality" was so brilliantly made and struck such responsive chords in the experience and emotions of all of us that it dominated our thinking about the early life situation.

There is no question that the feeding process is the primary event both in the biological existence of the newborn and in its emerging psychological and social life. It is the context in which communication between the infant and the mother— that person whom the child quickly learns will support his life style as well as his life—first occurs. It is no wonder, therefore, that there develops a confusion and fusion about the nature of food and security that is to last throughout life. We understood when we read Freud's early cases why eating becomes the first line of defense against anxiety and boredom; why obesity is the general sickness of our tense society; and why cigarette smoking persists in the face of the awareness that it is a slow poison destroying the respiratory apparatus on which the very breath of life depends.

Thus it is not surprising that before the 1960s psychologists as diverse as behaviorists and psychoanalysts still conceptualized early infancy as being dominated by the feeding situation. But even the term "the feeding situation" implies more than just the mechanical ingestion of nutrients. If one visualizes the feeding situation, it is a complex orchestration that involves the soothing ingestion of food commingled with, and inseparable from, a wide variety of primarily tactile sensations. Feeding the infant involves embrace, pressure, contact, flesh-to-flesh engagement, fondling, cooing, tickling, talking, stroking, squeezing. It involves the transmission of warmth from one body to another, the rhythmic pulsation of a mother's heart, the brushing of her lips, the smell of her secretions.

Of course all of this was early recognized; it did not take psychologists to point out that there was a special physical communication between the mother and child during this period. It also was apparent to some that the gestures inherent in the feeding situation must also eventually become associated with love and security. But there was a tendency among the professionals, and a logical one at that, to think that these activities became pleasurable only *because* of their association with feeding. In other words, it was Pavlov's bell. If the bell always rang at the moment of serving food, the bell itself would have an excitatory influence on the gastrointestinal tract. We salivate for the bell not because the bell itself has a primary deliciousness but because the bell is associated in our minds with the imminent delivery of food. Touching and embracing were seen as secondary elaborations.

Primary nurture was seen as exclusively an oral phenomenon. It was food that was necessary for survival, and the pleasures of the first year were visualized exclusively in terms of oral apparatus—the lips, the mouth, the upper digestive tract.

The lesson should have been learned from the observations of animal life that those adjunctive performances were not as random or casual or incidental as they might have seemed, but had a primary significance of their own. Unfortunately, during this period there was a sharp separation between animal psychologists, pediatricians, clinical psychiatrists, anthropologists, and ethologists. It was only in the 1950s, partly by accident and partly by the confluence of three different types of research associated with the names of Spitz, Bowlby, and Harlow, that we began to see our kinship in this respect with the lower mammals and to recognize the enormous complexity of the nature of nurture and caring. Harry Harlow, an experimental psychologist, had been working with monkeys, and over an extended period of years he produced amazing bodies of research on mothering in animals that transformed our concept of the caring situation. He established that even when these monkeys were supplied "all" of their physiological needs—nutrients (sufficient calories, proteins, vitamins, and so on), warmth, shelter, and safety from predators—they failed to develop properly if they were isolated from contact with the traditional parents and group. They developed into bizarre and strange creatures, as unlike the traditional monkey as a hebephrenic, back-ward, psychotic patient is to a healthy human being. All of the essentials (as then understood) of life had been supplied except for contact with their kind, and what developed was not a monkey but an incomplete and lesser creature.

Further refinements of the tests were devised to focus on precisely what else was necessary for true development into a whole person—or, in this case, monkey. Harlow offered one group of monkeys a wire-mesh "mother" which on demand supplied all the food the infant required. At the same time, the monkeys were supplied a warm, cuddly, terry-cloth mother who offered no life-sustaining foods. The small baby monkeys not only preferred the terry-cloth monkeys to the life-sustaining wire-mesh monkeys, but in moments of panic and dread they ran to the terry-cloth surrogates for protection, identifying them as the primary, caring creatures in their lives.

Parallel with this, John Bowlby was studying the effects of early separation on the children evacuated from London during the blitz, and René Spitz was taking his keen observer's eye into institutions of caring for the sick or abandoned child— the pediatric wards of hospitals, orphanages, and the like. Both of them confirmed something in the human condition quite similar to the experimental condition with animals. No amount of clean, sterile, scientifically measured dispensing of food and medications would allow for normal development if there were deficiencies in contact—indeed, *physical* contact—with one's own kind.

This led us to a massive re-evaluation of some of the social institutions that had been created by our previous infatuation with "scientific" child-rearing. It became apparent that even a lesser foster home might be better than a "good" institution. It also became apparent that what constituted a good institution went beyond expensiveness of architecture and technical facilities. We became more tolerant of the good home—and defined it with less dependence on certain economic standards. This re-evaluation was the precursor—for good and bad—of the current passion for deinstitutionalization in all areas.

We have long known—well before any scientific study of child development—that the capacity to be affectionate and to accept affection is a gift from those who have treated us affectionately. Demonstrative and caring parents are most likely to produce children of the same order. We are now learning that in a peculiar and reversed way the infant may determine the affectionate capacities of the mother! We are beginning to discover biological factors that influence the capacity of mothers to treat their children with overt demonstrations of affection—beyond the cultural directives we have long accepted. Even the simple caressing factor, it is found, is part of the mechanism of interrelationship between child and parent which has a biological fixity long recognized in animals but presumed absent in an animal like *Homo sapiens,* so free of biological directives.

Studies of certain herding animals—sheep and goats, particularly—pointed out that just as there was a necessity for the infant animal to be exposed to the mother for certain traits to develop, there was equally a necessity for the mother to be exposed to the baby for her maternal attitudes to be triggered. If the mother goat or sheep is allowed normal contact with her baby in the first few days and is then separated from it, she will inevitably return to her suckling nurturing role when the infant is restored to her presence. She will only accept her own infant. She will butt or reject or even kick to death any strange kid or lamb placed before her. If, however, the infant is only allowed to remain in her presence for a few hours, then separated, sufficient stimulation of the mother instinct will occur, but it will not be specific to her infant. It will have a non-specific quality; she is incapable of distinguishing her infant from others, and she will indiscriminately accept for nurture any infant offered to her. If, however, she is deprived of the infant immediately post partum, she will reject, butt, or kick her own infant as well as a strange one. She will be unprepared to allow even the act of nursing, which is essential for relief of her own distress.

Something in the presence of the infant seems biologically essential to trigger the mothering responses that are essential for the infant's survival. Drawing on this material, Marshall Klaus and his colleagues in Cleveland began to be concerned about the enforced separation of the typical premature infant in a nursery of a modern hospital. It has long been known that certain infants in premature nurseries who are handled do better than those not touched as often. Dr. Klaus himself had pioneered in insisting that every baby in the premature nursery—for good reason or no reason—be picked up and handled periodically by the nurses who cared for them. It was demonstrated that such random and seemingly purposeless touching and contact had a felicitous effect on the survival rates in the nurseries.

They then began to be concerned about what the separation might do to mothering aspects of the future parent, and contrived a method for enriching the typical amount of parental involvement with the premature baby by devising a heat shield which allowed the premature baby to be taken out of the nursery and placed into the arms of its mother. The incredible result of this research showed that there was a significant statistical difference between the treatment of babies by mothers who were allowed this immediate contact and those who had undergone the traditional deprivation characteristic of premature nurseries.

Up to two years later, follow-up showed, by almost any measurement, an increased intense caring on the part of the enriched mothers. But for our purposes perhaps the most fascinating fact was that the mothers who were given immediate contact with their babies began to touch them with their fingertips and very quickly moved on to full palm body caressing.

A significant number of those mothers deprived of their infant in the immediate post-partum period never graduated from fingertip touching, never went on to full palm body stroking. The caressing and stroking activity, which is the actual symbol of being loved and touched, is therefore seen to go beyond the learning process and to be a basic and essential biological function in the human species.

The importance of human *contact*, in the most basic meaning of that word, "the coming together, or touching," was dramatically demonstrated by experiences in a totally different form of institution, the intensive care unit. In an age of scientific medicine, we began to supplement and replace the subjective experiences of physician and nurse with the more accurate and objective capacity of mechanical instrumentation. We recognized that the human eye was fallible in a way that certain scanning machines were not. We began to design monitoring services of the most sophisticated sorts. After all, a nurse could only feel the pulse in her free moments, and even then was limited by the fallibility of the human monitor. Electrocardiograms attached to the body of the sick patient would give us a constant flow of accurate, precise information.

What gradually evolved was an environment for our sickest patients, totally free of human contamination, where the patients were tended by devices which supplied continual mechanical attention. With the corruption of language that seems so specific to medicine, we labeled these places "intensive care units." To the chagrin of many of the designers, the death rate for acute coronary patients in some such units at major institutions rose rather than fell. These intensive care units, with their constant surveillance, their television eye, their electrodes, their monitors, and their computers, were isolating patients from direct human contact. It quickly became apparent that the isolation and mechanization was terrifying to the patient at a time when alleviation of anxiety is a critical therapeutic measure. At this time particularly, we need the reassurance that we are being cared for. We need care—and the primary dictionary meaning of that word is "worry"—anxious concern. And no machine feels that. No machine feels anything; nor, more importantly, will a patient feel the reassurance of emotional contact with his kind.

Scientific medicine for years has been replacing the general practitioner and his bedside care with the specialist who served parts instead of persons, and who eschewed the laying on of hands. Medicine had become sterile in more than just the good sense of that word. So great was the suspicion of body contact that it had almost disappeared from the general relationships of patient to doctor, except in a few significant probes of the diagnostic examination. What caressing, stroking, massaging, or rubbing remained was left in the hands of the nurse.

The turning to chiropractics by so much of the population was a product of the neglect, indeed derogation, of the mechanical factors of the body until the birth of physical medicine in the post-World War II era. During that same period, World War II, one of the most devastating diseases of childhood was poliomyelitis. Before the current vaccines were available, it was the scourge of late summer, terrifying parents well beyond the statistical significance of the disease itself. There was no prevention known and seemingly little treatment. In Australia, Sister Kenny had developed the one effective treatment that was available. While it could not protect the child against the disease, it had remarkable impact in minimizing the permanent paralysis that was often the vestige of the acute phase. Sister Kenny's treatment was simplicity itself. It demanded forced rest of the musculature during the period of acute inflammation along with the application of warm packs. Then, with the gradual subsidence of the acute inflammation, a program of massage and passive exercise was instituted. This involved manual manipulation of the body of the patient by the therapist. The medical hierarchy at that time had nothing but contempt for Sister Kenny. Actions so simple as touching, massage, and exercise seemed inappropriate in the scientific age of medicine. It was only with the accretion of such massive evidence of the effectiveness of her treatment that American medicine reluctantly adopted it.

Beyond that, I suspect that the anxiety of the typical male physician in our Anglo-Saxon tradition about physical contact made the whole procedure an uncomfortable one. I do not think it is chance that the person who discovered and pioneered the treatment was both a nurse and a woman.

The right, and therefore the capacity, to display physical affection has been severely limited in men. By labeling emotion, tenderness, softness, and sensuality as "feminine" traits, we have deprived our insecure male population of the easy pleasures of physical affection. This is particularly constricting in male-to-male contact. Here the dread of latent homosexuality compounds the restrictions. Most American men are conditioned to avoid tender physical contact with one another after a certain age.

I became keenly aware of the awkward complications of these taboos in recent years with the marriage of my elder daughter. For twenty-five years my experience was limited to daughters. From the day they were born, my natural inclinations were supported by unstated social rules which sanctioned the demonstrating of my love for them by physical contact. A caressing, kissing, hugging, stroking, cuddling physical language of affection evolved. Of course, with age, the nature and time of such affectionate displays—the conditioning of acceptability—varied dramatically. How could the very same child who only yesterday demanded my hand at all times in public situations today shun such contact as a social humiliation? Is that cold adolescent creature really the extension of that adoring prepubescent who preceded her?

Even bearing the vicissitudes of maturation, easy affection is the privilege of a father-daughter relationship. The reaching for a hand, the unexpected rush of fingers across a cheek, the soft stroking of hair are the statements that someone who loves is nearby. When physical contact is deemed inadvisable, we are free to use words and epithets of endearment. "Honey," "sweetheart," "darling," "love," and the personal and idiosyncratic variations of the same are like verbal caresses.

When faced, therefore, with that alien creature—a new "child" (in the form of my son-in-law) who was an adult male—stereotyped and unconscious behavior patterns which had served for years proved inappropriate and disturbing. Since given names were reserved for formal and generally disapproving conversations, the appropriate form of address around a restaurant table would be as follows: "What are you having for the first course, love?" "And how about you, dear?" "And you, honey?" Such address which had been acceptable and unnoticed for years became startling, both within the family and to the eavesdropper at the nearby table, when the "honey," "dear," or "love" inadvertently was directed to a twenty-five-year-old man. But after enough embarrassments, one begins to learn.

Harder to handle, however, are moments of joy and greeting. The return from an absence, the announcement of a success, the occasions of approval and gratitude have traditionally been accompanied by a hug, an embrace, a kiss. Nothing sloppy, mind you, or excessive—simply the appropriate loving, physical contact. How, now, with a strange male child? In American society the only substitute that we have so far found acceptable has been the handshake and smile. But ironically the handshake—the only physical contact which seems acceptable at this point—is traditionally the symbol of a relationship among strangers. It is the greeting that one gives to the individual with whom one has the *least* in common, not the most. It signifies, if anything, an absence of affection and emotional involvement. This avoidance of physical contact between males, even fathers and sons, in our culture is not by accident, but by training and design. From early infancy fathers treat sons differently from daughters. The full stroking and lilting language addressed to the little girl is replaced by a staccato, infantile version of the punch in the ribs and the sock on the arm.

The intolerance for physical affection seems to have expanded in the last forty years. One notices an intriguing difference when watching old-style movies; the degree of physical affection between men which was tolerable forty or fifty years ago would no longer be admissible in modern movies. In one touching scene in *Wings,* a World War I aviator embraces, caresses, and kisses his dying buddy in a way that would embarrass modern audiences. It would threaten too many of the male members of the audience. We have hardened our gender stereotypes to such a point where "being a man" seems to imply an immunity to all affection and emotion. Perhaps with the re-evaluation of values initiated by the women's movement, we will begin to open the doors to physical affection from men, and among men. There is a sense of change; we are learning to avoid the patterning which reinforces unacceptable gender stereotypes.

Of course, the opportunities for tender and affectionate physical contact are minimized in general with adulthood. We miss them and we find symbolic alternatives. The vulgar use of the word "stroking" to mean ingratiating or complimenting is a testament to our recognition of this frustrated need. The importance of touch as a sign of love has therefore been transmitted into the language, so that being touched no longer has a tactile connotation, but rather implies merely the awareness that someone cares.

The fact that so many adults are isolated from emotions by culture or individual treatment that they cannot feel touched in real life, and are often embarrassed by open displays of affection, and ashamed of their hunger for it or response to it, explains the role of sentimental art forms. There is often almost a reverse correlation between the capacity to feel directly in one's life and the capacity to respond to what is known as cheap sentiment. The individual who is deprived by his environment or his personal character traits from appreciation of direct touching is more likely to be touched by the singing of the anthem, the passing of the flag, the television soap opera, or even the involvement with animal surrogates.

All of us come from the common experience of helplessness in which we depend for our pleasures and survival on caring individuals. With those we love, we assume the care and accept it like the warmth of our environment and the air that sustains us. Such caring supports our energy and efforts with quiet nourishment. It enters our emotional life most consciously when it is withdrawn or in moments of renewed reminder of its presence. With our loved ones, we are rarely touched even by their touch. We are touched by a new and surprising source of caring. All of us in one way or another will carry reminders within us of our once and future need for caring, and all of us therefore are touched when we are delightedly and unexpectedly reminded that someone cares. When we are deprived of the caring that we have accepted and expected from those whose lives we share, we will feel "hurt."

Hurt, of course, means injury or damage. It is the experiencing of pain. When I say my back hurts, whether your back has ever hurt or not, you know approximately what I mean. Yet this so physical word when utilized in terms of feelings has never had physical connotations. If I tell you that yesterday I was so hurt, you do not ask in what part of my body I experienced the pain. If I inform you that I am feeling guilty because I hurt my mother, you do not ask where I struck her—on the head or across the arm. We all understand that to feel hurt is not to feel physical pain. It means that psychologically and emotionally we are feeling distress, or pain, and that the cause is a psychic injury.

But what specifically is the injury in feeling hurt? In many ways it is, as was suggested, the polar phenomenon to being touched. If we are generally touched by behavior that does more for us than we had a right to expect, we are hurt by behavior that we feel gives us less than our due. This is why we are so often touched by strangers and so invariably hurt by those we love. And of course to inflict hurt on one we love, even unwittingly, suffuses us with guilt. Similarly our hurt is often used effectively to induce guilt in a neglectful or wanton lover. We punish those who have hurt us by making them feel guilty; they are particularly vulnerable to guilt, since it is the shared, loving experience that makes both guilt and hurt especially elicitable in the context of that relationship.

Examine this delightful interplay between Tom and Maggie Tulliver, a brother and sister. They have broken a jam tart in two pieces. Maggie offers to eat the smaller part but Tom, affecting a paternal manly role that exceeds his capacity, generously insists that she take the larger, with results that surprise them both.

Maggie, thinking it was no use to contend further, began too, and ate her half puff with considerable relish as well as rapidity. But Tom had finished first, and had to look on while Maggie ate her last morsel or two, feeling in himself a capacity for more.

Maggie didn't know Tom was looking at her; she was seesawing on the elder bough, lost to almost everything but a vague sense of jam and idleness.

"O, you greedy thing!" said Tom, when she had swallowed the last morsel. He was conscious of having acted very fairly, and thought she ought to have considered this, and made up to him for it. He would have refused a bit of hers beforehand, but one is naturally at a different point of view before and after one's own share of puff is swallowed.

Maggie turned quite pale. "O, Tom, why didn't you ask me?" "I wasn't going to ask you for a bit, you greedy. You might have thought of it without, when you knew I gave you the best bit." "But I wanted you to have it—you know I did," said Maggie, in an injured tone.

"Yes, but I wasn't going to do what wasn't fair. . . ." Maggie, gifted with that superior power of misery which distinguishes the human being . . . sat still on her bough, and gave herself up to the keen sense of unmerited reproach. She would have given the world not to have eaten all her puff, and to have saved some of it for Tom. Not but that the puff was very nice, but she would have gone without it many times over, sooner than Tom should call her greedy and be cross with her. And he had said he wouldn't have it—and she ate it without thinking—how could she help it? The tears flowed so plentifully that Maggie saw nothing around her for the next ten minutes.*

Poor Tom. He would so have liked to be up to his generosity, but it was a fantasy which could only survive with the assumption that it would not have been taken literally. If life only followed fantasy, Maggie would have been touched by the nobility and generosity of Tom's offer and forthrightly refused it. Tom would then have been allowed a delightful but rare repast. He would have been able to have his cake and eat it, too.

We tend to be touched by solicitude and hurt by the lack of it. We are touched by the fact that a chance acquaintance remembers it is our birthday, just as we are hurt by the fact that our spouse has totally forgotten it. Just as being touched represents the delightful surprise in finding someone caring where it had not been anticipated, feeling hurt is the distressing omission of an attitude or gesture of love where we feel expectant of it, and entitled to it.

Obviously, even on the psychological and emotional level, to feel hurt is a slight emotion, with little sense of deep or permanent damage. It is most abundantly the emotion of children and adolescents. When an adult feels hurt, he is often chagrined by the emotion, as though it remined him of an adolescent aspect still alive beneath his manly posture and experience.

A pure example of hurt is the reaction of Tom Sawyer after he has been ignored by his girl friend Becky Thatcher.

---

* George Eliot, *The Mill on the Floss* (Boston: Houghton Mifflin Co., Riverside Editions, 1961), p. 42.

Tom's mind was made up now. He was gloomy and desperate. He was a forsaken, friendless boy, he said; nobody loved him; when they found out what they had driven him to, perhaps they would be sorry; he had tried to do right and get along, but they would not let him; since nothing would do them but to be rid of him, let it be so; and let them blame him for the consequences—why shouldn't they? What right had the friendless to complain?*

I am not at all worried that anyone reading this passage will be depressed or worried over Tom's gloom and despair. Obviously, to feel hurt does not carry with it the burden of anguish. If anything, there is a self-pitying quality about hurt, so that when it is publicly announced or inadvertently exposed, it tends to elicit a condescending or patronizing response rather than true sympathy and compassion. With the young, however, we suffer their sensitivities through our own reminiscences, and in the situation with the Tullivers, identification and love permit the sharing of their mutual hurt.

As with "touched," one can speak of feeling "deeply hurt," but again that modifier only supports the notion that hurt is more normally used in a superficial way. Examine this scene from *King Lear*. Lear, turned out into a bitter storm by his ungrateful daughters Regan and Goneril, describes his feelings.

LEAR: Thou think'st much that this contentious storm
Invades us to the skin: so 'tis to thee;
But where the greater malady is fix't,
The lesser is scarce felt. Thou'ldst shun a bear;
But if thy flight lay toward the roaring sea,
Thou'ldst meet the bear i' the mouth. When the mind's free,
The body's delicate: the tempest in my mind
Doth from my senses take all feeling else
Save what beats there—Filial ingratitude!
Is it not as this mouth should tear this hand
For lifting food to 't?—But I will punish home:—
No, I will weep no more.—In such a night

---

* Mark Twain, *The Adventures of Tom Sawyer* (New York: New American Library, Signet Classics, 1959), p. 88.

To shut me out!—Pour on; I will endure:—
In such a night as this! O Regan, Goneril!
Your old kind father, whose frank heart gave all,—
O, that way madness lies; let me shun that;
No more of that.

KENT: Good my lord, enter here.

LEAR: Prithee, go in thyself; seek thine own ease:
This tempest will not give me leave to ponder
On things would hurt me more.*

Even though the word "hurt" appears in the final line of
this quotation, I doubt that anyone would discuss this passage
as a section where King Lear "felt hurt" at his treatment by
his daughters. The implications of the term are too trivial and
transitory to serve the gravity of this scene. We would reach
for more profound words which might be extensions from hurt
but carry a greater sense of damage. We might say he felt
wounded, injured, crushed. The nobility of the character, his
fusion with the elements and storm belie the quality and quantity of pain involved in simply "being hurt."

Hurt, then, like being touched, is a small emotion. It is also
an emotion of surprise—in this case, however, of disappointment rather than delight. It is almost inevitably associated with
response to the action of another person. We do not, for example, speak of being hurt by the fact that it rained on our parade.
Disappointed, angry, or upset, but certainly not hurt.

It is an emotion felt most closely and most frequently in
relationship to those whom we care about and who normally
care for us. To feel hurt, then, occurs with a failure in caring.
It represents our vulnerability through the various attachments
of life, and is a sign of how important is our need to feel cared
for. The relationship between feeling touched and feeling hurt
is interestingly demonstrated in the fact that one of the most

---

* *King Lear,* Act III, Scene 4, lines 6–26

common causes of our feeling hurt is a tact ("touch") less statement from a loved one.

The close affinity of being hurt to loving relationships can best be seen when one considers the closely related emotion of feeling slighted. The very types of situations which would lead to hurt when they arise as part of the loving relationship would lead to feeling "slighted" when occurring in a more casual relationship. When you have not been invited to the wedding, your emotion will range from hurt to slight, depending on how close you perceive your relationship with the participants. It is presumptuous and silly to feel hurt in a relationship where one should feel slighted. It does happen, and it happens most with individuals who confuse respect or esteem with love.

We feel slighted when another's behavior indicates less esteem, less value, for us than we presumed they held. We feel hurt with the absence of anticipated love. To feel slighted is to feel that one has been made less of, is less appreciated. One is slighted if one is not included in an honors group and not mentioned for one's contribution to some victory or success. We have been made small, reduced and made less of.

To return to the example of the wedding party; if the business associates on a professional level are invited and the secretarial staff ignored, the latter will have a right then to feel slighted. One presumes the degree of intimacy and love is no greater in either direction, but the invitation is seen as having been made on standards of value, because the failure to receive an invitation is a reflection of a judgment of diminished worth. The bride's parents are most likely to receive announcements of "hurt" in reference to the groom's sisters, and his cousins, and his aunts—particularly the aunts!

The talk of a slight occurs most often in intellectual and social circles, not within the structure of the family or of caring institutions. In some professional relationships, however, where love is not involved but caring often is, one is more apt to hear the word "hurt" used than "slight." A patient feels hurt—

not slighted—if a psychiatrist forgets an appointment. Again, what he is concerned about receiving from the doctor is not particularly evaluation, but care, a form of concern closely related to love. Of course he may want the respect of the doctor, but that is not the urgent need out of that relationship. Medicine is, after all (or has been labeled), a "caring" profession.

Slights occur in the world of footnotes and acknowledgments, of pecking orders and titles, of daises and distances, of sizes of offices and seatings at tables. Hurt occurs at parties and celebrations, in bedrooms and parlors. It is a family emotion in much the same way as guilt is, although the direction of flow is reversed. Our parents are more likely to generate guilt; and we are more likely to hurt them.

A special form of hurt centers around ingratitude, the primary "sin" of children—at least according to their parents. The parent expects gratitude—the "appreciative awareness and thankfulness . . . for kindness shown or something received."* Obviously, we can only expect gratefulness from those whom we have served, given to, and sacrificed for. It is logical, then, that parents expect gratitude from children. But children accustomed to continuing services—which, if anything, diminish as the child progresses out of infancy and total dependence—see the services as usual and unnoteworthy. It is ironic that parental demands for signs of gratitude increase as the child needs less and less of parental services. It is the threat that the parent will no longer be needed at all, and if unneeded will be unloved, that drives him to demand special reassurances. Gratitude is desired not in response to past services but as reassurance for a future in which the parent may need the child.

Ingratitude may be experienced in any relationship of service, and precipitates hurt. When the tutor Karl Ivanitch hears that "now the children are grown up, they must study in ear-

---

*American Heritage Dictionary, 1st ed., s.v. "gratitude."

nest" and will therefore be sent off to school, he is hurt and takes his "proper revenge" in the classroom:

" 'Of all pas-sions the most re-volt-ing is,' have you written that?" Here he paused slowly, took a pinch of snuff, and continued with renewed energy,—" 'the most revolting is In-grat-i-tude' . . . a capital I."
I looked at him after writing the last word, in expectation of more. "Period," said he.*

In this quotation, we glimpse the secret ingredient of hurt— anger. So often is an element of anger included with hurt that some reductionists insist that hurt is merely a euphemism for an anger which the individual is reluctant to acknowledge.

Certainly the conditions under which hurt is provoked are as likely to produce anger and resentment. To have served someone well over a period of years—to have loved them, or even sacrificed for them—and then to find a deficit in the reciprocity of feelings, a lack of appreciation, an indifference, a callousness, or even hostility, can surely produce anger. It is so grossly unfair! Despite the fact that there seems to be a general acknowledgment these days among men in high places that life is not fair, the confrontation with the fact inevitably arouses bitterness and a sense of injustice—particularly on the part of the deprived or disadvantaged. We want to assume that virtue is rewarded, that kindness returns kindness, and that our treatment *by* others will mirror our treatment of them.

The fact that hurt typically occurs within the context of loving relationships does not, as it might seem, mitigate the probability of anger. Quite the contrary. Who else are we usually angry with—except those we love? The reservoirs of anger we have toward our loved ones are always larger than what is available toward those we do not know. It is a traditional false assumption that love and hate are polar phenomena. In

---

* Leo Tolstoy, *Childhood, Boyhood and Youth* (New York: Lear Publishers, 1949), p. 16.

a polarity the absence of one is the presence of another. Heat and cold are polar phenomena—if you gradually reduce the quantity of heat, you produce cold. Love and hate, if anything, are linked in their antonyms. They are primary passions. The most likely opposite—at least of love—is indifference. To love someone means to be involved with, to identify with, to engage with, to suffer with and for them, and to share their joys.

Anger, too, thrives on intimacy. Certainly flashes of anger can be felt at the rude intruder in the line or the public figure who betrays a trust. Even when we do feel anger toward a stranger, it is usually ephemeral, and during the short spasm of feeling, the very quality of the emotion will bind us to the hated individual. Prolonged anger can be experienced toward an outrageous public villain, an Idi Amin or a Richard Nixon. In the latter cases, even though the feeling is not transient, it is still not quite the depth of anger that we feel toward those with whom we have some intimate involvement. Anger requires energy and intimacy, and it flourishes in a relationship of interdependency—children, parents, employers, room-mates, partners, and neighbors.

If it is logical and reasonable to feel anger toward those we are closest to, why the covert nature of anger associated with hurt? Why do we hide from it? It is precisely because of the complications of these close relationships. The concept that we are angry with people we love can be confused in our minds with the absence of love, and can produce an enormous sense of guilt. To protect against the guilty feeling, we will deny the anger. With children particularly, the parent recog-nizes—intellectually, at least—that the services are the due of the child, and that no reciprocity is really conceivable. Each parent disproportionately gives to his child, who will return only a small percentage; but then, in his time, he will dispropor-tionately give to his child. It is a system of linear justice biologi-cally determined and intellectually—if not emotionally—ac-knowledged by most parents. The feeling that we desire

gratitude and equal return makes us feel smaller and less adequate. Therefore the emotion of anger that signals that desire
must be suppressed. It betrays a lack of generosity and unselfishness.

Similarly, fear will mask the emotion of anger. With the
growth of the child, we sense the approaching shift of the
scale to the point—in our culture, at least—where the child
emerges from dependence on the parent as the parent slips
into dependence on the child. In this period, anger on the
part of the parent is frightening and dangerous. It may antago-
nize the very individual on whom he is becoming dependent.
Here, of course, I am using dependence not in the exclusive
terms of supplying survival needs—whether money, clothes,
or shelter—but in the terms of emotional dependence on the
presence of the other for our pleasure and happiness.

Where the dependent relationship is one of intimacy without
love, as in the case of employee to employer, the rage *must*
be controlled, for a real threat to direct survival needs exists.
But here we are most likely to feel impotent rage. We *know*
we are angry. We suppress the emotion, we do not repress
it. It is part of our consciousness, but unexposed. We do not
feel guilty; if anything, we feel righteous and frustrated in our
inability to redress the grievance. More often than not, such
impotent rage drives out hurt. There can be hurt in relationship
to an employer, as there was with Karl Ivanitch, but the hurt
indicates the affectionate ties that existed and the emotion dis-
creetly modifies even the feeling of anger. With hurt we usually
go beyond suppression; we deny the existence of the emotion
of anger. To see hurt only as a euphemism for anger is to
miss the peculiar amalgam of love and disappointment and
pain and anxiety that forms this complex emotion.

Feeling hurt, like being touched, is testament to our involvement with other human beings, and our need for them. Both
signal some aspect of caring relationships but with opposite
valences: feeling touched is the response to the unexpected

bonus; feeling hurt is the result of the entitlement not received. Yet interestingly, the two words derive semantically from such entirely different roots as to suggest that there are fundamental differences in the implications of the small accretions or subtractions of affection. What we subtract is more threatening than what we add.

Being touched may have no implication except for the lovely reminder that serendipity does exist, and that even mundane occasions may produce delightful surprises. To be treated kindly by someone who is not primarily involved in the structure of our life, on whose care we are not dependent, is like a stroke or caress. Unnecessary, unexpected, but delightful.

On the other hand, even when feeling hurt involves a small matter, it has a large portent. To be neglected by someone who should be caring for us carries with it the threat of real damage. We are thrust into this world helpless and dependent, and the earliest lesson learned is that our very existence depends on the loving concern of others. We do not forget these early lessons—even when the conditions of life make their message less relevant. Approval from a stranger is still a luxury; care from a loved one may ultimately be a matter of survival— if not at the moment we sense its absence, then at some future moment when we are more vulnerable, when the demands are more urgent and omissions more serious. If this individual with whom my fate is linked can be thoughtless at this moment, what then if the situation were not of a jam tart but of real hunger?

Being touched is the awareness of an unexpected sign of love, or identification with us, from an unexpected source. It is a sign that someone who need not care does, but whether he cares or not is of minor relevance. We are not bound to him. There is no legitimate potential for real harm in the discontinuation of that affection. But we can be harmed by the withdrawal of love from members of that supporting network of friends and family on whom we all depend for our emotional survival. "Hurt" is the right modality for that emotional contest. We can really be hurt (damaged) by situations signaled by the feeling of hurt. That feeling signals the absence of such caring and identification from one who ought to be displaying them. If it is a parent, we recognize that at some future time we may depend on that caring for our very survival. It therefore does indeed "hurt" us to perceive even a mild lapse.

We are extraordinarily sensitive in conditions central to survival—and we survive in great part through our loving relations. Our "receptors" for feeling hurt are therefore generally finely tuned and low-threshold mechanisms. When such hurts occur too frequently, they demand an examination of ourselves and those with whom we share a common fate. Either we are getting less from our loved ones than we are entitled to or we are expecting too much.

Touch and hurt testify to and motivate toward affectionate bonds. While rooted in survival needs of childhood, they extend beyond that age and outgrow that purpose. They guide us—beyond mere utility—toward the affectionate and joyous aspects of involvements with our kind. People need people not simply to survive but to embroider and enrich that survival.

⊰§ 11

Feeling Moved

M OVED" IS ANOTHER EMOTION closely linked with "touched." Here the two are often confused with each other, used synonymously, and, as typical with similar emotions, are often semantically fudged. They are different. Again, since we are dealing with a subjective aspect in which each man is the master of his own experience, no one can dictate what is right and what is wrong. Nonetheless I do feel that for purposes of clarity and refinement it is worth separating out these two sets of feelings.

Touched is generally a light emotion, although we do experience feelings of being deeply touched. The fact that we speak of it so (and it is not considered redundant) merely affirms the sense of touch as being a gentle feeling. The caress is its symbol. It arises almost inevitably in terms of something that is done for us by someone. It is a person-to-person emotion.

Being moved, on the other hand, is a deep and intense emotion and it rarely relates to a transaction between people. More often than not, the feeling of being moved is in relationship to certain abstractions, events, concepts, and sensations.

Before we approach the specific contexts in which we are moved, we should acknowledge the generic sense, in which we use "moved" to mean brought to an emotional state. We find a play "moving," meaning that it generates emotions in general. We similarly tend to use "touching" in this way. Yet even here, were we to tell a friend to see a certain play, and then say that it was either touching or moving, a quite different, albeit undefinable distinction would exist. And to my perceptions, at least, there is a greater depth and a more fundamental or primal quality to being moved.

Many have never felt "moved." In addition, the areas which elicit the feeling of being moved vary dramatically among people. The most common experience of being moved is in relationship to some encounter with grandeur. As such, we most commonly have this feeling in terms of interaction with nature.

> O world, I cannot hold thee close enough!
>   Thy winds, thy wide grey skies!
>   Thy mists, that roll and rise!
> Thy woods, this autumn day, that ache and sag
> And all but cry with colour! That gaunt crag
> To crush! To lift the lean of that black bluff!
> World, world, I cannot get thee close enough!
>
> Long have I known a glory in it all,
>   But never knew I this:
>   Here such a passion is
> As stretcheth me apart,—Lord, I do fear
> Thou'st made the world too beautiful this year;
> My soul is all but out of me,—let fall
> No burning leaf; prithee, let no bird call.*

---

* Edna St. Vincent Millay, "God's World," in *Collected Lyrics* of Edna St. Vincent Millay (New York: Harper & Row, 1939), p. 32.

There is a physical feeling implicit in the very name of the emotion "being moved." We do tend to feel "transported" by this emotion; "the heart leaps up" when we behold the rainbow in the sky, or the sunset, or the breaking dawn. The actual physical sense of being raised, lifted, stretched, pressed, elevated is so common a part of the sensate experience that it dominates the language and poetry of being moved in the face of nature's beauty.

It may well be that this lifting up expresses the feeling of our being lifted out of ourselves and characterizes that which is unique in this feeling. While so many emotions deal with our relations self-to-self, or our relations self-to-others, this is the one emotion which tends to take us out of our struggle for survival and even out of our search for gratifications. It affirms our relationships above and beyond even the limits of our body. It establishes an identification of ourself as a part of something bigger. It is the emotion of spiritual communion and, as such, may be the essential feeling of the religious experience.

In almost every poetic example of being moved, one finds the sense of awe and grandeur that one associates with the religious feeling. In addition, such writing is filled with actual references to God or nature as a generalization, independent of the specific events of nature.

> i thank You God for most this amazing
> day; for the leaping greenly spirits of trees
> and a blue true dream of sky; and for everything
> which is natural which is infinite which is yes
>
> (i who have died am alive again today,
> and this is the sun's birthday; this is the birth
> day of life and of love and wings; and of the gay
> great happening illimitably earth)
>
> how should tasting touching hearing seeing
> breathing any—lifted from the no
> of all nothing—and human merely being
> doubt unimaginable You?

(now the ears of my ears awake and
now the eyes of my eyes are opened)*

The Cummings poem specifically states that this contact with
the larger transcends all the sensate pleasures of daily existence,
and yet even while Cummings is stating so, the poem is filled
with the stretching, reaching, sensual, almost sexual feeling
of moving and experiencing.

It is a peculiar quality of being moved that even as we are
being "lifted out of ourselves" we experience the greatest sense
of self. It is as though being rid of *specific* feelings allows pure
feeling to come through. Being moved, then, is the transcendental emotion that brings us a sense of what we are in essence,
beyond measurement and specificity. This may explain why
we experience it at its purest in the non-literary forms of the
arts: in music, dance, fine arts. There is a feeling tone beyond
cognition—unattached to ideas, thoughts, or perceptions.

Those of you who have felt moved by music know precisely
what I mean. If you have not, I can only compare it to that
which you have felt with exposure to the beauty of natural
phenomena. There are certain notes and combinations of notes
that have nothing to do with intellect, rationality, ideation and
that inevitably cause a kind of chill to be felt across the back
of my neck and give me almost a literal feeling of being lifted
out of my seat. They produce the result with such regularity
that when I am half listening to music in the background while
doing other things—working, reading, writing; really "not listening at all"—I experience a strong alerting of consciousness.
The notes just prior to the sections to which I am particularly
vulnerable intrude into awareness and interrupt the flow of
concentration on the primary activity, and draw my attention
to the music.

This lifting out—experiencing self by escape from self—is
what some feel only with drugs or alcohol. Thomas Wolfe de-

_____

* e. e. cummings, *Poems 1923–1954* (New York: Harcourt, Brace & World),
p. 464.

scribed, in *Look Homeward, Angel,* his first experience with
drunkenness as an incredible sense of freedom, escape, and
liberation.

. . . It was, he knew, one of the great moments in his life—he
lay, greedily watching the mastery of the grape over his virgin flesh,
like a girl for the first time in the embrace of her lover. . . . He
exulted in the great length of his limbs and his body, through which
the mighty liquor could better work its wizardry. In all the earth
there was no other like him, no other fitted to be so sublimely and
magnificently drunken. It was greater than all the music he had ever
heard; it was as great as the highest poetry. Why had he never been
told? Why had no one ever written adequately about it? Why, when
it was possible to buy a god in a bottle, and drink him off, and become
a god oneself, were men not forever drunken?

He had a moment of great wonder—the magnificent wonder with
which we discover the simple and unspeakable things that lie buried
and known, but unconfessed, in us. So might a man feel if he wakened
after death and found himself in Heaven.*

It is hard to write about so non-literary, non-cognitive, and
non-specific a feeling. With anxiety, I can describe a specific
context in which almost every reader will have experienced
the emotion. Not so with feeling moved. Although the feeling
is very specific in its quality, it is not so in its context. It is
difficult to communicate about being moved across diverse experience. It is so dependent on the nature of our sensations
and the nature of our experiences that I cannot be sure whether
my personal response is universal or merely an idiosyncrasy
of my life and associations. The emotion itself is not (like fear,
guilt, et al.) specifically linked to the universal life experiences
that we all have shared: dependency, separation anxiety, discovery, and mastery. These universal experiences permit me
to abstract from them, to supply a general context in which
the most elemental feelings—the "vital signs," such as fear,
pride, and so on—are likely to occur for all.

With feeling moved, I am least confident when saying to

---

* Thomas Wolfe, *Look Homeward, Angel* (New York: Modern Library, 1929),
p. 493.

the reader, "You know how you feel when . . ." You may not
enjoy the same kind of music or, even if you "enjoy" it, you
may not respond to the same music in the specific way I just
described. It may be that painting performs this function for
you. It has always struck me as strange that I personally so
seldom respond this way to a painting, particularly since I am
essentially more sophisticated, knowledgeble, and interested
in painting than I am in music. Once I had thought that perhaps
it was my particular ignorance with technical music that allowed the pure emotion to come through there; whereas with
painting I am likely to be intrigued, captivated, and sidetracked
by the kinds of intellectual and technical judgments that dilute
pure feeling. I have since found that there is no relationship
between "feeling moved" and technical knowledge. Sophistication may simply make one more discriminating in response—
but probably enhances the depth of response. There may be
some hidden experiential or genetic factors which dictate the
capacity and context of this feeling.

When I respond to the visual arts with this feeling of being
moved, it is most frequently with architecture. I think of my
incredible first view of Chartres. It was a gloomy, foggy, rainy
day that by obscuring vision managed to obliterate all observation of the twentieth-century surroundings, so that out of the
flatness of the landscape this Gothic and medieval sight
emerged almost like a ghost from the past.

Literature (except poetry) rarely produces in me this feeling
of being moved. This is not to say that I am not *moved* by
literature, but here it is in the secondary sense of being brought
to emotion—that is, to some specific emotion. There are, however, times in which I do feel moved by literature (and this
same mechanism, in seeming contradiction to what I said before, allows us to be "moved" by acts of people). When that
does happen, I suspect it signifies that the literal act which
has reached us has brought us into direct emotional resonance
with the general feeling of which it is only a part; a concrete

act of being loved will remind us of the glorious *abstraction* of love and loving. It is when specific and literal scenes are so well portrayed—so poetically expressed—that they stand for the universal emotion. Just as in certain moments in life to feel loved by someone is to feel more than that; it is to be reminded of the nature of love; it is to be brought once again in contact with the generalization "love."

If being touched is to be made to feel good *within* our relationships, then being moved is to be made to feel good *beyond* our relationships. Those passages of literature that are most likely to move us are those that—beyond describing or eliciting specific emotions—affirm the very existence of love, compassion, beauty, and so on. That may be why poetry, with its concentration of imagery and economy of form, is the most likely source of literature for "feeling moved." (With poetry, we can in addition be moved by its "music.")

Even in poetry, freedom from intellectual trappings will often enhance the emotional pull. The poetry which moves me most is that in which the specific meanings are obscured in language, mood, or imagery; where ideas serve mood; where messages—if present—are unobtrusive and elliptic. The very obscurity that offends many readers and disturbs their sense of rationality and logic may serve the primary purpose of bending everything to the evoked feeling. Idea is clouded to better serve the feeling—which still may carry the idea! When the impressionistic fusions of meanings and half-meanings, of tones and sounds, all blend in one orchestral effect where it is difficult to tease out the specific instruments of mood, it is then that poetry becomes a form of music through words. It is this which I feel in "The Waking," which introduces this book.

It is not, however, the kind of poetry I have chosen to quote in the illustrative examples of the book. I do not trust the universality of its capacity to elicit that feeling. In this kind of poetry, I am less sure that what I am feeling is what you will be feeling. I have therefore selected those quotations from literature which not only express but also describe the feeling of being moved, and which do so in the most universal language, in the most generally experienced of situations.

Birth, renewal, rebirth are the stuff of wonder. In nature, particularly, springtime surely must be close to a universal source of awe in all of us. The renascence, the perpetual rejuvenation that is spring—the "breeding lilacs out of dead land"—tends to remind us of our own capacity to be aroused, to be reborn out of torpor and despair into elation and joy. In the following passage from *Zorba the Greek,* Kazantzakis describes this encounter with spring:

It seemed to me that the world had been transformed overnight. Opposite me on the sand, a small clump of thorny bushes, which had been a miserable dull color the day before, was now covered with tiny white blossoms. In the air hung a sweet, haunting perfume of lemon and orange trees in flower. I walked out a few steps. I could never see too much of this ever-recurring miracle.

Suddenly I heard a happy cry behind me. Zorba had risen and rushed to the door, half-naked. He, too, was thrilled by this sight of spring.

"What is that?" he asked stupefied. "That miracle over there, that moving blue, what do they call it? Sea? Sea? And what's that wearing a flowered green apron? Earth? Who was the artist who did it? It's the first time I've seen that, I swear!"

His eyes were brimming over.

"Zorba!" I cried. "Have you gone off your head?"

"What are you laughing at? Don't you see? There's magic behind all that."

He rushed outside, began dancing and rolling in the grass like a foal in spring.*

Zorba, experiencing the transcending feeling of spring, is moved. And he translates the metaphoric feeling of being moved into literally moving. He allows his body to experience

---

* Nikos Kazantzakis, *Zorba the Greek,* trans. Carl Wildman (New York: Simon & Schuster, Touchstone Books, 1952), p. 228.

and to express concretely the emotions felt. He abandons himself; he moves as he is moved.

Remember all the clichés spurned by the jaded and you
will know what it means to be moved—beyond any specificity
of ideas or named feelings. Remember the first sight of the
sea, remember a New England October day, remember the
first sight of your child—all of the confrontations with the
"goodness" of life capable of moving us.

It is possible that the "joy" that comes out of the simple,
physical experience of childhood is made up of expressions
of the newness and awareness of the pleasures themselves.
Spring may not have the same symbolic meaning to the child
as to Zorba, but some freedom—beyond specific fun—some
larger feeling is experienced.

> in Just-
> spring   when the world is mud-
> luscious the little
> lame balloonman
>
> whistles   far   and wee
>
> and eddieandbill come
> running from marbles and
> piracies and it's
> spring
>
> when the world is puddle-wonderful*

Even the grousing middle-aged commuter made miserable
by inconveniences and spring rains may recall a time when
the world was "mud-luscious," when the world was "puddle-
wonderful." Being moved may be the adult's version of the
sheer pleasure of first discovery in childhood—our reminder
of an existential joy that lies trapped beneath the confining
layers of routine existence.

---

* Cummings, *Poems*, p. 21.

~§ 12

Feeling Good

THERE COMES A MOMENT—often transitory at first—when a patient who has been mired in depression begins to emerge from the disease. With the alleviation of that oppressive sense of alive deadness that is called depression, the patient once again simply, but exultantly, "fees good." As a psychiatrist struggling to help patients with depression, I can recognize the moment when it happens before the patient has said a word, often before he is aware of what is happening, in a fleeting moment on catching sight of the patient—his facial expression, his body tone, his movement and posture.

What is that feeling of goodness? It is not just the relief that the depression is lifting. It is not just the absence of the pain that preceded it. Some believe that—with drug treatment, particularly—it is the emotional feeling which begins to cause the despair to lift. At any rate, the emotional feeling and the lifting of despair occur so simultaneously that the patient cannot distinguish one from the other. The patient feels the relief, joy, and optimism related to the sense of having won a battle, a joust with his sickness, and also the wonder of that non-specific "feeling good" again, after not having felt so for weeks.

"Feeling good" is generic and vague. Whenever questioned, any individual will find "reasons" why he feels good, but the emotion itself eludes specific cause and specific description. Lightness, buoyancy, aliveness, enthusiasm, optimism, peace, relaxation, hope, involvement—all are words that have been used to amplify the specific feeling of feeling good. All of us know that feeling good can be independent of a right to feel so, and can irrationally occur in the midst of problems. A day dawns like any other and we wake up "feeling good."

In one sense, feeling good is the opposite of despair; in another sense, it is the opposite of feeling upset. The major ingredients of feeling good are the antitheses and antidotes of those negative feelings. To feel good is to have a sense of hope, mastery, self-confidence, and self-esteem.

Part of the difficulty in defining or describing what the feeling is lies in our general ignorance in detailing the mechanisms of pleasure. Psychiatry, of course, has always been more successful in dealing with pain than pleasure, sickness than health. I suspect that in most fields of scholarship it is easier to analyze what has gone wrong than what went right. Failure is analyzed, while success is merely enjoyed. Rightness is therefore understood in terms of the absence of things gone wrong.

But there is a positive sense of pleasure. And surely there must be some concept that relates one form of pleasure to another—that defines the entity. We can feel different forms of pleasure in relationship to different kinds of stimuli. Still there must be something of the nature of pleasure that binds the individual experiences together. And whatever that is must define the generic sensation of feeling good.

It is with reluctance that I begin an analysis of pleasure. Almost inevitably, like an analysis of humor, it is heavy-handed work. Some things are meant to be experienced, relished, without analysis—indeed without cognition of any sort. Distress ought to be analyzed. The mere intellectual exercise reduces the distress. But to try to say why a joke is funny or why fun is fun almost ordains a certain resentment against the analyst. In the practice of psychoanalysis we know better. We rarely, if ever, analyze success for our patients. Health is its own excuse for being, and is accepted gratefully by both the parties.

Joy stems from an altered sense of self and, in turn, alters our view of our world and the way we are viewed. In the following quotation, Flush, a cocker spaniel, with some amazement and not a little jealousy, observes the transforming impact of a strange man on his ailing and unhappy mistress:

> Flush lay with his eyes wide open, listening. Though he could make no sense of the little words . . . he could detect with terrible accuracy that the tone of the words was changing. Miss Barrett's voice had been forced and unnaturally lively at first. Now it had gained a warmth and an ease that he had never heard in it before. And every time the man came, some new sound came into their voices.*

The change Flush first senses only in his mistress's tone will eventually transform her perceptions, her behavior, and the world she inhabits.

If Flush had changed, so had Miss Barrett. It was not merely that she called herself Mrs. Browning now; that she flashed the gold ring on her hand in the sun; she was changed, as much as Flush was changed. Flush heard her say, "Robert," "my husband," fifty times a day, and always with a ring of pride that made his hackles rise and his heart jump. But it was not her language only that had changed. She was a different person altogether. Now, for instance, instead of sipping a thimbleful of port and complaining of the headache, she tossed off a tumbler of Chianti and slept the sounder. There was a flowering branch of oranges on the dinner-table instead of one de-

---

* Virginia Woolf, *Flush* (New York: Harcourt Brace Jovanovich, Harvest Books, 1976), p. 68.

nuded sour, yellow fruit. Then instead of driving in a barouche landau to Regent's Park she pulled on her thick boots and scrambled over rocks. Instead of sitting in a carriage and rumbling along Oxford Street, they rattled off in a ramshackle fly to the borders of a lake and looked at mountains; and when she tired she did not hail another cab; she sat on a stone and watched the lizards. She delighted in the sun; she delighted in the cold.*

If there is a common ingredient to the various sources and forms of pleasure, the only one that I can identify is that they all seem to contribute to an enhanced sense of self. Pleasurable events either intensify our sense of ourselves or enlarge our view of ourselves. We tend to stretch to our limits, and satiation and easy gratification ultimately destroy pleasure. Samuel Johnson recognized this when he said:

> . . . [The Pyramid] seems to have been erected only in compliance with *that hunger of imagination which preys incessantly upon life.* . . . Those who have already all that they can enjoy, must enlarge their desires. He that has built for use, till use is supplied, must begin to build for vanity. . . . I *consider this mighty structure as a monument to the insufficiency of human enjoyments.*†

To analyze pleasure, it is probably best to start with the basic and the physical. The first, and simplest, source of pleasure arises out of stimulation—the pleasure of our senses: of touching and being touched—and the joys of tastes, smells, sounds, and sights.

> After a hearty New England breakfast,
> I weigh two hundred pounds
> this morning. Cock of the walk,
> I strut in my turtle-necked French sailor's jersey. . . .‡

Our senses are our primary instruments of pleasure and mediate our simplest forms of pleasurable experience. Perhaps calling it "the simplest" does a disservice to the importance

---

* Ibid., p. 122.
† W. Jackson Bate, *Samuel Johnson* (New York: Harcourt Brace Jovanovich, 1977), p. 299.
‡ Lowell, "Waking in the Blue," *Life Studies,* p. 82.

of sensate pleasure. "Elemental" is probably a more accurate description, and some would see it as at the core of living:

> The greatest poverty is not to live
> In a physical world, to feel that one's desire
> Is too difficult to tell from despair. Perhaps,
> After death, the non-physical people, in paradise,
> Itself non-physical, may, by chance, observe
> The green corn gleaming and experience
> The minor of what we feel. . . .*

A second category of pleasures—beyond particularly physical sensation, invoking our total self as person—is discovery. I have already discussed the sheer joy of the child on finding something new; observe his pleasure even in the pursuit of the unknown—in poking, examining, and exploring. Discovery takes us beyond mere stimlation. It allows us by using our distance perceptors, combined with our intelligence, to produce a form of pleasure that fuses the sensate with the intellectual.

Discovery can even abandon sensation and still produce pleasure. There is the form of pure discovery in the intellectual world. To those who have not experienced the pleasure of immersion in the world of knowledge and ideas, the phenomenon will be as impossible to communicate as to explain music to the deaf. There are people who have never developed intellectual pleasure. Obviously, an author is reasonably secure in the knowledge that the mere fact someone is reading his book means that whether the reader is getting pleasure in this specific book or not, he has an awareness of intellectual pleasure. There is something in the learning experience, independent of usefulness, that seems to give us joy. And it is again the concept of the enlargement of self. Our intellect extends our horizons. It frees us from the limits of our own experience. It allows us to transcend our own world, our own time, and our own identity.

---

* Stevens, "Esthétique du Mal," *Poems*, p. 124.

The whole book of Canticles used to be pleasant to me, and I used to be much in reading it . . . and found, from time to time, an inward sweetness that would carry me away in my contemplations. This I know not how to express otherwise than by a calm, sweet abstraction of soul from all the concerns of this world. . . . The sense I had of divine things would often of a sudden kindle up, as it were, a sweet burning in my heart; an ardor of soul, that I know not how to express.*

All individuals originally have joy in discovery. It is part of the common developmental experience. Discovery is an essential ingredient in the separation process which leads a child away from the protection of the maternal environment into the large world. The two-year-old is a bundle of intellectual curiosity. He is explorer, adventurer, philosopher, and scientist. What in heaven's name happens to this questing creature? How is it that as our sensate pleasures expand through adolescence, so many of us lose this other source of joy? Surely they need not be alternative sources. Is there a natural attrition of pleasure in discovery—particularly intellectual discovery—with aging, or is it some dreadful artifact of our educational and cultural systems? I suspect that the latter must play some part. To have delivered to an educational system such an incredibly curious creature as the average five-year-old, and to have delivered back to us, after twelve years of education, the average seventeen-year-old, seems to imply certain complicity in the educational process. Even allowing that there may be a natural attrition in delight in life (necessitated by our eventual need to abandon existence), seventeen seems too early an age for the processes to have started!

I do believe that the capacity for all pleasure diminishes with age, and that diminution serves a purpose. The acceptance of death, intolerable as it now is, would be too unbearable if we carried into our seventies the intensity and passion of sixteen or seventeen. It would be too much to ask that we give

---

* Jonathan Edwards: *Selections, Personal Narrative* (New York: Hill & Wang), p. 6.

up a food so nourishing. But later, when much of the experience of life is tinged with pain, when we are left with the dry residue of unfulfilled hopes and the remembrance of powers that are lost, friends that are gone, and sensations that are no longer— an end can at least be contemplated if not accepted.

A third category of pleasure, closely related to discovery, is the concept of expansion and mastery. We enjoy the sense of growth, of improvement. There is incredible pleasure in the smooth, unhurried, perfectly timed backhand passing shot, when it is executed. There is an elation in any athletic endeavor when one has the sense of one's body having done well. A thrill can be experienced merely by the sense of our own muscles, sinew and tendon perfectly timed and perfectly executing an action. The fact that it comes so rarely to most of us only enlarges the pleasure of mastery.

Mastery also occurs with mental processes. Mastery is the capacity to say, "I did it," with pride. The intellectual aspects of pleasure then go well beyond just discovery. Think of the joy of using your mind, independent of any useful purposes or accretion of knowledge. Think of problem-solving. There is a delight for many in mathematics, in logical reasoning, or in the efforts of the kind of thinking associated with solving puzzles. It is a mental exercise. What we enjoy is the nimbleness of our mind. It is the pleasure of sensing our minds in operation. It is in every way an enhancement of the sense of self, if only the intellectual self.

Obviously, we do many things perfectly which we do not comment about. We are all master breathers, and the mechanics of breathing is intricate and magnificent. The moving of the diaphragm, which creates a negative vacuum, which allows for the influx of air; the stretching of the intercostal muscles between the ribs, which allows for the expansion of the rib cage and the dilatation of the lungs and the biological and chemical transactions across the lung membrane—all exercised so beautifully many times a minute, yet producing no pride or pleasure. Pleasure comes with the *sense* of enlargement or enrichment, and it must involve awareness of change from other conditions.

One of the real confusions about pleasure is the assumption that it is the opposite of pain. This confusion can be best resolved by considering mastery. In this category we can readily see that most things that involve great pleasure also involve pain. Here, without the pain, there would be no pleasure. The "I did it" phenomenon is significant only when there is the sense that what was done was difficult to do. Otherwise, where is the achievement? There is pleasure in attending a beautiful play. There has to be infinitely greater pleasure in having written one. The pleasure of seeing a superbly executed piece of cabinetry is far exceeded by the creativity of having made it. Part of the joy to the woodworker involves the hundreds of hours of painstaking, boring, painful sanding and finishing necessary to produce the perfection of fit and finish that goes into a beautiful cabinet. It is only because of the awareness of the sweat, toil, perseverance, and agony involved that the words "I did it!" have so rewarding a quality. The implication is: "It was not easy; and having done it, I have proved something about myself and my nature."

The cabinetmaking is, in fact, an example of a fourth category of pleasure that follows closely on mastery—and is simply an extension of it. That is creativity. The fact of having done something well is expanded in joy when it is more than a graceful turn on the ski slope, but actually a production of something of worth.

To make something, to be a maker of things, is a worthy pursuit. In that pursuit we often experience a fifth form of pleasure—immersion. To be totally immersed in something, to have lost the sense of time, perception, and seemingly sense of self, is obviously a joyous experience. This at first may seem contrary to the principle of expansion of self. I think not. The immersion of ourselves in an activity allows us to transcend our awareness of bodily needs, pain, trivial sensate pleasure. Immersion is profound involvement of thing with self. It allows us to sense ourselves in a new environment like floating in water; the environment of the activity allows for a new awareness of ourselves through a new surrounding medium.

Closely related to the idea of immersion in things is the idea of fusion with people—our sixth category. What does one make of the pleasure that is achieved by playing in an ensemble or orchestra, singing in a choir, being a part of team activity? Here the individual's effort is not isolatable from the effect of the total group. This is the distinction between the soloist with the choir and the choir singer. Surely this, then, beyond immersion may be seen as a denial of self. But here again I think not. Rather than disappearing into the crowd, we are allowed by the pleasure of fusion to enlarge ourselves in identifying with the larger body. That we—knowing the limitations of our own voice—are part of that glorious sound emerging from the chorus is awesome and thrilling. We have found a form of enlargement through joining with our fellows. We are not lost in the group, intimidated by the mass, as when we are part of an inchoate crowd. That mighty sound of the chorus is *our* voice. We are the group. This is the thrill one gets in all cooperative effort. It is the excitement of sitting in a scull, pulling together, where your own backbreaking effort is indistinguishable from those fore and aft of you. The sense of power and motion is compounded by the fact that you are pulling all together, and at times the whole scull seems to be moving by your own individual effort. Fusion activities of all sorts are profound delights.

Fusion is a bridge in helping us understand our seventh category of pleasurable experience. For want of a better word, I will call it the transcendental experience. This is the form of pleasure specifically discussed in the chapter on being moved. The transcendental experience is that sense of feeling lifted out of oneself. In the same way that immersion in an activity or fusion with a group allows us to expand the limits of self by including the activity or the others in our sense of self, the transcendent feeling allows for an even larger attachment beyond groups, things, people, world. When we are moved by some transcendental experience, we are reminded that we are a part of something even larger than the course and activities of our life. It is our sense of continuity beyond existence. To be a part of the cosmos, to affirm our place in the larger order of things, excites us. It is for this reason that confrontation with nature is the most common source of this experience.

My categories of pleasure are undoubtedly incomplete. Each individual may have unique sources of pleasure unto himself, and each will dictate different sets of categorization. In every list will be discovered, however, that enlargement of self which goes into feeling good. Was it chance that I uncovered seven? Or was it the magic of the number intruding on the unconscious of a hedonist and an optimist? It is nice to balance the seven deadly sins and the seven cardinal virtues with seven sources of pleasure.

There are specific qualities of feeling good, however, that are unrelated to pleasure. There is a form of feeling good related to the alleviation of distress. There is the feeling good that follows reassurance. In this sense, the feeling of goodness is related not to pleasure but to the removal of a threat. We feel good, independent of what pleasure there may be in our life, when we are told that the sickness from which we are still suffering is not the cancer we suspected. This is feeling good even while in a state of misery.

All feeling good, therefore, does not necessarily tie to pleasure—even in its broadest sense. The term is too vague. A sense of well-being may come into play with a removal of pain or a revival of hope.

Then, beyond all rationality, there is the pure and existential feeling good simply related to being alive. Considering the impact of existentialism on our society, and the amount of thought devoted to existential anxiety, it is incredible how little thinking has been devoted to existential pleasure. Directly analogous to the fact that there is an anxiety that is simply a function of our existence, there is also a pleasure that is simply a function of our existence. Nowhere is this better expressed than by that forerunner of twentieth-century existentialism, Fyodor Dostoievski:

> . . . and I seem to have such strength in me now, that I think I could stand anything, any suffering only to be able to say and to repeat to myself every moment, "I exist." In thousands of agonies— I exist. I am tormented on the rack—but I exist! Though I sit alone in a pillary—I exist! I see the sun, and if I don't see the sun, I know it's there. And there's a whole life in that, in knowing that the sun is there.*

With a perversity typical of his genius, Dostoievski affirms his joy in life through symbols of pain and humiliation. It is because of the pain, and despite the pain, that existence has its value and its joy. The existential feeling of good often bears no relationship to anything except the sense that we are alive and there is a passion in that alone.

At the opposite end of the literary spectrum, Emily Dickinson manages to express this feeling of existential joy even while living the reclusive life that separated her from the traditional sensate pleasures to which so much joy is traditionally related.

> I taste a liquor never brewed,
> From tankards scooped in pearl;
> Not all the vats upon the Rhine
> Yield such an alcohol!
>
> Inebriate of air am I,
> And debauchee of dew,
> Reeling, through endless summer days,
> From inns of molten blue.†

---

* Fyodor Dostoievski. This quote is from a journal I kept during World War II in which I made no citations. I have been unable to locate the source.

† Emily Dickinson, "I Taste a Liquor Never Brewed," from *The Complete Poems of Emily Dickinson*, ed. T. H. Johnson (Boston: Little, Brown and Company, 1960), p.98.

Despite the references to nature, Emily Dickinson is not here discussing any sense of being moved by a specific and natural event. It is not a response to anything, but life itself. It is a response to air and dew and summer days—and being alive.

We are so aware—we have been made so aware—that the very nature of our existence involves travail and pain that it is good to be reminded we endure that pain, we endure those hardships we encounter, not through some perversity or masochistic nature but because also innate to that existence is a sweetness and joy. It is that which allows us to endure. It is that which dictates that we depart from life—with all its hardships—reluctantly and with grief.

It is absurd to have to remind people there is joy in life. Joy is defined in living. And it is the purpose of feelings not just to facilitate survival but to celebrate the sense of purpose and goodness in that survival.

Feeling good and feeling bad are not necessarily opposites. Both, at least, involve feeling. Any feeling is a reminder of life. The worst "feeling" evidently is non-feeling. This phenomenon is described by schizophrenics and is commonly known as anhdonia. It is a concept I have struggled with and something that I understand only suggestively and faintly. The pain of anhedonia—non-feeling—is so unbearable that schizophrenics are prepared to endure physical pain rather than the feeling of deadness. It explains, beyond some psychological meanings of self-punishment, why schizophrenics often burn themselves with cigarettes and lacerate themselves with razors. It is the need to have some feeling! And while pain is as painful to them as it is to us, it is one stage above the death that is anhedonia.

To most of us, the worst that we are likely to feel is despair. While it is not anhedonia, it has something of its quality. In despair we have a reduced sense of self; a reduced sense of our worth, of our hopes, and of our capacities. To most of us, despair is close to an antithesis of feeling good. All feeling is a reminder that we exist, and all good is defined in the existence of ourselves and our species.

When we "feel good," we carry the feeling so tightly to our senses that we are often unaware of its existence. Like the fluid movements of a healthy body, we most often accept the value of feeling good without acknowledging its existence. But that sense of good feeling, whether exploited for other purposes or enjoyed directly, is the sole support of the value of living in this world. It is, at any rate, good to "feel good."

~§ 13

Feelings and Emotions

I T WAS FREUD, more than anyone, who translated the theoretical ideas of philosophical idealism into a language for laymen. No one, he announced, lives in the real world. We occupy a space of our own creation—a collage compounded of bits and pieces of actuality arranged into a design determined by our internal perceptions, our hopes, our fears, our memories, and our anticipations. This "reality" we live in—half fact, half fantasy—is as much the product of our emotions (*more,* Freud would probably have said) as our rationality.

If the perceived world is fabricated partly on emotion, certainly our response to it is dominated by feeling. It is not the event but the meaning interpreted through our emotions that distinguishes the good from the bad. The snow that is cursed by the commuter is blessed by the skier.

217

It is the emotional imbalance of pain and pleasure that drives one to a psychiatrist. People come to treatment for failures in function and emotional complaints. One would have expected dynamic psychiatry—given the reality of its past and present—to have been absorbed in the problems of feeling. Yet, ironically, emotions and feelings until very recently had not played a central role in psychoanalytic theory or study. Beguiled by the unconscious and the psychodynamic processes, psychiatrists have been most intrigued by ideas and thoughts. Insight has dominated analytic thinking and therapy. "Conflict" has been the key word, and emotion simply the sign of it.

Of course, anxiety was one emotion that was not totally excluded. But even this emotion was never viewed as central in traditional psychoanalytic theory until very recent times. Fear and anxiety were seen as derivative phenomena, the products, if you will, of repressed sexual appetite. Only in the last creative years of his life did Freud reverse the process and decide that fear was primary, a warning signal, and that it *led* to repression of sexual drive. To this day, however, when they do deal theoretically with emotions, psychiatrists are most likely to be concerned with the measurable and quantifiable, observable or physiological aspects of emotion rather than the feelings.

Psychologists have, of course, paid even less attention. While psychoanalysts may be embarrassed by the omission of feelings in their learned discourse, the psychologists have rationalized the neglect. In this country, at least, psychologists are for the most part behaviorists. They can live without emotions, and indeed prefer to do so. It is behavior which intrigues them.

In addition, as one psychologist, R. S. Peters, has pointed out, there is a good historical reason why emotion has fared so poorly in the hands of modern psychologists.

The tendency of psychologists in the behaviorist tradition to confine their work to animals as a matter of fact left them little alternative; for most emotions—for instance, pride, shame, regret, grief—are not experienced by animals because the appraisals involved in them presuppose a conceptual scheme beyond the range of animals other than man.*

Despite all this, there is still a considerable literature about emotions. However, if you examine this corpus in search of feelings, you generally seek in vain. It is possible to plow through an entire book (let alone an article) on emotions without encountering a single feeling—as though passion had no place in the orderly charts, statistics, and physiological measurements that have come to represent the academic world of emotion. Again there is good historical reason for the neglect of feelings. The two major streams that feed the current of twentieth-century psychology originated in those two mountainous nineteenth-century men: William James and Sigmund Freud.

Freud, as I previously mentioned, was primarily interested in unconscious motives and purposes. In addition, he emerged from a solidly biomedical research background which was just beginning to gain scientific stature, and this through the rigor and discipline of the German laboratory. The total answer to emotions was what he wanted, and that would be found scientifically by examining the very stuff of which they were composed. He wanted to know their chemical and physical origin, and the complex interrelationship within the human being of the physiology and the affects of the emotions.

Recoiling—like James—from a tradition in which the emotions were relegated to philosophical discourse, he attempted to bring scientific rigor to the evaluation of emotions. Science, in those optimistic early days, implied "objectivity," measurable events, and laboratory data. The subjective was suspect.

Freud, however, was first and foremost a clinician, and his theoretical analyses were constantly modified by exposure to

---

* R. S. Peters, "The Education of the Emotions," in *Feelings and Emotions: The Loyola Symposium,* ed. M. B. Arnold (New York: Academic Press, 1970), p. 189.

the sensitivities of suffering human beings, and to his own incredible perceptivity in relationship to this.

James, straddling the fields of philosophy and psychology,
at a time when psychology was blossoming in the empiric laboratories of such nineteenth-century giants as Wundt and Helm-
holtz, opted, of course, for the scientific approach to emotions.
Much influenced by the Danish physiologist C. Lange, James
evolved a theory of emotion and interpretation of the bodily
changes mobilized by the exciting factor. So if something dangerous comes along, it excites physiological change to handle
the danger, and the feeling is our almost incidental awareness
of our bodily reactions. Poetic and descriptive concern about
feelings is foolish.

"The trouble with emotions in psychology is that they are
regarded too much as absolutely individual things," James says.
He asks us to forgo our cataloguing "their separate characters,
points and effects." Now that we know that feelings are only
"subsidiary" to the physical changes, we can ignore them.
"Having the goose which lays the golden eggs, the description
of each egg already laid is a minor matter."

From that time down to the present, psychologists have been
busily dissecting that goose. Yet people—ordinary people—continued to have feelings, not just physiological reactions. And
patients had feelings and complained of their feelings, and
the psychiatrist on a day-to-day level was forced to deal with
the feelings, whether the theory allowed for them or not. In
that sense, the clinical world is always safer from self-deception
than the world of the laboratory or the study.

Soon, however, even the laboratory caught up, and today
the James-Lange theory that saw feelings as only incidental,
and perhaps accidental, products of physiology is discredited
and generally abandoned. But the damage was done when
James said:

Unfortunately there is little psychological writing about the emotions which is not merely descriptive. . . .

Is there no way out from this level of individual description in the case of emotions? I believe there is a way out but fear that few will take it.*

James, of course, was wrong. His way became the way, and they (psychologists and psychiatrists) took it wit a vengeance.

Today, seventy-five years later, I am complaining that there are so few descriptive studies of emotions, that feelings have been slighted by the entire psychological community.

It is an acknowledged cliché (and, like most clichés, true) that were Freud alive today he would certainly not have been a "Freudian." It is the curse of the great geniuses of change that their fresh and revolutionary examinations become solidified by their followers into orthodoxies that would likely exclude the very people they revere if the geniuses were to reappear unrecognized to challenge the crystallized tenets of their past thinking.

Freud questioned everything, particularly his own propositions, and changed them constantly through a life of ideas that was as creative as it was contradictory. While emotion and feeling were never central to his theories, he, above all, drove us to a recognition that emotions are central to our lives. It was Freud who insisted that human beings and human endeavor are less rational than most of us had dared to recognize.

Similarly, what a wonderful contradiction is expressed in the work of James. The James-Lange *theory* trivialized the subjective feeling, while James the philosopher and psychologist went on to become a prophet of "experience." He wrote with feeling and *about feelings* in a way that would embarrass many of his most respectful disciples. He demanded that we recognize the distinction between "knowing about" and "knowledge of" something. In so doing he pointed out that the latter, the subjective experiencing, allows for a truth that will never be recog-

---

* William James, *The Principles of Psychology* (New York: Henry Holt and Co., 1890), Vol. 2, pp.448, 449.

nized by the mere accretion of facts and their analysis. He would, I suspect, have heartily acknowledged that

> One might have thought of sight, but who could think
> Of what it sees, for all the ill it sees?
> Speech found the ear, for all the evil sound,
> But the dark italics it could not propound.
> And out of what one sees and hears and out
> Of what one feels, who could have thought to make
> So many selves, so many sensuous worlds,
> As if the air, the mid-day air, was swarming
> With the metaphysical changes that occur,
> Merely in living as and where we live.*

Neither Freud nor James, then, was as responsible for the neglect of feelings as was the nature of the movements influenced by them in a period which was ready to model all behavioral sciences on the natural sciences.

The scientific revolution that ushered in the twentieth century profoundly influenced all areas of intellectual and creative endeavor. Method became everything; even in the arts, the subjective was suspect. The natural sciences so intimidated the poor social sciences that in attempting to adopt their methodology of data-collecting, objectivity, measurement, and statistics, the social sciences abandoned their own grand tradition of insight and imagination. Since sociology could never achieve the exactness of the laboratories, this methodological mimicry earned little respect from the natural scientists, who, ironically—during the same period—were learning the ephemeral and relative nature of "objectivity" and "scientific truth."

We must not be too hard on James and Freud. For their time they were right, and their corrective influence was probably good for us. With that grand scientific optimism that existed at the turn of the century, why should they not have attempted to go the whole way to solve the complete riddle of the mind and body, and fusion of the two, and do so with the assumption

---

* Stevens, "Esthétique du Mal," *Poems*, p. 125.

that it, like all other riddles, would be solved with the measuring devices of the laboratory? And, indeed, someday that may be true. But not yet. Today we are less confident about our ability to find ultimate answers. We are less confident that there even *are* ultimate answers, and where human behavior is concerned we are learning humility. Even were we capable of dissecting emotions to their biochemical components, this would not abrogate the need for a descriptive analysis of feelings. The two are not competitive. To borrow Franz Alexander's metaphor from music—were we to perfect the science of sound, it might be possible to reduce a Beethoven symphony to its component elements of tones, modulations, overtones, frequencies, resonances, and the like, but it is questionable whether we would understand the *Eroica* more that way than by simply listening to it.

In addressing myself exclusively to feelings, I intend no slight to the broader aspect of emotions. The recent discoveries in the pharmacology of emotions are perhaps the most promising aspect of modern psychiatry. The subjective aspect of the emotions has priority over the objective only in my current attention—not in my general respect. I am simply trying to redress a balance. We have neglected feelings, and have failed to grasp the value of their directives. It is time to change.

Bibliography

Index to Bibliography

1954	G. Ryle	1967	A. White
1956	T. Benedek	1968	*M. Goldstein
1956	S. Rado	1969, 1973	*J. Bowlby
1957	T. Szasz	1969	J. Davitz
1959	S. Arieti	1970	*W. Fischer
1959	R. DeSaussure	1970	R. Lazarus
1960	*M. Arnold	1970	R. Peters
1960	L. Eidelberg	1970	*R. Plutchik
1960	*J. Hillman	1970	S. Schachter
1960	O. Mowrer	1970	D. Stanley-Jones
1963	E. Erikson	1973	*K. Strongman
1963	A. Kenny	1974	C. Brenner
1963	P. Knapp	1974	*W. Shibles
1964	H. Hartmann	1975	*W. Knoff
1966	L. Spiegel	1976	R. Schafer
1967	J. Millenson	1977	R. Soloman

* Works in which one finds a review of theories on emotion.

II.   SURVEY OF LITERATURE ON SPECIFIC EMOTIONS.

On feeling tired, depressed, fatigued, helpless, hopeless: Abraham, Alexander, Arieti, Beck, Beigel, Benedek, Bibring, Bonime, Cameron, Cohen, Donnelly, Fabrega, Freud (1917), Friedman, Gaylin (1968), Guntrip, Jacobson, James, Knoff, Lesse, Mendelson, Meyersburg, Nacht, Pilowsky, Rado, Rosenfeld, Rosenthal, Rycroft, Schmale, Siggins, Szasz, Weissman, Zetzel.

On feeling bored: Berlyne, Fenichel, Fromm, Greenson, Hill, Siassi.

On feeling frustrated: Amsel, Dollard, Lowenfeld, Maier.

On feeling anxious, fearful—of solitude, of failure, of death, of separation, of loss, of women, of men: Abraham, Alexander, Bibring, Birney, Bowlby, Cattell, Chasseguet-Smirgel, Erikson, Eysenck, Fenichel, Fischer, Freud (1893, 1909, 1926), Glover, Goldstein, Grinker, Guntrip, Harlow, Horney, James, Jones, Klein, Lerner, May, Ramzy, Rosen, Stolorow, Sullivan, Teevan, Tillich, Winnicott, Zetzel.

On feeling perplexed, confused: Searles.

On feeling worried: Challman.

On feeling "pain" (as a sensory/affective modality in itself): Melzack, Niederland, Ramzy.

On feeling angry, aggressive, hostile, and guilty (for feeling angry and hostile): Abraham, Alexander, Bandura, Bychowski, Dollard, Fenichel, Glover, James, Klein, Lerner, Lewis, Maher, Meyersburg, Miller, Mosher, Piers, Rosen, Weissman.

Bibliography

Abraham, K. "Notes on the psychoanalytical investigation and treatment of manic-depressive insanity and allied conditions" (1911). In *Selected Papers of Karl Abraham*. London: Hogarth Press, 1927. Pp. 137–56.

———. "A short study of the development of the libido, viewed in the light of mental disorders" (1924). Ibid., pp. 418–501.

Adorno, T. W., et al. *The Authoritarian Personality*. New York: W. W. Norton & Co., 1969.

Alexander, F. *Fundamentals of Psychoanalysis*. New York: W. W. Norton & Co., 1963. Copyright 1948.

Amsel, A., and Roussel, J. "Motivational properties of frustration: I. Effect on a running response of the addition of frustration to the motivational complex." *Journal of Experimental Psychology* 43 (1952):363–68.

Apsler, R. "Effects of embarrassment on behavior toward others." *Journal of Personality and Social Psychology* 32, no. 1 (1975):145–53.

Arieti, S. "Manic-depressive psychosis." In *American Handbook of Psychiatry*, vol. 1, edited by S. Arieti. New York: Basic Books, 1959. Pp. 419–54.

Aristotle. *De Anima* (1:1, 403a,b). Version of William of Moerbeke. New Haven: Yale University Press, 1951.

Arlow, J. "On smugness." *International Journal of Psychoanalysis* 38 (1957):1–8.

Arnold, M. B. *Emotion and Personality*, vol. 1. New York: Columbia University Press, 1960.

———, ed. *Feelings and Emotions: The Loyola Symposium.* New York: Academic Press, 1970.

Balint, M. *Thrills and Regressions.* New York: International Universities Press, 1959.

Bandura, A., and McDonald, F. J. "The influence of social reinforcement and the behavior of models in shaping children's moral judgments." *Journal of Abnormal Social Psychology* 67 (1963):274–81.

———; Ross, D.; and Ross, S. A. "Transmission of aggression through imitation of aggressive models." *Journal of Abnormal Social Psychology* 63 (1961):575–82.

Beck, A. T. *Depression: Clinical, Experimental, and Theoretical Aspects.* New York: Harper & Row, 1967.

———, et al. "Hopelessness and suicidal behavior: An overview." *Journal of the American Medical Association* 234, no. 11 (1975):1146–49.

Beigel, A., and Murphy, D. L. "Unipolar and bipolar affective illness: Differences in clinical characteristics accompanying depression." *Archives of General Psychiatry* 24 (1971):215–20.

Benedek, T. "On the organization of psychic energy: Instincts, drives and affects." In *Mid-century Psychiatry*, edited by R. R. Grinker. Springfield, Ill.: C. C. Thomas, 1953. Pp. 60–75.

———. "Toward the biology of the depressive constellation." *Journal of the American Psychoanalytic Association* 4 (1956):389–427.

Bergler, E. *Curable and Incurable Neurotics.* New York: Liveright, 1961.

Berlyne, D. E. *Conflict, Arousal and Curiosity.* New York: McGraw-Hill, 1960.

Bibring, E. "The mechanism of depression." In *Affective Disorders*, edited by P. Greenacre. New York: International Universities Press, 1953. Also in *The Meaning of Despair*, ed. W. Gaylin.

Birney, R. C., et al. *Fear of Failure.* New York: Van Nostrand-Reinhold, 1969.

Bonime, W. "The psychodynamics of neurotic depression." In *American Handbook of Psychiatry*, vol. 3, ed. S. Arieti. Pp. 239–55.

Bowlby, J. *Attachment and Loss*. Vol. 1: *Attachment*. New York: Basic Books, 1969. Vol. 2: *Separation, Anxiety and Anger*. Ibid., 1973.

Brenner, C. "On the nature and development of affects: A unified theory." *Psychoanalytic Quarterly* 43, no. 4 (1974):532–56.

Brierley, M. "Affects in theory and practice." *International Journal of Psychoanalysis* 18 (1937):256–68.

Brown, N. O. *Life Against Death: The Psychoanalytical Meaning of History*. New York: Random House, 1959.

Buber, M. *The Knowledge of Man*. London: George Allen & Unwin, 1965. Pp. 123–36.

Buchenholz, B. "The motivating action of pleasure." *Journal of Nervous and Mental Disease* 124 (1956):569–77.

_____, and Naumburg, G. W. "The pleasure process." *Journal of Nervous and Mental Disease* 125 (1957):396–402.

Bull, N. *The Attitude Theory of Emotion*. New York: Association of Nervous and Mental Disorder Monograph, 1951.

_____. "Towards a clarification of the concept of emotion." *Psychosomatic Medicine* 7 (1945):210–14.

Bychowski, G. "Patterns of anger." *Psychoanalytic Study of the Child* 21 (1966):172–92.

Cameron, C. "A theory of fatigue." In *Man Under Stress*, edited by A. T. Welford. New York: John Wiley & Sons, 1974.

Cannon, W. B. *Bodily Changes in Panic, Hunger, Fear and Rage*. New York: Appleton-Century, 1915.

Cattell, R. B. "The nature and measurement of anxiety." In *Contemporary Psychology*. New York: W. H. Freeman & Co., 1971. Pp. 358–65.

_____, and Scheier, I. H. *The Meaning and Measurement of Neuroticism and Anxiety*. New York: Ronald Press, 1961.

Challman, A. "The empirical nature of worry." *American Journal of Psychiatry* 131, no. 10 (1974):1140–41.

Chasseguet-Smirgel, J. "Feminine guilt and the Oedipus complex." In *Female Sexuality: New Psychoanalytic Views*, edited by J. Chasseguet-Smirgel et al. Ann Arbor: University of Michigan Press, 1970. Pp. 94–134.

Cohen, M. B., et al. "An intensive study of twelve cases of manic-depressive psychosis." *Psychiatry* 17 (1954):103–37.

Darrow, C. W. "Emotion as relative functional decortication: The role of conflict." *Psychoanalytic Review* 42 (1935):566–78.

Darwin, C. W. *The Expression of Emotions in Man and Animals.* New York: Appleton, 1873.

Davitz, J. R. *The Language of Emotion.* New York: Academic Press, 1969.

———. "A dictionary and grammar of emotion." In *Feelings and Emotions,* ed. M. B. Arnold.

DeForest, I. "The self-dedication of the psychoneurotic sufferer to hostile protest and revenge." *Psychiatric Quarterly* 24 (1950): 706–15.

DeSaussure, R. "The metapsychology of pleasure." *International Journal of Psychoanalysis* 40 (1959):81–93.

Descartes, René. *Les passions de l'âme* (Art. 36). Paris: Henri Le Gras, 1649.

Dewey, John. "The theory of emotion. I: Emotional attitudes." *Psychoanalytic Review* 1 (1894):553–69.

———. "The theory of emotion. II: The significance of emotions." *Psychoanalytic Review* 2 (1895):13–32.

Dollard, J.; Miller, N. E., et al. *Frustration and Aggression.* New Haven: Yale University Press, 1939.

Donnelly, E. F., et al. "Perception and cognition in patients with bipolar and unipolar depressive disorders: A study in Rorschach responding." *Archives of General Psychiatry* 32, no. 9 (1975): 1128–31.

Ducey, C., and Galinsky, M. D. "The metapsychology of pleasure." *Journal of the American Psychoanalytic Association* 21, no. 3 (1973):495–525.

Easser, R. "Empathic inhibition and psychoanalytic technique." *Psychoanalytic Quarterly* 43, no. 4 (1974):557–80.

Eidelberg, L. "A contribution to the study of the unpleasure-pleasure principle." *Psychiatric Quarterly* 36 (1962):312–16.

———, and Kanzer, M. "The structural description of pleasure." *International Journal of Psychoanalysis* 41 (1960):368–71.

Ellis, H. *Psychology of Sex.* New York: Emerson Books, 1938.

English, F. "Shame and social control." *Transactional Analysis Journal* 5, no. 1 (1975):21–28.

Erikson, E. H. *Childhood and Society.* New York: W. W. Norton & Co., 1963.

Evans, W. N. "The eye of jealousy and envy." *Psychoanalytic Review* 62, no. 3 (1975):481–92.

Eysenck, H. J. *The Dynamics of Anxiety and Hysteria.* London: Routledge & Kegan Paul, 1957.

———. "Psychological aspects of anxiety." In *Studies of Anxiety*, edited by M. H. Lader. Ashford, England: Headley Bros., 1969. Pp. 7–20.

Fabrega, Horacio. "Problems implicit in the cultural and social study of depression." *Psychosomatic Medicine* 36, no. 5 (1974):377–98.

Fenichel, O. *The Collected Papers of Otto Fenichel, First Series.* New York: W. W. Norton & Co., 1953.

———. *The Psychoanalytic Theory of Neurosis.* New York: W. W. Norton & Co., 1945.

Fischer, W. F. *Theories of Anxiety.* New York: Harper & Row, 1970.

Freud, S. *Standard Edition.* London: Hogarth Press, 1955. *Figures refer to volume and page number in this edition.*

Studies in Hysteria (1893–95) 2:1

Character and Anal Eroticism (1908) 9:167

Analysis of a Phobia in a Five-Year-Old Boy (1909) 10:3

Psychoanalytic Notes Upon an Autobiographical Account of a Case of Paranoia (1911) 12:3

Totem and Taboo (1913) 13:1

Mourning and Melancholia (1917) 14:237

Inhibitions, Symptoms and Anxieties (1926) 20:77

Civilization and Its Discontents (1930) 21:59

Friedman, R. J., and Katz, M. M., eds. *The Psychology of Depression: Contemporary Theory and Research.* New York: Halsted Press, 1974.

Fromm, E. *The Art of Loving.* New York: Harper & Row, 1956.

———. *Psychoanalysis and Religion.* New Haven: Yale University Press, 1950.

———. *The Sane Society.* New York: Rinehart & Co., 1955.

Gaylin, W. *Caring.* New York: Alfred A. Knopf, 1976.

———. *The Meaning of Despair.* New York: Science House, 1968.

Gemelli, A. "Orienting concepts in the study of affective states. Part I." *Journal of Nervous and Mental Disease* 110 (1949):198–214.

Glover, E. *Psycho-analysis.* London: Staples Press, 1949.

———. "The psycho-analysis of affects." *International Journal of Psycho-analysis* 20 (1939):299.

Goffman, E. *The Presentation of Self in Everyday Life.* New York: Doubleday, 1959.

———. "On facework." *Psychiatry* 18 (1955):213–31.

Goldstein, K. "On emotions: Considerations from the organismic point of view." *Journal of Psychology* 31 (1951):37–49.

Goldstein, M. L. "Physiological theories of emotion: A critical historical review from the standpoint of behavior theory." *Psychology Bulletin* 69 (1968):23–40.

Greaves, George. "Toward an existential theory of drug dependence." *Journal of Nervous and Mental Disease* 159, no. 4 (1974):263–74.

Greenacre, P. "Experiences of awe in childhood." *Psychoanalytic Study of the Child* 11 (1956):9–30.

————. "Penis awe and its relation to penis envy." In *Drives, Affects, Behavior,* edited by R. M. Loewenstein. New York: International Universities Press, 1953.

Greenson, Ralph. "On boredom." *Journal of the American Psychoanalytic Association,* 1 (1953):7–21.

Grinker, R. R., Sr. "The psychosomatic aspects of anxiety." In *Anxiety and Behavior,* edited by G. D. Spielberger. New York: Academic Press, 1966. Pp. 129–42.

Guntrip, H. "The manic-depressive problem in the light of the schizoid process." *Schizoid Phenomena, Object Relations and the Self,* edited by H. Guntrip. New York: International Universities Press, 1969. Pp. 132–64.

Harlow, H. F. "The nature of love." *American Psychologist* 13 (1958):673–85.

Harrison, I. B. "On the maternal origins of awe." *Psychoanalytic Study of the Child* 30 (1975):181ff.

Hartmann, H. "The mutual influences in the development of ego and id." *Essays on Ego Psychology: Selected Problems in Psychoanalytic Theory.* New York: International Universities Press, 1964. Pp. 155–81.

Heimann, P. "A combination of defense mechanisms in paranoid states." In *New Directions in Psychoanalysis,* edited by M. Klein, P. Heimann, and R. E. Money-Kryle. New York: Basic Books, 1955.

Hekmat, H; Khajavi, F.; and Mehryar, A. "Some personality correlates of empathy." *Journal of Consulting and Clinical Psychology* 43, no. 1 (1975):89.

Hendrick, I. "Work and the pleasure principle." *Psychoanalytic Quarterly* 12 (1943):311–29.

Hill, A. B. "Extraversion and variety-seeking in a monotonous task." *British Journal of Psychology* 66 (1975):9–13.

Hillman, J. *Emotion: A Comprehensive Phenomenology of Theories and Their Meanings for Therapy.* London, 1960.

———. "C. G. Jung's contributions to 'feelings and emotions': Synopsis and implications." In *Feelings and emotions,* ed. M. B. Arnold. Pp. 125–34.

Horney, K. "The dread of women." *International Journal of Psychoanalysis* 13 (1932):348–60.

———. "The value of vindictiveness." *American Journal of Psychoanalysis* 8 (1948):3–12.

Hull, C. L. *Principles of Behavior.* New York: Appleton-Century, 1943.

Jacobson, E. *Depression.* New York: International Universities Press, 1971.

———. "Problems in the psychoanalytic theory of affects." *Psychoanalytic Quarterly* 21 (1952):459–60.

James, W. *The Principles of Psychology.* New York: Henry Holt & Co., 1890.

———, and Lange, C. G. *The Emotions.* (1884–85) Baltimore: Williams & Wilkins, 1922.

Joffe, W. G. "A critical review of the status of the envy concept." *International Journal of Psycho-analysis* 50 (1969):532–545.

Jones, E. *Papers on Psychoanalysis.* 5th ed. London: Bailliere, Tindall & Cox, 1948.

Katan, M. "A psychoanalytic approach to the diagnosis of paranoia." *Psychoanalytic Study of the Child* 24 (1969):328–57.

Kaufman, G. "The meaning of shame: Toward a self-affirming identity." *Journal of Counseling Psychology* 21, no. 6 (1974):568–74.

Kenny, A. *Action, Emotion and Will.* London: Routledge & Kegan Paul, 1963.

Klein, G. S. "The vital pleasures." *Psychoanalysis and Contemporary Science* 1 (1972):181–205.

Klein, M. *Contributions to Psychoanalysis.* London: Hogarth Press, 1948.

———. *Envy and Gratitude.* New York: Basic Books, 1957.

Knapp, P. H., ed. *Expressions of the Emotions in Man.* New York: International Universities Press, 1963.

Knoff, W. F. "Depression: A historical overview." *American Journal of Psychoanalysis* 35 (1975):41–46.

Koestler, A. *The Act of Creation.* New York: Dell Publishing Co., 1967.

Kris, E. *Psychoanalytic Explorations in Art.* New York: International Universities Press, 1952.

Lazarus, R. S.; Averill, J. R.; and Opton, E. M., Jr. "Towards a cognitive theory of emotion." In *Feelings and Emotions,* ed. M. B. Arnold.

Lee, J. A. "The styles of loving." *Psychology Today* 8, no. 5 (1974):43–50.

Leeper, R. W. "The motivational and perceptual properties of emotions as indicating their fundamental character and role." In *Feelings and Emotions*, ed. M. B. Arnold. Pp. 151–68.

———. "A motivational theory of emotion to replace 'emotion as disorganized response.'" *Psychoanalytic Review* 55 (1948):5–21.

Lerner, H. E. "Early origins of envy and devaluation of women: Implications for sex role stereotypes." *Bulletin of the Menninger Clinic* 38, no. 6 (1974):538–53.

Lesse, S. "Depression masked by acting-out behavior patterns." *American Journal of Psychotherapy* 28, no. 3 (1974):352–61.

Lewin, B. D. *The Psychoanalysis of Elation*. New York: W. W. Norton & Co., 1950.

Lewis, Helen B. *Shame and Guilt in Neurosis*. New York: International Universities Press, 1974.

Lowenfeld, H. "Notes on frustration." *Psychoanalytic Quarterly* 44, no. 1 (1975):127–38.

Maher, Brendan, ed. *Clinical Psychology and Personality: The Selected Papers of George Kelly*. New York: John Wiley & Sons, 1969.

Maier, N. R. F. *Frustration—the Study of Behavior Without a Goal*. New York: McGraw-Hill, 1949.

Maslow, A. H. *Toward a Psychology of Being*. 2nd ed. Princeton, N.J.: D. Van Nostrand Co., 1968.

May, Rollo. *The Meaning of Anxiety*. New York: Ronald Press, 1950.

McDougall, W. *An Introduction to Social Psychology*. Rev. ed. Boston: Luce, 1926.

———. "Emotion and feeling distinguished" (1928). In *Feelings and Emotions* (Wittenberg), ed. M. L. Reymert.

Melzack, R., and Casey, K. L. "The affective dimension of pain." In *Feelings and Emotions*, ed. M. B. Arnold. Pp. 55–68.

Mendelson, M. *Psychoanalytic Concepts of Depression*. New York: Spectrum, 1974.

Meyersburg, H. A.; Ablon, S. L.; and Kotin, J. "A reverberating psychic mechanism in the depressive processes." *Psychiatry* 37 (1974):372–86.

Michotte, A. E. "The emotions regarded as functional connections" (1950). In *Feelings and Emotions: The Moosehart Symposium* edited by M. L. Reymert. New York: McGraw-Hill, 1950.

Millenson, J. R. *Principles of Behavior Analysis*. New York: Macmillan Co., 1967.

Miller, F. "Anger anhedonia, and the borderline syndrome." *Journal of Psychoanalysis* 35 (1975):157–61.

Mosher, D. "The development and multitrait-multimethod matrix analysis of three measures of three aspects of guilt." *Journal of Consulting Psychology* 30 (1966):25–29.

Mowrer, O. H. *Learning Theory and Behavior*. N.Y.: John Wiley & Sons, 1960.

Nacht, S., and Racamier, P. C. "Depressive states." *International Journal of Psychoanalysis* 41 (1960):481ff.

Niederland, W. G. "Psychoanalytic approaches to artistic creativity." *Psychoanalytic Quarterly* 45, no. 2 (1976).

Papez, J. W. "A proposed mechanism of emotion." *Archives of Neurological Psychiatry* 38 (1937):725–43.

Peters, R. S. "The education of the emotions." In *Feelings and Emotions,* ed. M. B. Arnold. Pp. 187–204.

Piers, G., and Singer, M. B. *Shame and Guilt*. Springfield, Ill.: C. C. Thomas, 1953.

Pilowsky, I., and Spence, N. D. "Hostility and depressive illness." *Archives of General Psychiatry* 32, no. 9 (1975):1154–59.

Plutchik, R. "Emotions, evolution, and adaptive processes." In *Feelings and Emotions,* ed. M. B. Arnold. Pp. 3–24.

Rado, S. *Psychoanalysis of Behavior*. New York: Grune & Stratton, 1956.

———. "Psychodynamics of depression from the etiologic point of view." *Psychosomatic Medicine* 13 (1951):51ff.

Ramzy, I., and Wallerstein, R. S. "Pain, fear and anxiety: A study in their interrelationships." *Psychoanalytic Study of the Child* 13 (1958):147–89.

Rapaport, D. *Emotions and Memory*. New York: International Universities Press, 1950.

———. "On the psychoanalytic theory of affects." *International Journal of Psychoanalysis* 34 (1953):1–22.

Reymert, M. L., ed. *Feelings and Emotions, the Wittenberg Symposium*. Worcester, Mass.: Clark University Press, 1928.

Rivera, J. de. *A Structural Theory of Emotions*. New York: International Universities Press, 1977.

Robbins, M. D. "On the psychology of artistic creativity." *Psychoanalytic Study of the Child* 24 (1969):227–31.

Rosen, M. "A dual model of obsessional neurosis." *Journal of Consulting and Clinical Psychology* 43, no. 4 (1975):453–59.

Rosen, V. H. "On mathematical 'illumination' and the mathematical thought process: A contribution to the genetic development and metapsychology of abstract thinking." *Psychoanalytic Study of the Child* 8 (1953):127–54.

Rosenfeld, H. "A note on the precipitating factor in depressive illness." *International Journal of Psycho-analysis* 41 (1960):512–13.

Rosenthal, B. G. "The psychology of compassion." *Human Context* 4, no. 3 (1972):500–607.

Rosenthal, S. H., and Gudeman, J. E. "The self-pitying constellation in depression." *British Journal of Psychiatry* 113 (1967):485–89.

Rycroft, C. "Two notes on idealization, illusion and disillusion as normal and abnormal psychological processes." *International Journal of Psychoanalysis* 36 (1955):81–87.

Ryle, G. "Feelings." In *Aesthetics and Language,* edited by W. Elton. New York: Philosophical Library, 1954. Pp. 56–72.

Sartre, J. P. *The Emotions: Outline of a Theory.* Translated by Bernard Frechtman. New York: Philosophical Library, 1948.

Satler, J. "A theoretical development and clinical investigation of embarrassment." *Genetic Psychology Monographs* 71 (1965):19–59.

Schachter, S. "The assumption of identity and peripheralist-centralist controversies in motivation and emotion." In *Feelings and Emotions,* ed. M. B. Arnold.

Schafer, R. *A New Language for Psychoanalysis.* New Haven: Yale University Press, 1976.

Schatzman, M. "Paranoia or persecution: The case of Schreber." *History of Childhood Quarterly: The Journal of Psychohistory* 1, no. 1 (1973):62–88.

Scheler, M. *Ressentiment.* New York: Schocken Books, 1972.

Schmale, A. H., Jr. "A genetic view of affects: With special reference to the genesis of helplessness and hopelessness." *Psychoanalytic Study of the Child* 19 (1964):287–310.

Schneider, C. D. *Shame, Exposure and Privacy.* Boston: Beacon Press, 1977.

Schoeck, H. *Envy: A Theory of Social Behavior.* New York: Harcourt, Brace, 1970.

Schutz, W. C. *Joy, Expanding Human Awareness.* New York: Grove Press, 1967.

Schwartz, M. M. "Leontes' jealousy in *The Winter's Tale*." *American Imago* 30, no. 3 (1973):250–73.

Searles, H. F. *Collected Papers on Schizophrenia and Related Subjects*. New York: International Universities Press, 1965.

Segal, H. "A psycho-analytical approach to aesthetics." *International Journal of Psychoanalysis* 33 (1952):196–207.

Shibles, Warren. *Emotion: The Method of Philosophical Therapy*. Whitewater, Wis.: Language Press, 1974.

Siassi, I; Crocetti, G.; and Spiro, H. R. "Loneliness and dissatisfaction in a blue collar population." *Archives of General Psychiatry* 30, no. 2 (1974):261–65.

Siggins, L. D. "Mourning: A critical survey of the literature." *International Journal of Psycho-analysis* 47 (1966):14–25.

Soloman, R. *The Passions*. Garden City, N.Y.: Anchor Press, 1977.

Sorokin, P. A., ed. *Explorations in Altruistic Love and Behavior*. Boston: Beacon Press, 1950.

Spiegel, L. A. "Affects in relation to self and object: A model for the derivation of desire, longing, pain, anxiety, humiliation, and shame." *Psychoanalytic Study of the Child* 21 (1966):69–92.

Spielman, P. "Envy and jealousy: An attempt at clarification." *Psychoanalytic Quarterly* 40 (1971):59–82.

Stanley-Jones, D. "The biological origin of love and hate." In *Feelings and Emotions*, ed. M. B. Arnold. Pp. 25–36.

Stolorow, Robert D. "Perspectives on death anxiety: A review." *Psychiatric Quarterly* 47, no. 4 (1973):473–86.

Strasser, S. "Feeling as basis of knowing and recognizing the other as an ego." In *Feelings and Emotions*, ed. M. B. Arnold. Pp. 291–306.

Straus, E. *Phenomenological Psychology*. New York: Basic Books, 1966.

Strongman, K. T. *The Psychology of Emotion*. New York: John Wiley & Sons, 1973.

Sullivan, H. S. *The Interpersonal Theory of Psychiatry*. New York: W. W. Norton & Co., 1953.

Suttie, I. D. *Origins of Love and Hate*. New York: Julian Press, 1935.

Szasz, T. *The Myth of Mental Illness*. New York: Hoeber-Harper, 1961. Esp. pp. 280–293.

_____. *Pain and Pleasure: A Study of Bodily Feelings*. New York: Basic Books, 1957.

Teevan, Richard C., and Smith, B. D. "Relationships of fear-of-failure and need achievement motivation to a confirming-interval measure of aspirational levels." *Psychological Reports* 36, no. 3 (1975):967–76.

Tellenbach, Hubert. "On the nature of jealousy." *Journal of Phenomenological Psychology* 4, no. 2 (1974):461–68.

Tillich, Paul. *The Courage to Be.* New Haven: Yale University Press, 1952. Pp. 35–36.

Tolman, E. C. *Purposive Behavior in Animals and Men.* New York: Century, 1932.

*Torok, Maria. "The significance of penis envy in women." In *Female Sexuality,* ed. J. Chasseguet-Smirgel et al. Pp. 135–70.

Watson, J. B. *Psychology from the Standpoint of a Behaviorist.* 3rd ed. Philadelphia: J. B. Lippincott Co., 1929.

Weinberg, M. S. "Embarrassment: Its variable and invariable aspects." *Social Forces* 46 (1968):382–88.

Weissman, M. M.; Klerman, G. L.; and Paykel, E. S. "Clinical evaluation of hostility in depression." *American Journal of Psychiatry,* 128 (1971):261–66.

White, A. R. *The Philosophy of Mind.* New York: Random House, 1967.

Winnicott, D. W. *The Maturational Processes and the Facilitating Environment.* New York: International Universities Press, 1965.

———. "Fear of breakdown." *International Review of Psychoanalysis* 1, nos. 1–2 (1974):103–107.

Yachnes, E. "Neurotic pride." *American Journal of Psychoanalysis* 35 (1975):27–32.

Yorburg, B. "Psychoanalysis and women's liberation." *Psychoanalytic Review* 61, no. 1 (1974):71–77.

Young, P. T. "Emotion as disorganized response—a reply to Prof. Leeper." *Psychoanalytic Review* 56 (1949):184–91.

Zetzel, E. R. *The Capacity for Emotional Growth.* London: Hogarth Press and the Institute of Psychoanalysis, 1970.

Index

Index

COPYRIGHT ACKNOWLEDGMENTS

Grateful acknowledgment is made for permission to reprint:

Excerpt from *Feelings and Emotions: The Loyola Symposium* by R. S. Peters and Edited by M. B. Arnold. Reprinted by permission of R. S. Peters and Academic Press, Inc.

Excerpt from *Call It Sleep* by Henry Roth. Reprinted by permission of Cooper Square Publishers.

Excerpt from *Go Tell It on the Mountain* by James Baldwin. Copyright 1952, 1953 by James Baldwin. Reprinted by permission of The Dial Press.

"The Waking" from *The Collected Poems of Theodore Roethke*. Copyright 1953 by Theodore Roethke. Reprinted by permission of Doubleday & Company, Inc.

A selection from "Skunk Hour" from *Life Studies* by Robert Lowell. Copyright © 1956, 1959 by Robert Lowell. Reprinted with the permission of Farrar, Straus & Giroux, Inc.

Poem from *Complete Poems 1913–1962* by e. e. cummings. Copyright 1947 by e. e. cummings; renewed 1975 by Nancy T. Andrews. Reprinted by permission of Harcourt Brace Jovanovich, Inc.

Excerpt from *Flush* by Virginia Woolf. Reprinted by permission of Harcourt Brace Jovanovich, Inc., the Author's Literary Estate and The Hogarth Press.

Excerpt from *Samuel Johnson* by W. Jackson Bate. Reprinted by permission of Harcourt Brace Jovanovich, Inc.

"God's World" by Edna St. Vincent Millay. Copyright 1917, 1946 by Edna St. Vincent Millay (Harper & Row, Publishers, Inc.). Reprinted by permission of Norma Millay Ellis.

Excerpt from "In Just" from *Tulips & Chimneys* by e. e. cummings is reprinted with the permission of the Liveright Publishing Corporation. Copyright © 1923, 1925 and renewed 1951, 1953 by E. E. Cummings. Copyright © 1973, 1976 by Nancy T. Andrews. Copyright © 1973, 1976 by George James Firmage. Copyright © 1976 by Richard S. Kennedy.

Excerpt from the book review of "The Psychopathic God: Adolf Hitler," by Robert G. L. Waite from the August 29, 1977 issue of *The New Yorker*. Reprinted by permission of The New Yorker.

"Monotony" and excerpt from "The City" from *C. P. Cavafy: Collected Poems* translated by Edmund Keeley and Philip Sherrard, edited by George Savidis. Translation © 1975 by Edmund Keeley and Philip Sherrard. Published by Princeton University Press. Reprinted by permission of Princeton University Press.

Lines from "Bantams in Pine-Woods" from *The Collected Poems of Wallace Stevens* by Wallace Stevens. Copyright 1923 by Wallace Stevens; renewed 1951 by Wallace Stevens. Reprinted by permission of Random House, Inc.

Excerpt from *Portnoy's Complaint* by Philip Roth. Copyright © 1967, 1968, 1969 by Philip Roth. Reprinted by permission of Random House, Inc.

Excerpt from *The Woman Warrior: Memoirs of a Girlhood Among Ghosts* by Maxine Hong Kingston. Copyright © 1975, 1976 by Maxine Hong Kingston. Reprinted by permission of Alfred A. Knopf, Inc.

Excerpt from "Death in the Soul" from *Lyrical and Critical Essays* by Albert Camus, translated by Philip Thody. Copyright © 1968 by Alfred A. Knopf, Inc. Copyright © 1967 by Hamish Hamilton, Ltd. and Alfred A. Knopf, Inc.

Excerpt from "The Ghost's Leavetaking" from *The Colossus and Other Poems* by Sylvia Plath. Copyright © 1959 by Sylvia Plath. Reprinted by permission of Alfred A. Knopf, Inc.

Excerpt from *Zorba the Greek* by Nikos Kazantzakis. Copyright 1952 by Simon & Schuster, Inc. Reprinted by permission of Simon & Schuster, a Division of Gulf & Western Corporation.

Excerpt from *Dubliners* by James Joyce. Originally published by B. W. Huebsch, Inc. in 1916. Copyright © 1967 by the Estate of James Joyce. Reprinted by permission of The Viking Press.

Lines from "For Anne Gregory" from *Collected Poems* by William Butler Yeats. Copyright 1933 by Macmillan Publishing Co., Inc.; renewed 1961 by Bertha Georgie Yeats. Reprinted with permission of Macmillan Publishing Co., Inc., M. B. Yeats, Miss Ann Yeats and the Macmillan Co. of London and Basingstoke.

Excerpt from *Ressentiments* by Max Scheler. Copyright © 1961 by The Free Press, a Corporation. Reprinted by permission of Macmillan Publishing Co., Inc.